ISLAMIC GLOBALIZATION

Pilgrimage, Capitalism, Democracy, and Diplomacy

ISLAMIC GLOBALIZATION

Pilgrimage, Capitalism, Democracy, and Diplomacy

Robert R Bianchi

Middle East Institute, National University of Singapore, Singapore

World Scientific

NEW JERSEY • LONDON • SINGAPORE • BEIJING • SHANGHAI • HONG KONG • TAIPEI • CHENNAI

Published by

World Scientific Publishing Co. Pte. Ltd.
5 Toh Tuck Link, Singapore 596224
USA office: 27 Warren Street, Suite 401-402, Hackensack, NJ 07601
UK office: 57 Shelton Street, Covent Garden, London WC2H 9HE

Library of Congress Cataloging-in-Publication Data
Bianchi, Robert, 1945–
Islamic globalization pilgrimage, capitalism, democracy, and diplomacy / Robert R. Bianchi.
pages cm
ISBN 978-9814508438 (hardback : alk. paper) -- ISBN 978-9814508445 (ebook) --
ISBN 978-9814508452
1. Globalization. 2. Islamic modernism 3. Muslim pilgrims and pilgrimages.
4. Finance--Religious aspects--Islam. 5. Globalization--Political aspects. I. Title.
JZ1318.B534 2014
303.48'21767--dc23
2013008278

British Library Cataloguing-in-Publication Data
A catalogue record for this book is available from the British Library.

Front cover image credit: "Egyptian Elections" by Svitalsky Bros

In-house Editor: Chye Shu Wen

Printed in Singapore by World Scientific Printers.

For Lenny and the memory of Fazl

Acknowledgments

Several of the essays in this collection have also appeared in other publications in different versions or with different titles. Below are the citations to the original sources with grateful acknowledgement of the publications and conference organizers in each case.

Chapter 2

"The Hajj in Everyday Life," In *Everyday Life in the Muslim Middle East*, 3rd Edition, Donna Lee Bowen, Evelyn A. Early, and Becky Schulthies, eds. (2013). The material appears courtesy of Indiana University Press.

Chapter 3

"Hajj," In *The Oxford Encyclopedia of the Modern Islamic World*. Editor in Chief: Esposito, John (2007). By permission of Oxford University Press, USA.

Chapter 4

Reprinted from "The Hajj," In *The Encyclopedia of Global Human Migration*, Immanuel Ness and Peter Bellwood, eds. (2013). With permission from Wiley & Sons, USA.

Chapter 5

"Hajj, Women's Patronage of: Contemporary Practice" by Robert Bianchi *from Oxford Encyclopedia of Islam and Women*. Editor in Chief: Delong, Bas, Natana; Series Editor: Esposito, John (2013). By permission of Oxford University Press, USA.

Chapter 6

"Travel and Travellers: Travel for Religious Purposes" by Robert Bianchi from *The Oxford Encyclopedia of the Modern Islamic World*. Editor in Chief: Esposito, John (2007). By permission of Oxford University Press, USA.

Chapter 7

"Capitalism and Islam" by Robert Bianchi from *The Oxford Encyclopedia of the Modern Islamic World.* Editor in Chief: Esposito, John (2007). By permission of Oxford University Press, USA.

Chapter 8

Reprinted from "The Battle for the Soul of Islamic Finance—If it Has One," *Islamic Finance*, September 2007.

Chapter 9

Reprinted from "The Revolution in Islamic Finance," *The Chicago Journal of International Law*, 7(1), January 2007.

Chapter 10

Reprinted from "Islamic Finance and the International System: Integration without Colonialism," In *Integrating Islamic Finance into the Mainstream: Regulation, Standardization, and Transparency*, S. Nazim Ali (ed.), Copyright (2007), with permission from Harvard Law School, Islamic Legal Studies Program, Islamic Finance Project.

Chapter 11

Reprinted from "Egypt's Revolutionary Elections," *The Singapore Middle East Papers*, Copyright (2012), with permission from Middle East Institute, National University of Singapore.

Chapter 12

Reprinted from "The Socioeconomic Bases of Ennahdha Power: Khaldunian and Tocquevillian Reflections on the Tunisian Elections," *The Singapore Middle East Papers*, Copyright (2013), with permission from National University of Singapore, Middle East Institute.

Chapter 13

Reprinted from "On Liberty and Human Interests in the Work of Iliya Harik," *Journal of New Media Studies in MENA*, Issue 2, Copyright (2013).

Chapter 14

Reprinted from "Leonard Binder's, 'Islamic Liberalism: A Critique of Developmental Ideologies,'" *Journal of Near Eastern Studies*, 51(4), Copyright (1992), with permission from University of Chicago Press.

Chapter 15

"Philosophers, Lawyers, and Journalists: Arab and Turkish Ventures in Modernist Islam," Paper presented to the conference on *The Arab State of Islam*, University of California at Los Angeles, Center for Near Eastern Studies, October 2004.

Chapter 16

Reprinted from "Morsi in Beijing: Implications for America's Relations with China and the Islamic World," *Middle East Institute Insights*, September 12, 2012, with permission from Middle East Institute, National University of Singapore.

Chapter 17

Originally published in *China Report*, Vol. 49, No. 1. Copyright 2013 © Centre for the Study of Developing Societies, New Delhi. All rights reserved. Reproduced with the permission of the copyright holders and the publishers, Sage Publications India Pvt. Ltd, New Delhi.

Contents

III. Democracy and Islamic Modernism

IV. Diplomacy and Great Power Politics

List of Tables

List of Figures

List of Maps

Chapter 1

Introduction: Islamic Globalization

This collection of essays examines an emerging pattern of transnational modernization that I call Islamic globalization. It is a distinctively Muslim approach to globalization rooted in four mutually reinforcing transformations—international pilgrimage and religious travel, capitalist economic development, political and religious democratization, and growing assertiveness in world diplomacy.

These are long-term trends that are gaining force throughout the Islamic world as a whole. They suggest far more positive and encouraging views of diverse Muslim societies in Asia and Africa than we are accustomed to hearing from journalistic accounts that focus on terrorism and the daily crises of the Middle East. By adopting a wider historical and geographic perspective, we can see that Muslims are some of the most active participants in globalization and that they are contributing to its creative adaptations in a wide variety of non-Western settings.

It is fitting to speak of Islamic globalization because religion has stimulated much of the progress in Muslim countries and because the growth of capitalism and democracy is promoting more open-minded approaches to religion and greater interest in balance of power diplomacy. These interaction effects give Islamic globalization an additive and cumulative dimension—perhaps even a potential for self-sustaining innovation if it engages with similar experiments in other non-European civilizations, particularly China, India, and Latin America.

Like reformers in other great world civilizations, Islamic modernists frequently move back and forth between conflicting assessments of tradition and its future relevance. Many view Islamic globalization as the natural evolution of a living multicultural heritage with ancient roots. Others insist on a revolutionary break with repressive authority and Western neocolonialism. And many others see themselves as continuing a historic pursuit of ideals that have animated and eluded every generation since the dawn of Islam. Nonetheless, educated Muslims generally agree that Islam rests on a vast body of learning and general principles that is open to constant reinterpretation by all believers rather than a handful of fixed rules that can be monopolized by a clerical caste or an authoritarian state.

Against this background of socioeconomic development and political-religious reform, the leading countries of the Islamic world have joined the mainstream of modern life and are exerting a profound and growing influence in every aspect of global affairs. Turkey, Egypt, Iran, Saudi Arabia and the Persian Gulf states, Indonesia, Malaysia, Pakistan, and Nigeria—these are the current and emerging powers that are carving out major roles not only in their neighboring regions, but throughout the Muslim world and the wider international system. In varying degrees, each of them has experienced a series of remarkable—and often tumultuous—transformations in nation-building, economic development, social re-stratification, cultural pluralism, democratic reform, and foreign policy.

Their economies have industrialized and diversified, they have become firmly integrated into international trade and financial networks, and they dominate the land and sea lifelines of natural resource supplies that sustain both developed and developing markets. Their societies are highly urbanized and educated, spawning a new generation of middle class consumers, entrepreneurs, and professionals who are spearheading a vigorous associational life and a more assertive civil society.

Democratic reforms and revolutions have toppled dictators, monarchs, and military rulers spreading multiparty competition and parliamentary rule in one country after another. Cultural and religious modernization have severely eroded the authority of traditional religious leaders, particularly of the ‘ulama (classical legal scholars), promoting broad individual freedom to interpret Islamic texts and heritages for lay people of all ages and genders with modern education in the sciences, the professions, and the business world.

Islamic nations are both strengthening and challenging the current architecture of international organizations and diplomacy. In addition, they have created unique international regimes to manage the global surge in pilgrimage and the transnational boom in Islamic financial services.

Both individually and collectively, these countries have already become a key force in global capitalism and diplomacy. They lead efforts to mediate regional conflicts that can quickly escalate into international confrontations. In an increasingly multipolar balance of power system, they operate as swing votes and quasi-allies of the Great Powers, particularly the United States and China. And they are bound to play a pivotal role in a wide range of future efforts to reform global governance, including banking regulation, controlling climate change, reorganizing the United Nations Security Council, limiting nuclear proliferation, and insuring equitable access to vital resources of energy, water, and food.

Pilgrimage and Religious Travel

In many respects, the Hajj—the annual pilgrimage to Mecca—is the hallmark of Islamic globalization. Newly independent nations quickly removed colonial restrictions on pilgrimage and subsidized modern jet travel for newly prosperous middle class and rural populations with growing disposable incomes. Rival political parties outbid one another in expanding Hajj services to win the support of Muslim voters in newly democratizing systems. Virtually every country's pilgrimage contingent included higher proportions of women, young people, urbanites, and graduates of secondary schools and universities. Private tourist agencies offered an array of Hajj packages to Muslim submarkets with different income levels and religious preferences. Modernist and reformist writers filled much of the new mass demand for literature about Hajj rituals and symbolism with interpretations that connect the pilgrimage to the problems of daily life and the injustices of rapidly changing societies.

The Organization of the Islamic Conference—the so-called United Nations of the Muslim world—established a novel international regime that set national quotas for the size of pilgrimage contingents and devolved broad administrative powers to government-run Hajj bureaucracies throughout Asia, Africa, Europe, and the Americas. Consequently, for the first time in history, about 80 percent of today's pilgrims come from the non-Arab countries of Asia and Africa instead of the nearby Arab states that dominated Hajj activities for more than a millennium. Thus, the Hajj has become much more representative of the diversity and modernity of Muslim societies, more enmeshed with global markets, technology, and migration flows, and more deeply politicized at both national and international levels.

Capitalism and Islamic Finance

Economic development in the Islamic world has moved decisively into the capitalist mainstream. Even countries that previously experimented with state-led import substitution and autarky are now driven largely by private and foreign firms producing for export and tied to international finance and transport. The long debate over whether Islam is compatible with capitalist development seems to have been resolved with a resounding verdict in the affirmative. Instead, attention has shifted to the rapid emergence of a specialized industry of Islamic financial services tailored to the religious tastes and nationalist sentiments of hundreds of millions of middle class consumers, savers, and investors.

Islamic finance is blossoming into a distinctive type of capitalism where a multitude of Muslim and non-Muslim institutions compete for market share by inventing and branding products that claim to offer all of the conveniences of conventional banking while also complying with the principles of Islamic law. The potential profits are astronomical, the risks are incalculable, and rising competitors are likely to sweep the current leaders from the field in the coming decades. The Organization of Islamic Cooperation[1] has established specialized agencies to regulate the industry in line with central bank and Basel Club rules for disclosure and capital adequacy. Nonetheless, fierce rivalries remain between regional centers in Kuala Lumpur, Dubai, and London who cater to divergent cultural and religious markets. Worse yet, there are no uniform professional standards to prevent glaring conflicts of interest among the burgeoning class of "financial 'ulama" who hold themselves out as objective jurists while also serving as highly paid

[1] The Organization of Islamic Cooperation was formerly known as the Organization of the Islamic Conference. It assumed its current name on 28 June 2011.

directors and consultants of the very institutions they are supposed to monitor.

Democracy and Islamic Modernism

Capitalist development has encouraged democratic politics and both, in turn, have promoted more pluralist and liberal religious currents. Majority rule has triggered profound and permanent power shifts from big cities to provincial towns and villages, from military officers and intellectuals to business people and middle class professionals, and from Westernized secular elites to more pious common citizens.

Political freedom has stimulated a steady proliferation of competing parties, interest groups, and ideologies. Open and vigorous debate has created greater room for diverse interpretations of Islam with modernist and liberal tendencies gaining ground against conservative and extremist views. The recent victories of Islamic liberals in Egypt and Tunisia followed earlier breakthroughs in Turkey and Indonesia, assembling similar multiclass coalitions and interregional alliances.

The essays in this section examine the social and intellectual bases of modernist Islamic movements, particularly in Egypt and Turkey both before and after the revolutions of the Arab Spring. They highlight the electoral strategies of Muslim democrats in Egypt and Tunisia as well as the central role of professionals and lay people in broadening the understanding of Islamic heritage to include far more than the conventional legal schools.

Diplomacy and Great Power Politics

Islamic countries have adopted a newly assertive and independent role in international politics. They operate as pivotal balancers in regional conflicts, as quasi-allies that pragmatically hedge support for Chinese and American rivals, and as collective advocates of more inclusive institutions of global governance. Diplomats in Turkey and Indonesia have emerged as particularly skillful and influential mediators in the volatile Middle Eastern and Asia-Pacific regions. Saudi Arabia and Pakistan have drifted far beyond their earlier pro-American orbits, leveraging their economic and geostrategic advantages to win stronger Chinese backing against their archenemies in Iran and India. Even Egypt—a virtual American dependency for three decades—is eager to regain its leading role as a power broker in Arab, Islamic, and global arenas.

China's deepening relations with the Islamic world are helping Beijing to integrate its own Muslim minorities while building a network of partnerships that traverses the breadth of Eurasia as well as the Indian Ocean basin. The Obama administration's "pivot to the Pacific" is a belated—and probably futile—effort to reverse this momentum and to put China on the defensive by encircling it with hostile neighbors. The United States seeks to disengage from Middle Eastern quagmires and refocus its attention on Pacific economic opportunities. However, it is more likely that Obama and his successors will become embroiled in simultaneous Middle Eastern and Pacific crises that can quickly aggravate one another and escalate beyond control.

Western strategy can pursue a wiser and more effective course. Instead of trying to undermine the rising power of China and the Islamic world or working to turn them against one another, America and Europe would be better advised to offer both Chinese and Islamic leaders a greater share of power in helping to restore balance to an increasingly unstable multipolar system.

My views of Islamic globalization have coalesced from a series of research projects in many disciplines and countries over several years. I began with studies of associational life and interest group politics in Turkey and Egypt, shifting gradually to the international political ramifications of the Hajj in the Middle East, South Asia, Southeast Asia, and Africa. As I developed new interests in international law and legal pluralism, I examined the controversies surrounding Islamic finance and efforts to blend religious law with customary, Western, and international legal traditions. Most recently, extended residences in China, Qatar, and Singapore have allowed me to explore the wide overlap and longstanding interchange of Islamic and East Asian civilizations, giving me a new appreciation of their combined power in world politics.

As my interests broadened, I became evermore aware of my many debts to Leonard Binder and the late Fazlur Rahman, my teachers and colleagues at the University of Chicago. Whether I was focusing on religion or politics, on law or economics, or on regional or global questions, their contributions to Islam, the social sciences, and the humanities were always in mind and on point. I also had the good fortune to enjoy many years of debate and encouragement from Louis Cantori and Iliya Harik, my predecessors at Chicago and my dearest friends who were taken from us much too soon.

The research and fieldwork reflected in these pages were undertaken at several institutions—the University of Chicago (both the Department of Political Science and the Law School), the American University in Cairo, Middle East Technical University in Ankara, Qatar University, the Johns Hopkins-Nanjing University Center for Chinese and American Studies, and the National University of Singapore.

I: Pilgrimage and Religious Travel

Chapter 2

A Pilgrim's Eye View of the Hajj

When I went on the Hajj I soon discovered that I had to put aside most of what I had learned about it before hand. Nothing prepared me for what I saw—the maddening confusion and mass exhaustion, the daily brushes with death, and the stunning courage and kindness of countless strangers who held the world together when it was about to fly apart in all directions. I had thought that the Hajj was a religious ritual and that like other rituals it was a time and place outside of real life where people sought a fleeting touch of the supernatural and a glimpse of eternity. And then it would be finished. We'd leave the magic behind and get back to business. God would be in His proper place and humans would be in theirs.

Having assumed that the Hajj was a ritual, I also expected it to be ritualistic—standardized, lock step, and by the book with everyone going through the same motions whether they made sense or not. Everything pointed to that conclusion. The main goal was to fulfill Islam's most difficult religious obligation, a journey that God commanded of everyone able knowing that less than one percent of any generation had the health and savings to obey. An important side benefit would be forgiveness of all sins and the chance to face Judgment Day with a clean slate. But neither reward was guaranteed. God would decide to accept or reject every person's pilgrimage on a case-by-case basis depending on the purity of one's intention and the conformity of one's behavior to the multitude of special rules that make the Hajj the Hajj. Only God can decide if a particular pilgrimage is accepted or not and no human, including the Hajji, can ever know for sure what verdict God has given.

In fact, the pilgrims hardly ever follow a set script and they would find it impossible to do so even if they tried. They quickly learn that the only way to survive is to throw away the rule books and improvise their own coping strategies by building close-knit "families" in which everyone looks out for everyone else so they all scrape through safe and sound. Sooner or later, nearly all Hajjis realize that the formal institutions of pilgrimage management have failed them. Even before they arrive in Mecca, they can feel the system breaking down under the weight of cronyism, partisanship, and corruption. By the time they return home months later, they each have a special pack of tales about the abuse and neglect they've suffered at the hands of bureaucrats, tour agents, religious officials, hotel operators, police, guides, shopkeepers, thieves, doctors, drivers, shrine attendants, and litter bearers.

These experiences force pilgrims to confront the inherent flaws and biases of the elaborate government-sponsored Hajj networks in their home countries and in Saudi Arabia, including the powerful nexus of political, economic, and religious authorities that control them and profit from them. The inevitable result is a ceaseless worldwide debate over every aspect of the pilgrimage, thrusting Hajj issues to the forefront of public consciousness every day of the year as the cycle of preparation, mobilization, and criticism makes all months seem like phases of one seamless Hajj season that touches Muslims everywhere whether or not they ever go on pilgrimage themselves.

The globalized Hajj debate is producing far-reaching consequences. Instead of the old-fashioned notion that pilgrimage is a simple matter of conforming to unchanging rituals and unquestionable rules, today's Muslims commonly see every person's Hajj as a unique experience that even the same pilgrim could not relive at a later time. In this view, the Hajj is a deeply personal encounter with mysteries and holy symbols, open to infinite interpretations that can rival or contradict conventional meanings endorsed by clerics, governments, and social scientists.

In addition, Muslims increasingly see the pilgrimage in the contemporary contexts of earthly space and time rather than as a dream land or a suspended state divorced from the realities of this world. This change of perspective is steadily eroding Saudi Arabia's religious prestige and political legitimacy. All Muslims acknowledge that Mecca is the spiritual center of Islam and the site of God's symbolic "house," the ka'ba. But this does not mean that the Saudi state and ruling family automatically drink from the cup of divine grace as God's chosen agents.

On the contrary, nowadays Hajjis are more critical than ever of what they see in Saudi Arabia and more impressed by the greater power and vitality of non-Arab peoples who make up 80 percent of the pilgrims and an identical share of the global Muslim population. In terms of modern achievements in economic, democratic, and cultural development, Saudi Arabia is a backwater rather than a model or a center. Pilgrims from more open and cosmopolitan societies are convinced that *they* occupy and define the modern center of the Islamic world regardless of lingering stereotypes that they are historically or geographically peripheral.

A similar shift is occurring in popular views of the Hajj's temporal context. Traditional pilgrimage manuals often portray the Hajj as a reenactment of the legendary deeds of ancient prophets and spiritual ancestors from Muhammad, to Abraham and Adam, and even to the angels before Creation. Equally common is the future-looking focus on death and eternity—pilgrimage as a rehearsal for the Day of Judgment when all souls learn their fate in the afterlife. Such older preoccupations with the ancient and the eternal find less and less favor among today's pilgrims who are increasingly young, well-educated, urban, middle class, and female. These modern Hajjis are more attracted to the works of independent and reformist writers who stress pilgrimage's connections with contemporary social and political problems, particularly celebrated author's like Muhammad Iqbal and 'Ali Shari'ati who describe the Hajj as a spontaneous global conclave where Muslims from every land can share information and ideas about the current predicaments of Islam and its future contributions to human history. Throughout the Islamic world, nearly every bookstall or sidewalk kiosk has dust-laden copies of the old-fashioned official guide books and prayer manuals sitting side-by-side with local translations of the newer genre that connects the Hajj to real life and real time. Prospective pilgrims preparing for their sacred journeys eagerly scoop up both types according to their ages and tastes, but demographic changes are pushing the business steadily to more interpretive and socially relevant titles.

The Triumph of Experience over Ritual

Governments around the world have poured billions of dollars into efforts to make the Hajj convenient, affordable, safe, and orderly. Improved organization and infrastructure make it possible for larger crowds to flock to Mecca, overwhelming the city's narrow confines and ravaging the delicate desert ecology. Every time Hajj managers succeed in expanding the carrying capacity and surface area of the sacred precincts, they attract even greater numbers of pilgrims who quickly force the planners to undertake ever more costly and extravagant renovations. No matter how much money and technology governments throw at the problem, they find themselves on a quickening treadmill where they have to run harder and harder just to stay in the same place.

Pervasive hardship and confusion force pilgrims to improvise in order to compensate for the inevitable breakdowns in basic services and planning that dog them day in and day out. Most Hajjis eventually gravitate to small informal groups of about four to ten people who do virtually everything together for two or three weeks. They watch out for one another, alert to any danger from unruly crowds to speeding buses, tending to one another's needs for snacks and drinks, and watching for the slightest signs of sunstroke or dehydration that might require emergency treatment.

Soon the bonding and close quarters loosen tongues and spark imaginations. Family problems, politics, teasing, and grumbling help the time race by. The most animated discussions revolve around the Hajj—its mysteries, benefits, intricacies, and multiple meanings. "Are we doing the pilgrimage properly?" "Will our Hajjs be accepted?" "Why are other people doing things in different ways and different sequences?" "Have we done anything to spoil our pilgrimages and make them invalid?" "If we make mistakes and lapses, how do we compensate—by fasting, by offering an extra animal sacrifice, by giving alms?"

The hardest questions are about shortcuts in performing the main rituals. Sooner or later, nearly all pilgrims realize they cannot fully accomplish one rite or another they regard as mandatory. Nothing evokes greater pain in a Hajji's conscience than the prospect that all her efforts might be in vain, particularly when she sees that her sincere intentions can be defeated by circumstances beyond her control. The feelings of injustice and personal inadequacy can be overwhelming for the elderly and frail who have saved and sacrificed an entire lifetime to fulfill Islam's most sacred obligation.

Perhaps the greatest contribution of pilgrims' informal "family" groups is granting themselves permission to take shortcuts in dangerous situations where insisting on strict ritual compliance would invite physical injury or the risk of death. Often these are snap decisions the group must make on the spot. Inevitably, there is a dissenter who holds out in the name of doctrinal purity. "You're trying to spoil my Hajj," he'll say. "God has commanded this act and you have no authority to disobey." Of course, the dissenter is usually correct, but the rest of the group closes ranks to persuade him. "God does not expect pilgrims to commit suicide," they will say. "Islam is a religion of reason and God gives us reason because He loves us and wants us to prosper." And when all else fails, they can add, "We take full responsibility for your actions. If God wants to blame someone, He will blame us and not you."

Gradually, Hajjis become more confident. They stop looking for instructions and take control of their own movements and schedules, creating personalized pilgrimage experiences better than anything they had imagined. If a companion goes missing, his group phones the lost pilgrim camps to track him down and bring him back. If the water canisters in the Great Mosque are too far apart to serve all of the worshippers, small cups move hand to hand over hundreds of meters without spilling a drop. When a panicked crowd breaks into a human stampede, someone points the way to safety and people shield one another with their own bodies. Each day brings them in contact with a wider circle of pilgrims from other nations, races, classes, and cultures who might not share a common tongue. They learn to pool their language skills, translating between two or three languages at a time to exhange views about religion, work, and current events—and snapping endless photos until their batteries run down.

As the public Hajj of the rule books gives way to the private Hajjs of three million individuals, pilgrims grow more eager to reflect on their experiences, particularly as their time in the Holy Land winds down and they prepare for the return to normal life. During these last days—but most of all, at night—the magic of the Hajj is on full display. In the valleys outside of Mecca, the desert sky contains so many shooting stars it's impossible to keep count. From the roof top of the Grand Mosque, there is an unobstructed midnight view of the courtyard below—bathed in power lights and colored beams—where pin wheels of human specks swirl around the ka'ba for the last time.

Between Mecca and outlying shrines, a perpetual traffic jam in both directions forces exasperated Hajjis to abandon their taxis and walk to the last-minute rites. But now there is no rhyme to their dress. Most have cast off the seamless white towels required in the earlier phases, reverting to street clothes of a thousand climes and styles. Others decide to "go native," sporting crisp new Arabian robes and head dresses like the ones they're packed as souvenirs for friends back home. Some haphazardly mix and match all three genres—Hajj gear, national colors, and Bedouin fashion.

These last days in Mecca create a third type of pilgrimage alongside the public and private Hajjs that have paved its way. I would call it the "secret Hajj" because it unleashes profound introspection and unfettered speculation about every aspect of Islam, creation, and the human condition. One of the most common insights is that the ka'ba is meaningless. It is not really God's house because God lives in everyone's heart and soul no matter who they are or where they are. Why go to Mecca? To obey a divine command and in the process to learn what God probably intended us to know all along—that He guides every part of His creation, including the 99 percent of humanity that never makes a pilgrimage anywhere. Equally important, Hajjis now realize that their journey has succeeded because they made it succeed through their own ingenuity, patience, courage, and selflessness. Governments, companies, and clerics have done the best they could given their inherent shortcomings, but in the end they let everyone down—as usual. With this new confidence and wisdom in their heart of hearts, Hajjis frequently return home to positions of enhanced status and influence which they turn to good advantage in criticizing and rebuilding their communities in all corners of the Islamic world.

Dethroning Arabian Pretensions

For decades, Saudi Arabia has invested lavishly in Hajj projects, yet no nation has earned less gratitude from those who accept its generosity. Indeed, the longer pilgrims remain in the country the more negative their impressions become. Many people see no reason to praise governments for discharging their sacred duties to allow Muslims to obey God's commands. In this view, all sovereigns carry such a responsibility and the Saudis are no different except that fortuitous wealth has given them an added burden of having to use it for the common good. When the royal family gives itself glorious religious titles and poses as exemplary Muslims, it all seems quite over the top to anyone familiar with the brutality of their rule and the intolerance of their religious attitudes.

Each year, more and more pilgrims come to see Saudi control of the Hajj a classic case of mismanagement that should be corrected through greater internationalization of all decisions concerning the Holy Cities. Most of the grievances cluster around three very raw issues—destruction of the historical and ecological foundations of Mecca, heavy-handed suppression of Hajj practices that are popular among Muslims from many lands in Asia and Africa, and politically motivated manipulation of the quota system that allocates pilgrimage visas to every country in the world.

In the last sixty years, the annual number of overseas pilgrims to Mecca has soared from about 50,000 to 2 million. Several mutually reinforcing factors have driven this meteoric rise—the revolution in cheap commercial air travel, the steady growth throughout Asia and Africa of more prosperous middle class and working class communities with greater disposable income, the gradual demise of colonial rule in favor of independent nations whose governments actively promote Hajj participation instead of suppressing it, and the deliberate strategy of Saudi monarchs since King Faysal to cultivate the Hajj as a pillar of religious legitimacy at home and an instrument of diplomacy everywhere in the Islamic world. All of these changes are irreversible and in combination they virtually insure that Mecca's overburdened infrastructure and environment will come under even greater pressure every year.

A swelling tide of architects, planners, historians, preservationists, environmentalists, foreign governments, and common pilgrims deplores Saudi decisions to demolish revered landmarks, to encircle the Grand Mosque with shopping centers and high-rises, and to flood the valleys with diesel smoke from tour buses frozen in place by endless gridlock. The indictment is not that Saudi Arabia has planned poorly, but that it has planned destructively by willfully despoiling an irreplaceable resource that—unlike their oil wealth—belongs not to them, but to all Muslims and to all humanity, including generations not yet born.

Much of the problem stems from a fatal mismatch between Saudi Arabia's universal custodial duties, which make it responsible to all of Islam, and its idiosyncratic Wahhabi theology, which is contemptuous of many sentiments and customs that are dear to the 1.4 billion believers it must serve. Saudi clerics and officials harbor a deep suspicion of anything suggesting the veneration of humans, objects, or places because they fear that it undermines the direct and exclusive worship of God. From this perspective, some of the most popular practices of Sunnis, Sufis, and Shi'ites are borderline examples of idolatry and polytheism. Praying at tombs and cemeteries, retracing the footsteps of legendary Muslims, touching blessed objects, invoking miraculous powers, experiencing ecstatic states—all of these are regarded as ever-present vestiges of paganism and animism requiring constant police vigilance and public displays of physical force.

Sometimes, the sectarian bias of these measures is transparent—for example, when mainly Iranian Shi'ites are beaten for trying to enter the closely guarded cemetery in Medina where several of their holiest leaders are buried. More often, however, the policeman's lash falls on the backs of regular Sunnis and Sufis, including visitors to the tombs of the Prophet and early Caliphs who are so overcome by emotion that they try to pray at choke points and inadvertently crush the flow of pilgrims behind them.

The most provocative behavior of Saudi officials during the Hajj appears in punitive and callous acts that seem motivated by racism and ethnic discrimination. During the most tragic disaster in recent Hajj history, more than 1,400 pilgrims died in a 1990 human stampede in the mountain tunnel connecting Mecca and Mina. The victims were mainly Indonesians, Malaysians, Bangladeshis, and Indians. By the time their bodies were sent back home, they had been so dismembered and mutilated by earthmoving equipment that most were unidentifiable. Outraged publics in all of these countries saw a direct connection between disrespect for their martyred pilgrims and the daily mistreatment of their brothers and sisters who had migrated to Saudi Arabia to work for local firms and families. Resentment over Saudi racism against Asian Muslims during the Hajj and in the workplace have poisoned relations between these nations for more than two decades on both official and personal levels.

Complaints of racial discrimination are even more widespread among pilgrims from sub-Saharan Africa, particularly Nigeria. Nigeria's Hajjis are routinely detained and questioned over suspicions about carrying infectious diseases, drug peddling, currency smuggling, prostitution, illegal immigration, terrorism, vagrancy, public disorder, and every type of customs violation. For the ordinary pilgrims with no involvement in any of these things, their only offense would be the Saudi Arabian equivalent of "driving while black"—or, in this case, "making the Hajj while black." Saudi officials have forced Nigerian Hajj managers to implement an elaborate nationwide screening process for prospective pilgrims, including criminal background checks, medical exams, inoculations, letters of reference, personal interviews, non-refundable deposits and application fees, mandatory training sessions, and written tests on Islamic ritual obligations. No other country has erected so many barriers to pilgrimage—and so many payment points for corrupt bureaucrats and religious officials. As desperate security measures, these obstacles could have, at most, a temporary justification if properly targeted and tailored to local circumstances. Nonetheless, even then the system as a whole reflects a pervasive racial bias that violates Islam's core values and contradicts the Hajj's special embodiment of equality and universalism.

Despite important steps toward internationalizing Hajj management over the last 20 years, Saudi Arabia still wields considerable power because of its ability to increase or decrease each nation's annual contingent of pilgrims. The Organization of Islamic Cooperation

(OIC)—the so-called Islamic United Nations—has mandated a global system of quotas that allots each nation about 1,000 pilgrimage slots for every 1 million people. The original intent was to stabilize the aggregate level of overseas pilgrims at about 1.4 million per year—roughly the average for the period just before and after 1980.

The Saudis were desperate for quotas because Mecca was being overwhelmed by massive numbers of Iranian pilgrims—over 100,000 per year—during the heyday of the Islamic Revolution. Under Ayatollah Khomeini's direction, Iranian Hajjis organized mass marches denouncing Saudi Arabian claims to sovereignty over the Holy Cities and demanding an international regime to administer them on behalf of all Muslims. The Saudis could—and did—slaughter hundreds of Iranian protesters inside the Grand Mosque itself, but they knew they had no authority to prohibit sincere pilgrims from entering the country because Islamic custom and law insist on free access for all Muslims seeking to fulfill their religious obligations.

In panic, Saudi Arabia pleaded for the largest and most powerful Sunni nations to vote in favor of its proposal to grant quota-making authority to the OIC, which would then supervise Saudi implementation. The Sunni governments eventually agreed, but they extracted an enormous price from the bargain. The quotas would be strictly per capita based, non-discriminatory, and permanent. Over night, the non-Arab Muslims of Asia and Africa, who comprise about 80 percent of Islam, leapfrogged ahead of all Arabs combined, who had previously dominated about 60 percent of the overseas pilgrimage contingents.

But the Hajj was just one part of a much larger bargain that shifted power and prestige from the oil rich Arab states—and the Arab countries in general—to the newly developing regional giants of Asia and Africa. Henceforth, OIC leaders would no longer be hand-picked by Saudi Arabia and its neighbors. They would be elected by delegates from every member state and leadership would rotate between three new blocks formed by members in Asia, Africa, and the Arab world. Once again, overnight the Saudis handed over the keys to the international organization they founded and funded in order to push back the Iranian assault that threatened their very existence.

Almost 30 years later, Saudi leaders are trying to claw back a bit of the power they had to trade away. With the quotas firmly established and the Iranian pilgrims back in the fold, Saudi Arabia has begun to tinker with the margins of the system in order to dispense and withhold favors in line with its foreign policy interests. Inherent ambiguities and inconsistencies in quota estimation give Saudi bureaucrats considerable leeway. Should calculations be based on a country's total population or just its Muslim population? Which censuses and surveys are the most accurate measures of either number? Should minority Muslim communities be intentionally over-represented to encourage their solidarity with the global mainstream? When can Saudi decision-makers grant exceptional, one-time only, please-don't-ever-ask-for-this-again increases?

Even when the stakes are comparatively small, overseas Hajj managers usually try to move up the pecking order instead of challenging its arbitrariness head-on. Nigeria, Malaysia, Singapore, and South Africa constantly fret that their quotas might be slashed to between one-half and one-twentieth of their current size. Turkey and Iran are always trying to institutionalize special increments awarded for good behavior in controlling their delegations. It's always helpful to have a fugitive pilgrim problem as a bargaining chip, particularly if both sides agree on the approximate number of violators. National Hajj managers reason this way: "If the Saudis cut our quota, then we can turn a blind eye to the illegal traffic and they are stuck with the free riders. If we shift to stricter enforcement, then they owe us more places on the legal side of the ledger because we're saving them the costs of apprehension and deportation." In this fashion, many countries try to ward off the threat of Saudi blackmail by applying a little of their own first.

After navigating the countless chambers of the global Hajj mill—from initial application to safe passage home—returned pilgrims have seen it all. The divine mysteries of pilgrimage are more awesome than ever, but there are few illusions about the religiosity of Saudi society or the networks of ambition and greed that connect it to Hajj agencies around the world. Saudi Arabia now appears not as the center of Islam, but as a self-sealed cocoon at the end of the earth waiting to drop off at any moment. As for Saudi Arabian models of Islam, they are vivid and unparalleled—but resoundingly negative and unsuitable back home in a modern and pluralistic society.

Bringing the Hajj Home

In retrospect, it seems natural that pilgrims would reverse their initial impressions about the Hajj's true location in space and time. When they departed for Mecca, they were convinced that they were going to a real country in the modern world in order to experience universal spiritual wonders that would suspend them in an eternal moment. But while explaining these events to others and to themselves, they learn the opposite—they've gone to a land of make believe in the middle of nowhere in order to develop wisdom and relationships with the most practical and profound value to their daily lives here and now. The Hajj is real and relevant whereas Arabia is an illusion and isolated.

How could they have been so misled as to have it exactly backwards in the beginning? Hadn't they been proper Muslims all their lives, praying and learning together from the same texts and teachers as Islam had required the world over throughout history? When Hajjis ask such questions, they chip away at the 'ulama's already crumbling claim to a monopoly of authority in religious interpretation. They help to expand the global conversation of Islam to include a host of scientists, professionals, journalists, women, youth, associations, academics, artists, and public opinion leaders whose specialized knowledge of modern life and all-embracing social connections vastly outweigh the meager resources of traditional religious scholars.

Debates about the meanings of the Hajj and the shortcomings in its current management inevitably spillover to include all of the interconnected institutions—political, economic, social, international, and transnational—that sustain and profit from global pilgrimage. The snowballing Hajj conversation becomes not only more critical, but also more democratic, more interdisciplinary, and more universal. And just like the pilgrimage of personal experience, it develops a life of its own beyond the control of earthly sovereigns and mandarins.

Because debates about the Hajj never take a day off, the pilgrimage remains at the forefront of popular imaginations year round.

In this sense, today's Hajj never stops. It no longer occupies a special season on the margins of everyday life. Instead, it embodies everyday life—both sacred and profane—magnifying all of its contradictions, hypocrisies, and unfulfilled promises.

As the Hajj becomes a metaphor that stimulates critical thinking about Islam and society, all Muslims become Hajjis whether or not they ever make the physical journey. They realize that because they have a vital stake in real life at home, they also have a stake in pilgrimage on the other side of the world. In this manner, all Muslims are with the Hajjis no matter where they are. And like the Hajjis, they also learn that the ka'ba is nothing more than a symbol of their own hearts—God's "real home" where, according to the Qur'an, He rests closer than the jugular vein in one's neck.

Chapter 3

The Contemporary Hajj

Unique among the world's great pilgrimages, the Hajj is in many ways also the most important. Even compared to the ancient and highly developed international pilgrimage systems of Christianity and Hinduism, the Hajj is remarkable in its doctrinal centrality, its geographic focus, and its historical continuity. The size and global coverage of the Hajj are unparalleled. It currently attracts about one and a half million overseas pilgrims from virtually every nation—about 50 percent of them from Asia, 35 percent from the Arab world, 10 percent from sub-Saharan Africa, and 5 percent from Europe and the Western Hemisphere. These are joined in Mecca by another million local pilgrims, mostly foreigners working in Saudi Arabia. The combined contingents form the largest and most culturally diverse assembly of humanity to gather in one place at one time.

As the Hajj has grown in size, the demographic characteristics of the pilgrims have changed substantially. Today's Hajjis are increasingly Asian, non-Arab, female, young, educated, and urban. In the last four decades, the proportion of women pilgrims has soared from less than one-third of the total to nearly half. In certain countries such as Indonesia, Malaysia, Singapore, and Lebanon, women usually constitute the majority of the national Hajj delegations. In many other countries, female pilgrims predominate in the most prosperous regions and ethnic communities such as Turks in western Anatolia, Punjabis in northeastern Pakistan, and Yorubas in southwestern Nigeria.

Characteristics

The Hajj is the annual pilgrimage to Mecca during the second week of Dhu al-Hijjah, the final month of the Islamic lunar calendar. All adult Muslims are required to perform the Hajj at least once in their lifetimes provided they possess adequate resources and their absence from home will not create unreasonable hardships for their families. No other pious journey may be equated with or substituted for the Hajj; this includes visits to the tombs of saints (ziyaras), to Muhammad's tomb in Medina, or to Mecca itself at other times of the year ('umra). Nor can the Hajj be replaced by a spiritual "inner pilgrimage" through meditation or mystical enlightenment.

The Hajj includes an intricate series of highly symbolic and emotional rituals performed in unison by all pilgrims. The sequence of rites observed today was determined by Muhammad shortly before his death and is regarded as a ritual reenactment of critical, faith-testing events in the lives of Abraham, the ancient founder of monotheism, his wife Hajar, and their son Isma'il. When Muslim pilgrims replicate Muhammad's movements, they recall not the pagan ceremonies of pre-Islamic Mecca (some of which were also known as Hajj), but the much older models of the earlier prophets.

Before the Hajj begins, all male pilgrims don a special garb (ihram) consisting merely of two white sheets or towels covering the upper and lower parts of the body. Female pilgrims have greater freedom of dress so long as they remain modest and tasteful. The primitiveness and uniformity of the ihram symbolizes the radical equality and humility of all believers before God regardless of worldly differences in race, nationality, class, age, gender, or culture. The ihram is a metaphor for how people will appear when they emerge from the grave on Judgment Day to confront their creator. Many pilgrims retain their ihram for years after the Hajj and use it as a burial shroud.

The initial rite of the Hajj, the tawaf, is performed at least twice—immediately upon arriving in Mecca and just before departing after the completion of all other rites. The tawaf is a sevenfold circumambulation of the ka'ba, the cube-shaped "House of God" first built by Abraham and Isma'il and the spiritual center of the world that all Muslims face during prayer. The ka'ba is often called an earthly counterpart to God's throne in heaven, and the tawaf is described as a human imitation of the angels' circling his throne in adoration. During the tawaf many pilgrims approach the corner of the ka'ba that holds the Black Stone, a mysterious "heavenly rock" resembling a meteorite whose origins and alleged powers are widely disputed. Most pilgrims merely salute the Black Stone from a short distance as a gesture of their renewed covenant with God. Others struggle to touch or kiss the Black Stone, believing that it physically absorbs sin.

The tawaf is followed immediately by the sa'y, in which the pilgrim runs back and forth seven times between two small hills close to the ka'ba. This recalls Hajar's frantic search for water after Abraham was forced to abandon her and Isma'il in the desert. After the exertion of the tawaf and sa'y most pilgrims wash and relax at the nearby well of Zamzam, which appeared miraculously to rescue Hajar and her son from death. Pilgrims drink Zamzam water throughout their stay in Mecca and frequently take home small flasks as souvenirs for friends and relatives who are unable to make the Hajj themselves.

The climax of the Hajj is the massive procession to the plain of 'Arafat just outside Mecca on the ninth day of Dhu al-Hijjah. Two million pilgrims from more than one hundred countries gather in tents that cover the valley and surrounding mountains as far as the eye can see. From just after noon until shortly after sunset they are absorbed in continuous prayer and conversation. Many believe that at this spot and time God's spirit descends closest to earth, making it easier for human prayers to attract his attention.

Some of the most devout pilgrims scale the sides of the Mount of Mercy where Muhammad delivered a famous sermon during his "farewell pilgrimage"; however, the vast majority remain in tents sheltered from the dangerous midday sun. The encamped congregation at 'Arafat is a beehive of activity, constantly exchanging news and ideas about the condition of Islam in every corner of the world. Each camp combines the air of a religious retreat, a country picnic, and a town meeting.

Promptly after sunset, more than two million people and a hundred thousand vehicles break camp and rush out of the valley, creating the world's largest traffic jam (nafrah). They inch their way through the narrow mountain pass of Muzdalifah, where they spend the night in the open under the starry desert sky. The complete lack of accommodations at Muzdalifah makes this one of the most ascetic phases of the Hajj, and for many Muzdalifah is the most inspiring and calming part of the pilgrimage. On the tenth day of Dhu al-Hijjah, at sunrise, pilgrims continue on to the adjacent valley of Mina, where another colossal tent city is erected between ‘Arafat and Mecca.

Mina is the site of two ritual dramas poignantly replicating Abraham’s crisis in fulfilling God’s command to sacrifice his son Isma‘il. Pilgrims reenact Abraham’s rejection of Satan’s temptation to disobey the divine order by hurling seven pebbles at a tall stone pillar (jamrah) representing the devil. The massive crush of humanity and flying stones about the pillar create the most frenzied and cathartic moments of the Hajj, as well as some of the most perilous. Because of frequent stampedes and hundreds of deaths during the stoning ritual, Saudi officials have built multitiered pedestrian bridges around the pillars and posted special police to help manage the crowds. After the stonings, each pilgrim offers an animal sacrifice (qurban) commemorating the sheep that God ultimately accepted from Abraham in place of his son. Muslims all over the world participate vicariously in this phase of the Hajj by simultaneously making their own sacrifices at home on ‘Id al-Adha, Islam’s most important holiday.

During the next two or three days, until the twelfth or thirteenth day of Dhu al-Hijjah, pilgrims constantly shuttle back and forth between Mina and Mecca via clogged highways and wide pedestrian tunnels cut through the mountains. Following a slightly more flexible schedule, they perform at least six more stonings in Mina and at least one more tawaf and sa‘y in Mecca. In the final few days of the ceremonies male pilgrims wear the ihram garb less frequently. Instead, they wear various combinations of their regular national costumes and local Arabian dress, signifying their gradual return to the profane world and their closer identification with Muhammad and his companions.

Symbols and Meanings

A properly performed Hajj creates spiritually reborn pilgrims absolved from all previous sins. At this point, elderly and infirm pilgrims sometimes express a readiness for death, particularly in Mecca, believing their purified souls will enter paradise immediately. However, a Hajj is only valid if God accepts it, and his judgment cannot be known with certainty by the pilgrim or anyone else. The hallmark of a valid pilgrimage is not performing each ritual with precision, but undertaking the entire journey with the sincere intention (niyah) of coming closer to God. If a pilgrim's intentions are spiritually sound, then all but the most flagrant breaches of ritual formality can be corrected by sacrificing additional animals in Mecca or by special acts of charity and fasting after returning home.

The Hajj is unique in its symbolic richness as well as its far-reaching political ramifications. The extraordinary interplay of symbolism, ritual, and power links pilgrims with one another and with Muslims around the world in a feeling of common destiny extending from the time of creation until Judgment Day. The dream of preserving and harnessing the unifying power of the Hajj has long fascinated and frightened elites in the Muslim world and beyond. The struggle to control the organization and interpretation of the pilgrimage has persisted throughout Islamic history and became a major religio-political conflict in the twentieth century. Since World War II, newly independent states throughout the Muslim world have adopted elaborate programs to manipulate the Hajj for political and economic gain. However, controlling the Hajj is far more difficult than the technocrats imagine; its pluralistic symbolism and multifunctional ritual defy the modern state's penchant for standardization and regimentation.

The symbolic structure of the Hajj contains numerous layers open to alternative interpretations. At each phase of the rites the pilgrim reenacts dramatic events associated with multiple, often overlapping characters. Any analysis of this symbolism soon becomes an investigation of archetypes derived not only from the Qur'an and sunnah but also from local legend and oral tradition. In many accounts Muhammad's association with shrines and sites is preceded not only by Abraham and his family (a pre-Islamic layer), but also by Noah and Adam (a prehistoric layer) and by Gabriel and other angels (a preterrestrial layer).

Interpretation of this sacred symbolism has always been pluralistic and controversial. Orientalists such as Gustave E. von Grunebaum have claimed that the rites have no meaning and that pilgrims perform the Hajj with no comprehension of their actions beyond blind obedience. In contrast, some esoteric writers see every place and persona as a profusion of signs pointing toward a unique truth for each pilgrim and each pilgrimage. Many pilgrims, literate or not, carry government-approved guide books that reveal the "secrets" or hidden meanings of the Hajj as though there were a single, standard message that could be decoded once and for all.

Muslim commentators generally acknowledge that the Hajj contains many mysteries that no human intellect grasps fully. However, they then proceed to interpret these latent themes in ways that reflect conventional differences among 'ulama, Sufis, Shi'ites, modernists, and fundamentalists. For many of these writers, the symbolism of the Hajj serves as a metalanguage inviting critical and creative thought, open to periodic reinterpretation and congenial to wide variations in culture, nationality, and politics. Even the government of Saudi Arabia, which tries to set the limits of respectable discourse and conduct during the Hajj, recognizes that such disagreements are inevitable and perhaps desirable.

The ritual functions of the pilgrimage are just as diverse as its symbolic structure. Anthropologists who specialize in the study of ritual commonly distinguish among rites of passage, rites of renewal, rites of reversal, and rites of affliction. Although these concepts generally describe discrete phenomena, each is appropriate in highlighting a different facet of the Hajj.

Pilgrimage frequently coincides with major turning points in the life cycle such as adulthood, marriage, career change, retirement, illness, and death. It may also serve as a flexible and repeatable initiation for people of any age, including new converts to Islam or those seeking spiritual rejuvenation after a personal crisis or loss. Viewed as a rite of passage, the Hajj appears capable of helping individuals adapt in various cultures and social structures, with generally conservative, system-supporting implications.

On the collective level, the Hajj celebrates the reunion and renewal of the ummah, the worldwide community of Muslims. Indeed, the pilgrimage is the symbolic rebirth of the ummah every year. It is the most powerful reminder of Islam's ideals of unity across cultures and its continuity over time. Pilgrims retrace the footsteps of the founders of monotheism and Islam. They discuss and debate the role of the ummah country by country, in the international system and in the course of world history. Afterward, they return home with a stronger sense of the transcendent, charismatic quality of the community—a sentiment shared and reaffirmed by neighbors and countrymen unable to perform the pilgrimage themselves.

By symbolically negating all status and hierarchy, the Hajj devalues the status quo in all its forms. It is true that the reversal of roles is only temporary and fictional. In fact, throughout their stay in the holy land pilgrims enjoy vastly different accommodations and comforts depending on their nationality and class. Nevertheless, repeated stress on the ultimate irrelevance of all distinctions among believers challenges the legitimacy of economic and political inequalities both nationally and internationally. As with other rites of status reversal, the Hajj has mixed implications for authority. It can produce either catharsis and acquiescence or empowerment and protest. Controversies over control of the Hajj reflect recurrent struggles between elites who favor these opposing goals.

Recent Political History

Since 1979, controversy has centered on Saudi Arabia's attempts to use the pilgrimage as a rite of reconciliation versus Iran's desire to turn it into a platform for revolution. King Faysal (r. 1964–1975) frequently told pilgrims that the Hajj should serve not only to heal their spiritual ailments but also to mend the political splits in the ummah as a whole so that it could become a more effective force in world affairs. He portrayed the Hajj as a period of reflection and self-criticism that should be institutionalized in a permanent international forum. Faysal lobbied Muslim heads of state attending the pilgrimage to found the Organization of the Islamic Conference (OIC) as a Muslim counterpart to the United Nations.

During the 1980s, when Iran's revolutionary government disrupted the Hajj and demanded its removal from Saudi supervision, the OIC provided decisive support for Faysal's successors. More than 40 member-states of the OIC not only reaffirmed Saudi protection of the holy cities but also endorsed an unprecedented quota system limiting the number of pilgrims in each nation's delegation. In an effort to centralize

Hajj management further, many Muslim technocrats have urged the OIC to establish an international agency to coordinate the burgeoning government bureaucracies that currently regulate all aspects of the pilgrimage in their respective countries.

On the global level, the OIC manages the Hajj through a unique international regime that tries to reconcile three conflicting demands on the Holy Cities of Mecca and Medina—Saudi Arabian claims to national sovereignty, the universal right of Muslims everywhere to free passage and unfettered worship, and the interest of future generations in preserving endangered historical sites and desert environments that belong to the common heritage of mankind. At the national level, each government regulates Hajj participation at its source by allocating the limited spaces designated under the OIC quotas and by providing a wide array of subsidized pilgrimage services that often includes discounted air fares, educational programs, visa services, hotel accommodations, medical care, and life insurance.

Many governments have tried to use the Hajj for political and economic gain, particularly by increasing pilgrimage services during election campaigns and by awarding lucrative contracts to selected businesses. These practices simultaneously reflect and aggravate the growing politicization of the Hajj, both nationally and internationally. Entrenched elites manipulate the pilgrimage at their own peril. Government sponsorship and control frequently swell into a virtual state monopoly over a lucrative Hajj enterprise. Such monopolies commonly breed favoritism, resentment, and heightened conflict among parties, regions, classes, and ethnic groups. This sort of pilgrimage policy not only threatens to undermine the political elites who wield it, but also ultimately contradicts the ideals of the Hajj.

The Hajj and Islamic Law

The most important legal controversies over the Hajj center on three key issues—limitations on the right of access to the holy cities, destruction of the environment and historical heritage, and regulations on the participation of women. The quota system has failed to resolve disputes over access because Saudi authorities have applied the rules inconsistently, relaxing the standards for many countries where Muslims are a minority (especially in Europe and North America) and granting or retracting extra places for governments depending on whether they support or criticize Saudi foreign policy. Alarm over urban sprawl and hyper-commercialization has reached unprecedented levels as traditional quarters and revered sites are demolished to make room for high-rise buildings and opulent shopping centers. Heavy-handed enforcement of requirements that women pilgrims be accompanied by male guardians often seem intentionally targeted at African and Asian countries, triggering accusations that the Saudis are discriminating against non-white Muslims.

For all of these issues, Saudi Arabia's stewardship is severely undermined by a striking mismatch between its lingering attachment to idiosyncratic religious doctrines and its growing responsibility to serve the universal interests of Muslims everywhere. Saudi officials and religious leaders often stress principles of state sovereignty, iconoclasm and patriarchy to a degree that clashes with the weight of scholarly opinion and popular sentiment in the wider Islamic world. In dealing with mounting demands for international supervision of the holy cities, for protecting historical sites associated with revered figures and sacred events, and for honoring the rights of women pilgrims, the Saudi government seems woefully out of touch with the people it is supposed to serve.

The OIC has not yet created a specialized body to consider Hajj-related legal matters, but such a step would be a sensible extension and deepening of the international regime for pilgrimage management that it established in the 1980s. An advisory judicial council that reflected the pluralistic views of Muslims around the world could help to set standards for Hajj policy in the same manner that agencies such as the Islamic Financial Services Board have done in the fast growing field of Islamic finance. A more institutionalized and transparent Hajj regime could mitigate some of the sectarian and political biases that have eroded Saudi Arabia's legitimacy as an impartial manager of pilgrims' affairs.

Chapter 4

The Hajj and Human Migration

The Hajj is the greatest gathering of humanity on earth. All Muslims who are physically and financially capable are required at least once in their lives to make this pilgrimage to visit "God's house" in Mecca, Saudi Arabia. For the three million Muslims from over one hundred countries who meet in and around Mecca every year, these three weeks of tumultuous rituals mark the peak of their spiritual lives and the renewal of Islam's historic identity as a universal community of believers.

In form, the Hajj remains firmly centered on the original rites and holy places that Muhammad consecrated fourteen centuries ago. But today's Hajj is vastly more important because its massive mobilization of people, money, and power is helping to transform social, economic, and political life throughout the Islamic world. Beyond its eternal role as Islam's most profound religious experience, the Hajj now reflects and energizes powerful forces of social revolution, global community, and poetic imagination.

Social Revolution

The contemporary Hajj is a result of the confluence of successive revolutions that have swept across the Middle East, Asia, and Africa since the end of World War II. The end of European colonialism and the rise of independent nations quickly ended a century of governmental restrictions on overseas travel. Colonial rulers from England, France, and the Netherlands were particularly eager to discourage Muslims from visiting Mecca because they feared pilgrims would be doubly contaminated by pan-Islamic sentiments sweeping the Ottoman empire and by infectious diseases carried from South Asia. Even when colonial administrations decided to sponsor Hajj contingents as a paternalistic gesture to mollify Muslim opposition, they were careful to limit the size of pilgrim contingents, to pack them with police and spies, and to impose onerous quarantines at the first rumor of threats to public health in the Arabian peninsula. Newly independent states in Muslim countries abolished most of these obstacles in the 1950s and 1960s while expanding the basic services that European administrations had provided for transport, medical care, and repatriating destitute pilgrims stranded in Mecca after the Hajj.

The rapid spread of civil aviation opened the Hajj as never before to Muslims from the most distant corners of Asia and Africa. The number of overseas pilgrims skyrocketed from about 80,000 in 1950 to 250,000 in 1964, 900,000 in 1974, and 1.5 million by 2005. In addition, the national and ethnic composition of the pilgrimages shifted dramatically. Before 1960, Arabs consistently dominated the Hajj, comprising 50 to 60 percent of all pilgrims, year in and year out, even though they made up only 20 percent of the world's Muslims. As more and more governments directed their national airlines to offer special Hajj flights with low-cost fares, distance from Mecca virtually disappeared as a barrier to pilgrimage. By the 1970s, non-Arab pilgrims equaled Arabs and since the 1980s the majority has come from Turkey, Iran, South Asia, and Southeast Asia. The Arab world's pilgrimage has experienced a similar shift in its center of gravity—from the wealthier Gulf and Fertile Crescent countries to the bigger and poorer societies of the Nile Valley and North Africa.

Economic development steadily emerged as the most important force propelling pilgrimage in all regions and cultures. As private savings spread beyond the big cities to provincial capitals and villages, thousands of newly prosperous middle-class and peasant families became the first in their communities to realize Hajj dreams that had been unattainable for previous generations. Wealthy oil-exporting countries had thriving pilgrimages, but their contingents were quickly joined and surpassed by countries with more diversified economies that benefited from green revolutions, manufacturing growth, and foreign worker remittances.

As the Hajj encompassed more nations and classes, the personal characteristics of pilgrims changed dramatically. Women and young people were the greatest beneficiaries, particularly urban, middle-class

Muslims who are more educated and connected to the information revolution. Worldwide, the number of female pilgrims nearly equaled males and in societies where female literacy and property ownership are widespread—such as Singapore, West Java, northern Pakistan, Lebanon, Palestine, western Turkey, and southeastern Nigeria—women regularly comprised the majority of Hajjis. Easier transportation and better accommodation made family pilgrimages common and women were quick to take advantage of new opportunities for group travel where a few male escorts accompanied large numbers of ladies.

Young people with diplomas and careers rejected the old-fashioned notion that the Hajj should be mainly for the elderly and infirm who wanted to prepare for the hereafter. They saw the pilgrimage as a badge of success and mobility carrying spiritual benefits they could enjoy for a lifetime. In just three or four decades, the average ages of Hajjis fell from around 65 to 45 or less in one country after another.

The greater accessibility of the Hajj was a powerful stimulus to the development of Islamic banking and finance. Muslims embraced long-term savings plans for financing future pilgrimages alongside the nest eggs they were creating for retirement and their children's educations. Malaysia pioneered the use of special Hajj accounts as the engine for an aggressive Islamic investment fund that allowed Muslim politicians to challenge the long Chinese dominance of the economy. Their success resonated not only in Indonesia, but also in Pakistan, Turkey, the Arab World, Europe, and North America where state, private, and foreign banks competed to expand the portfolio of Islamic financial products to include home mortgages, auto loans, mutual funds, and credit cards. Today, Islamic banking and Hajj savings are so intimately interconnected that many people have forgotten which came first.

The spread of democracy and multiparty politics has placed the issue of Hajj services near the top of the policy agenda in every country that enjoys even intermittent pluralism, including the democracies of Western Europe where Muslim diasporas are still disfavored minorities. Politicians of all ideological stripes try to outbid one another in providing government sponsored pilgrimages regardless of whether they describe themselves as "religious" or "secular," "capitalist" or "socialist." Using the Hajj to buy votes does not always work and sometimes it backfires. Muslims often express gratitude to politicians who use state agencies to organize and subsidize the pilgrimage. Nonetheless, just as frequently they criticize those services as inadequate or take them for granted, viewing them as basic duties of any modern government. Indeed, one of the surest ways to alienate Muslim voters is to debase the Hajj by implying that it is just another public good to be traded in the political marketplace.

Most importantly, the Hajj's remarkable growth is an integral part of the recurrent religious awakenings and searches for cultural authenticity that have spread throughout Islamic lands during the colonial and postcolonial eras. For at least two centuries, the Hajj has fueled the imaginations of every generation of reformers from Asia and Africa that returned home from Mecca determined to reshape their societies in successive campaigns of anti-imperialism, nationalism, modern education, economic development, and democracy. In each case, Muslim leaders and writers reinterpreted Islamic ideals to suit the particular blend of nationalist, religious, and Western initiatives they championed for their times and cultures. The common thread was the claim that pilgrimage brought them closer to Islam's origins and refreshed their understanding of its enduring principles now matter how they diverged in adapting those values to new circumstances. Thus, virtually all nationalist revolutions and mass movements in the Islamic world have revived and reworked religious traditions—including the multilayered symbolism of the Hajj—to distinguish themselves from the supposedly secular and materialist excesses of the West.

Global Community

The Hajj has always reminded Muslims around the world that they belong to a single community (ummah, in Arabic) with a common historical destiny and that this shared identity transcends differences of nationality, race, culture, class, and gender. Today's Hajj has enhanced this sense of community by promoting new international institutions as well as a greater appreciation for pluralism and diversity.

The Hajj's unprecedented cosmopolitanism vividly demonstrates the wide diffusion of wealth and power far beyond Islam's supposed Arabian heartland into thriving areas of Asia and Africa that once were regarded as the periphery and farther still into Europe and the Americas. Mecca remains the symbolic center of Islam, but it is outshone by dozens of newer centers of economic, political, and scientific achievement on every continent. Indeed, the contemporary Islamic world is so geographically universal and interconnected that it no longer has any discernible center or periphery.

The Hajj's explosive growth occurred hand in hand with the rise of international organizations and international regimes among Islamic countries. The Organization of the Islamic Conference (OIC) arose under Saudi sponsorship in the 1970s but it gradually developed a life of its own, operating as an Islamic United Nations where Arab, Asian, and African blocks share power and cooperate as a diplomatic lobby in world politics. During the 1980s the OIC created the world's first international regime for pilgrimage management. It adopted controls on participation in the Hajj by implementing a worldwide quota on the number of pilgrims that each nation could send to Mecca.

The national quotas were pegged to population size and designed to freeze overall participation at 1990 levels of about 1,000 Hajjis for every 1 million Muslims. In order to enforce these rules, every country had to create an official pilgrimage agency responsible for selecting, preparing, and escorting its allotted Hajj contingent. As these national agencies grew, they learned from one another and helped to shape pilgrimage policy in the OIC and the Saudi government. The result is a sophisticated global network of Hajj management that is of enormous interest to social scientists and international relations scholars because of its unique approach to reconciling the conflicting interests of national sovereignty, freedom of access to universally revered holy places, and preservation of the common heritage of mankind for future generations.

The new Hajj regime both reflects and encourages a profound shift in the balance of power between Islamic countries. It abolishes the historical underrepresentation of Asian and African Muslims in the pilgrimage and in Islamic diplomacy. Moreover, it stresses economic development and organizational capacity as the key determinants of influence and participation instead of relying on differences in culture and geography.

Nonetheless, many national Hajj agencies are plagued by favoritism and corruption. The economic and political stakes of pilgrimage management are so tempting that Hajj resources are commonly diverted to enrich cronies and to mobilize partisan allies. Ironically, these shortcomings at the national level not only threaten the fairness of the global Hajj regime, they also contradict the egalitarian and universalistic principles of Islam itself.

Poetic Imagination

The Hajj's invigoration of Islamic imaginations is even more far reaching than its contributions to social and institutional development. Contemporary Muslim writers have been exceptionally bold and creative in reinterpreting the rich symbolism of the Hajj in ways that encourage social criticism and political action. Nearly every street stall and bookstore in the Islamic world sells modernist depictions of the Hajj as a reenactment of ancient struggles against evil and as a dress rehearsal for looming battles to correct political, economic, and religious injustice.

The evocative works of Muhammad Iqbal in India, 'Ali Shari'ati in Iran, and Muhammad Arkoun from Algeria have inspired an entire generation of writers to use the Hajj as a metaphor for debating core Islamic principles and charting the future of the global Muslim community, including its relations with other world religions and civilizations. These writings have been translated into all of the major languages of the Islamic world and absorbed into a wide spectrum of religious and political outlooks. By elevating the Hajj from individual conformity with formal rituals to collective criticism of national and global community, Islamic modernists have helped to democratize religious interpretation and to undercut the authority of traditional Islamic scholars who still treat pilgrimage as a simple act of obedience that prepares Muslims for entering the next world instead of remaking this one.

Chapter 5

Women's Participation in the Hajj

Women's participation in the Hajj has risen dramatically in the last 40 years, particular among younger, better educated, and more urbanized groups. The trend is remarkably uniform at the global level and across virtually every region and nation. Between 1968 and 1993, the proportion of women among all overseas pilgrims increased from about 34 percent to 43 percent. In several countries—Indonesia, Singapore, Lebanon, and Palestine—women comprised the majority of Hajjis year after year.

Nonetheless, large disparities remain in female Hajj rates not only between countries but within them. Variations in women's pilgrimage are closely related to differences in education, income, and culture. Female education is a strong predictor of women's pilgrimage. Even primary school education—in either secular or Islamic institutions—expands young women's horizons and opportunities sufficiently to encourage high levels of pilgrimage. Income also promotes pilgrimage for women as for men, but women's rates are especially high in communities with strong traditions of female land ownership and with local commercial networks that are dominated by women merchants.

Patriarchal cultures continue to suppress women's pilgrimage, but patriarchy's effects vary enormously in different ecologies and economic environments. The greatest contrasts appear between cosmopolitan maritime zones, inland agricultural economies, and isolated mountain regions. Women Hajjis are most common in coastal regions with strong traditions of maritime commerce. Lower pilgrimage rates prevail in inland agricultural regions, with provincial capitals and villages often sending more women than richer metropolitan centers. Women are least likely to make the Hajj if they live in nomadic or mountainous regions, particularly if they belong to minority ethnic and tribal communities.

In Turkey, women regularly comprise the majority of Hajjis in the western coastal regions around the Sea of Marmara and along the shores of the Aegean Sea. These areas have the highest income, the greatest levels of female literacy, and the largest numbers of European immigrants. In Central Anatolia, female pilgrims are most common along the Mediterranean coast and least common near the more mountainous and isolated districts of the Black Sea. Eastern Turkey has by far the lowest frequency of women Hajjis, particularly the Kurdish provinces in the southeast where poverty, illiteracy, and ethnic segregation combine to severely limit women's abilities to engage in any type of travel except for permanent migration to big cities and foreign countries where job prospects are more promising.

In Pakistan, ethnic and economic differences create contrasting environments for women who want to make the Hajj. In the booming towns and villages of Punjab in northeast Pakistan, most pilgrims are women, particularly where Islamic primary and secondary schools for girls are widespread. Female pilgrimage is also common in the southern cities of Karachi and Hyderabad where educated northern Indian migrants are most concentrated. The lowest levels of female pilgrimage appear among the tribal societies of the Pashtuns in the northwest and the Balouchis in the southwest along the mountainous borders with Afghanistan and Iran. Pilgrimage is least popular for both men and women in the rural districts of Sindh where feudalism, tribalism, and poverty are the most intense.

In Indonesia, women Hajjis frequently make up the majority nationwide with particularly high rates in the capital city, Jakarta, and in the maritime trading centers of the Outer Islands. Female pilgrimage closely follows historical routes of international commerce—along the Makassar Straits in western and southern Sulawesi and eastern Kalimantan, near the Straits of Malacca in eastern and central Sumatra, and in the smaller islands of Nusa Tenggara to the east of Java. Female Hajjis are also dominant in Western Sumatra where the Minangkabau community retains long traditions of matrilineal inheritance, including land ownership.

Nigerian women have vastly different opportunities to make the Hajj depending on their ethnic background. Women are the majority of

Hajjis among the Yoruba of southwestern Nigeria, especially in central Lagos and Ibadan where female business networks control much of the retail trade. Yoruba men frequently delay their own pilgrimages until they have first saved enough money to send their mothers to Mecca. Only then do they make the journey themselves and whenever possible they also take their wives and daughters. In contrast, the Hausa regions of northern Nigeria have consistently lower levels of female pilgrimage even in the wealthier cities. In central Nigeria—also known as the Middle Belt—where Christians and Muslims live side by side in relatively equal numbers, there are competing pilgrimage campaigns to Jerusalem and Mecca, which boost female Hajj participation as well. This is the center of Nigeria's most violent and tenacious religious conflicts, and the pattern of dueling pilgrimages merely aggravates the problem.

Many aspects of the Hajj help to break down gender biases by strengthening the equality of the sexes and highlighting women's contributions to the development of Islam. Women are explicitly prohibited from veiling or covering their faces during the pilgrimage. They usually wear normal loose-fitting dress rather than the distinctive white towels that men don for the major rituals. At night, women sleep in rooms with their families or with other women, but throughout the day they are in close and casual contact with strangers from every corner of the world—both men and women—in ways that would be discouraged in daily life back home.

One of the most emotional and symbolically charged rites of the pilgrimage is the sa'y, in which Hajjis reenact the drama of Hagar, the wife of Ibrahim and the mother of Isma'il. Imitating Hagar's desperation after being left alone in the desert with her infant son, pilgrims run back and forth between two hills searching for water. Afterwards, like Hagar, they drink from the blessed well of Zamzam, which the angel Gabriel revealed to her just as she was tempted to abandon hope of survival. The famous Iranian writer, 'Ali Shari'ati, portrays Hagar as the central heroine not only of the Hajj but of monotheism in general. For Shari'ati, Hagar is an icon of struggle, faith, and liberation that every pilgrim should emulate during the Hajj and in their own communities where they should continue her fight for equality and justice.

Chapter 6

Religious Travel in Islam

Muslims participate in many types of travel that combine spiritual and mundane goals. For pious Muslims, nearly every journey has a religious dimension. Historically and currently, the most popular forms of religiously-inspired travel include the pilgrimage to Mecca (Hajj), shorter off-season trips to Mecca ('umra), visits to hundreds of holy places throughout Asia and Africa (ziyaras), study at Islamic schools and universities (madrassas), reunions of transnational mystical orders (tariqas), missionary activity among both Muslims and non-Muslims (da'wa), private business transactions guided by Shari'a principles, diplomacy representing Muslim governments and international organizations, and journeys of exploration surveying the global Islamic community (ummah) and assessing its role in world affairs.

A typical traveler often combines several of these activities in a multipurpose journey, especially when visiting several destinations over an extended period of time. For example, most pilgrims to Mecca (Hajjis) also visit Medina to pray at the Prophet's mosque and to see his tomb. Many people combine a Hajj with stopovers at other holy places along the way. Asian Hajjis frequently adjust their itineraries to include popular sites in Konya, Damascus, Jerusalem, Baghdad, Karbala, Shiraz, Mashhad, Multan, Ajmeer, Mazar-i-Sharif, Samarkand, Quanzhou, Demak, and Yogyakarta. For African pilgrims, the routes to and from Saudi Arabia often pass through Fez, Cairo, Kano, Touba, Capetown, Khartoum, and Harar. In all of these places, pilgrims are not merely worshipers but also traders, students, preachers, emissaries, demonstrators, explorers, and itinerant workers. Many also become fugitives, illegal immigrants or smugglers.

Religious travel in Islam reflects an extraordinary degree of intercontinental cooperation among constantly intersecting groups that perform overlapping functions. The general pattern resembles a web of interlacing and autonomous networks instead of a rigid hierarchy, spontaneous collaboration rather than central direction, and fluid process over fixed structure. This vast web encompasses Muslims in every part of the world, helping to create a universal Islamic identity that transcends nationality, race, gender, and class. The Hajj has always been the most powerful expression of Islamic unity and egalitarianism, and today its unprecedented size and diversity make it more important than ever.

Religious travel helps to sustain multi-tiered loyalties among Muslims allowing them to identify with universal, regional, and even parochial communities at the same time. By guaranteeing the continuous interplay of unity and diversity, the web of religious travel fosters simultaneous pride in a single worldwide faith, in multiple cosmopolitan cultures, and in dozens of ancient ethnicities. Students of Islamic civilization have long appreciated the inherent tensions between these identities and the need for every Muslim society to renegotiate them periodically. However, they have not always understood how religious travel helps to make this coexistence and accommodation possible.

Most religious travel, including the Hajj, is organized around linguistic and ethnic communities that participate in the global ummah while preserving a distinctive personality for diverse transnational cultures. The core groups define themselves in terms of common or closely related languages, particularly Arabic, Malay-Indonesian, Persian, Urdu, Turkish-Turkic, Hausa, Swahili, English, and French. All of the major languages of the Islamic world have evolved as a lingua franca facilitating the integration of multiethnic empires, intercontinental markets, and Diaspora communities. Many are hybrid languages and even when their structures differ widely they still share a vast vocabulary, particularly in religion, politics, and philosophy that reflects common ideals and experiences.

All of these communities have an intercontinental reach and most also predate the rise of Islam. They are smaller than the ummah but much larger than states and nationalities, and they have developed different relationships with non-Muslim neighbors and Western colonialists. Each core community has made a special contribution to the evolution of Islamic civilization, to the rise of modern nationalisms, and to widespread intercultural borrowing between Muslims and non-Muslims. Thus, Islamic civilization is an amalgam of amalgams—a pluralistic family of overlapping transcontinental communities in which a handful of dominant languages help to forge common identities among disparate ethnicities and subcultures. Religious travel is one of the linchpins that unites and rejuvenates Islam globally and regionally. The constant intersection of multiple networks of religious travel is the lifeblood of the universal ummah as well as the trans-cultural linguistic communities that comprise it.

Every region of the Islamic world has a handful of cities that are particularly important crossroads because they blend a host of religious activities and radiate multiple layers of symbolic meaning. Some of the most notable examples are Konya in central Turkey, Yogyakarta in south-central Java, Kano in northern Nigeria, and Kashgar in far western China. These regional hubs attract an enormous flow of travelers and ideas moving back and forth between their neighboring hinterlands and Mecca. They are critical meeting points where the primordial and the cosmopolitan collide and transform one another in countless ways every day.

Konya's soul lies in the emerald-domed mosque and mausoleum of Celaleddin Rumi, patriarch of the Mevlevi mystical order known throughout the world as the "whirling dervishes." The tomb of Mevlana ("our guide" or "our teacher") is the preeminent pilgrimage site in the Turkish-speaking world, but it also attracts non-Turkish Muslims who know Rumi's Sufi poetry in Persian as well as followers of many other religions who admire his ecumenical and humanistic spirit. Konya is an important educational center for both mainstream and mystical Islam and it hosts a thriving religious publishing industry. The confluence of rich agriculture and private industry has made it one of the leading "Anatolian Tiger" economies and all of the conservative political parties that have ruled Turkey in recent decades enjoy wide support there. Beyond its spiritual, economic, and political importance, Konya is a powerful force in reviving traditional Turkish culture, including handicrafts, folklore, music, and archeology. Konya's genius is its ability to display its religious vitality through multiple personalities—Anatolian and Turkish, pan-Islamic and trans-sectarian, pre-Ottoman and post-modern—managing their inherent contradictions while profiting from the global reach of their combined appeal.

Yogyakarta plays a similar role in linking rival Indonesian expressions of Islam with the international mainstream as well as with indigenous Javanese culture. The Sultan's palace is a traditional center of Sufi learning and a generous patron of local arts. The palace's ties with the rural population contrast with the urban middle-class following of the Muhammadiya, the modernist mass movement whose founders were inspired by Egyptian and Arabian reformers and whose branches extend to trading communities throughout Indonesia, including remote parts of the outer islands of Sumatra, Sulawesi, and Nusa Tenggara. Despite its relative poverty, Yogyakarta continues to compete with Jakarta both culturally and politically. Its publishing houses and bookshops offer the richest variety of religious and secular titles in the country. Together, the mysticism of the palace and the modernism of the Muhammadiya have encouraged record-breaking levels of pilgrimage in many forms—to local shrines in Yogyakarta, to the northern coastal cities that are resting places of the Wali Sanga (the "Nine Saints" who pioneered Islam in Java), and especially to Mecca for the Hajj and 'umra. Each year Indonesia sends the world's largest delegation of Hajjis to Mecca—about 200,000 annually—and many more make the 'umra. During the last 40 years, Yogyakarta has been a driving force behind the rapid spread of Islam in Java and the rest of Indonesia. Its religious, intellectual, and political leaders have contributed greatly to Indonesia's growing influence in international diplomacy in the Islamic world and beyond.

Kano sits astride a wide belt of Hausa settlement and trade stretching across the African savanna from the Atlantic Ocean to the Red Sea. Pilgrims of the Tijani and Qadiri mystical orders come to Kano from many countries, sometimes taking a long circular route via Egypt, Morocco, and Senegal before proceeding to Mecca and Medina. Kano enjoys a brisk traffic of illegal Hajjis from neighboring countries such as Niger and Burkina Faso who use Kano as their gateway because they can buy foreign exchange and import contraband more easily in Nigeria than in their homelands. Kano boasts the most pluralistic collection of Islamic organizations, business interests, and political parties in northern Nigeria. The combination of sectarian, economic, and ideological rivalry generates constant turmoil and creativity throughout Nigeria and sub-Saharan Africa. Saudi Arabian officials are more worried about trouble-making pilgrims from Nigeria than from any other country. The Saudi government regularly accuses Nigerian Hajjis of carrying infectious diseases, overstaying their visas, and belonging to international criminal gangs. In contrast to Indonesia where the pilgrimage boom has helped to increase diplomatic clout, Nigeria's rocky relations with Saudi Arabian Hajj authorities have undermined Abuja's efforts to play a stronger pan-African and pan-Islamic role.

Kashgar is an historic Silk Road entrepôt linking China and Central Asia to the Middle East that has benefited greatly from post-Mao China's increasing links to the Islamic world. Kashgar retains a majority Muslim population of Uighurs, Kyrgyz, Kazakhs, Tajiks, and Turkmen. Unlike Urumqi, the richer capital of Xinjiang province, Kashgar is not sharply polarized between dominant Han Chinese immigrants and a marginalized indigenous community that is mostly Uighur. Kashgar's multiethnic environment promotes a religious and cultural openness that is a striking contrast to Urumqi's communal tensions. New investment from the Middle East as well as Beijing has rebuilt the central business district around the majestic Id Gah Mosque. The media and schools are trying to promote a polyglot population and bookshops are teeming with bilingual and trilingual materials for all ages in Uighur, Chinese, and English. As Beijing encourages Islam domestically in order to strengthen its diplomatic and commercial ties with the Islamic world, Kashgar is poised to reemerge as a pan-Asian hub for religious and commercial travelers.

Each of these cities—and dozens more in the Arab world, Iran, and South Asia—exposes Muslims from all classes and cultures to multiple expressions of a common faith. Their constant interaction has helped to sustain a worldwide civilization for more than a millenium. Long before Western scholars discovered the importance of globalization and transnational networks, Muslims were experiencing them as concrete realities every time they left their homelands to worship and to explore a world that they have always viewed not as a shifting jumble of man-made nations, but as a seamless creation of God.

II: Capitalism and Islamic Finance

Chapter 7

Capitalism and Islam

Debates over Islam's economic implications are even more heated and inconclusive than debates over its social and political implications. Traditional texts and authorities provide countless blueprints for an ideal Muslim family and polity but not for an Islamic economy. The Qur'an explicitly endorses few economic values beyond private property, commercial honesty, and competition tempered by concern for the disadvantaged. The hadith extol the virtues of pious merchants in tones that would be familiar to any reader of *Poor Richard's Almanack*. Yet these adages hardly amount to a business-class creed or an Islamic counterpart to Calvinism. The shari'a (Islamic law) lays down firm rules both protecting personal wealth and discouraging excessive profits. However, the more rigid the rules, the more ingenious were the loopholes that judges devised to avoid enforcing them.

During the nineteenth and twentieth centuries, Muslims and Westerners have tried to articulate a clearer set of economic imperatives for Islam that could be either reconciled with or distinguished from competing models of capitalism, socialism, and communism. Pre-modern texts and practices are malleable enough to lend useful if inadequate support for many of these efforts. By and large, however, Islamic traditions have been most conducive to the development of indigenous capitalism and most hostile to the importation of communism. Sporadic enthusiasm has appeared for nascent theories of Islamic socialism in a few important countries, such as Egypt, Pakistan, Indonesia, and Iran. Yet even the most popular advocates of Islamic socialism are colored by secularist and heterodox reputations that severely limit their appeal to the Muslim mainstream.

Although most debates over Islamic economics have focused primarily on the relation between religion and capitalism, those debates have moved in three different directions. At first, attention focused on Western arguments that Islam is an obstacle to capitalism. Gradually,

Muslim and Western writers converged in viewing Islam as supporting a variety of capitalism. Most recently, Islamic modernists have combined a wide assortment of economic theories and religious programs to portray Islam as a superior alternative to capitalism.

Islam as an Obstacle to Capitalism

Both Orientalists and social scientists have emphasized Islam's supposed incompatibilities with capitalism, but their explanations typically diverge into theological versus institutional analysis. Orientalists tend to characterize Islam as inherently contradictory to capitalism because of basic and unchangeable doctrines such as fatalism, other worldliness, and disdain for lending money at interest. These polemics often reflect and reinforce crude popular prejudices against Islam by providing them with a patina of pseudoscientific authority.

Social scientists, on the other hand, focus on situational and perhaps temporary tensions between Islam and capitalism. They identify these tensions with particular historical conditions and structures such as feudalism, sultanism, and imperialism. Compared to Orientalists, social scientists are more likely to view conflicts between religion and economics as partial, not all–encompassing, as rooted in malleable institutions and relationships, not in mindless dogmas and dictums. Social scientists tend to think in terms of an adaptive, "historical Islam" rather than a formative, "ethical Islam." "Historical Islam" mirrors predominant cultures and ideologies, whereas "ethical Islam" actively tries to shape them. The former justifies ruling institutions and groups, the latter guides and limits them.

By viewing Islam as less powerful in molding the world, social scientists also portray it as less culpable in retarding capitalism. If Muslims lagged behind others in accumulating private wealth and investing it in more productive enterprises, this was not because of their religion's imagined hostility to economic progress. The most serious obstacle to capitalism was the inhospitable foundation of political, social, and economic institutions that would have stunted entrepreneurs no matter what their degree or brand of piety. Capricious sultans and intriguing concubines, greedy tax farmers and unruly mercenaries, absentee landlords and landless peasants, mosaic societies and frozen classes, integrated markets and ungovernable hinterlands, relentless warfare and foreign encroachment—these were the crippling weaknesses of the Muslim world, not the spiritual or moral shortcomings of its creed.

Whereas many social scientists can envision capitalist revolutions among Muslims who refashion their institutions, most Orientalists cannot. Because social scientists view religion as just one part of a complex Islamic civilization, they can imagine Islam adapting to capitalism and even promoting it in response to pressures from a changing environment. Because Orientalists view Islam as an immutable mentality that affects all other aspects of life, they expect it to distort and defeat capitalist impulses from any source, foreign or domestic.

Islam as a Variety of Capitalism

While Orientalists and social scientists counted and weighted religion's supposed burdens on development, economic historians began to turn the debate in a novel direction. They argued not only that capitalism in the Muslim world was more advanced and widespread than previously assumed, but that Islam itself deserved much of the credit for these achievements. Both Western and Muslim writers described a vibrant merchant capitalism linking the major cities of Asia and Africa in a vast intercontinental network stretching from the Silk Road to the Gold Coast, from the Sahara to the Spice Islands, from the Black Sea to the Cape of Good Hope.

Across city-states and multinational empires, in agrarian kingdoms and maritime principalities, Muslims shared a cosmopolitan culture that was carried not by the soldier or the bureaucrat but by the itinerant trader who often doubled as a mystical missionary. Particularly in non-Arab regions, the Sufi merchant became the very embodiment of international Islamic civilization, uniting religion and commerce, town and country, sober mysticism and flexible orthodoxy. In many ways Islam seemed to express the special ethos of a transnational, urban middle class that could most easily adapt to its lunar calendar and devotional rigors, its prudish manners and charitable bent. Muslim traders and preachers helped popularize prophetic traditions exhorting frugality, modesty, and diligence to the point where converting to Islam might have seemed like embracing capitalism as well.

Historians and economists frequently argue that this florescence of international commerce could have promoted industrial revolutions throughout the Islamic world if Muslims had been able to resist the onslaught of European imperialism. From this viewpoint, the decisive inhibitor of capitalist development was not the inherent weakness of Islamic thought or the rigidity of outmoded institutions, but the overpowering force of Western arms and avarice. Indeed, in many countries, Europe's commercial and colonial invasions shattered native crafts and manufacturing. Flooding one region after another with cheap, mass-produced goods, Western traders often deindustrialized the very economies they were integrating into the modern world market.

The sophisticated long-distance trade that for centuries had been both a fountain and a fruit of Islamic civilization could not survive the industrial revolution and the age of imperialism. As long as the power of rival regions was either remote or in check, Islam nourished a distinctive and durable form of international capitalism. However, once Europe's competitive advantages approached global hegemony, the rules and limits of economic development were no longer set by local actors and resources.

Islam as an Alternative to Capitalism

As capitalism became more firmly identified with foreign domination, it lost some of its appeal to Muslims. Rather than asking whether Islam obstructed capitalism, Muslim reformers and nationalists began to see Western economic models as blocking their own paths to independence and prosperity. Instead of stressing those aspects of Islam that had promoted capitalism in the past, they argued that a more authentic and coherent Islamic economics could surpass capitalism in the future.

Efforts to articulate a distinctive Islamic economics are quite recent, taking off during the petroleum boom of the 1970s. Thus far, the most interesting innovations have been not in theories but in structures and practices. The prevailing theoretical tendencies are unmistakably capitalist, stressing the primacy of private property and free enterprise.

There is a heightened emphasis on cooperation between the private sector and the state as well as between Muslim firms and governments internationally. There is considerable discussion of economic inequality in the Islamic world and of the need for a more just distribution of wealth both within and between Muslim nations. Moreover, there is a common assertion that ownership of land and natural resources is a public trust that must be safeguarded for the benefit of future generations. Hence, in the Muslim world, as elsewhere, contemporary economic thought is increasingly preoccupied with social harmony, global interdependence, and environmental preservation.

The hallmark of this emerging Islamic capitalism is an impressive array of new institutions that are strikingly multifunctional and multinational. The pivotal role belongs to a few dozen big, state-sponsored Islamic banks that seek to centralize investment and power while sharing risk and profit. To preserve their claim to an Islamic pedigree, the enterprises avoid paying interest at fixed rates. Instead, they generally offer depositors a share in realized gains and losses. Because they ask depositors to accept considerable risk, they often require borrowers to relinquish a degree of managerial control. Although these policies do not alter formal ownership, they nonetheless create a kind of involuntary partnership between depositor, lender, and debtor, who all become joint investors.

The Islamic banks blend the activities of accumulation, appreciation, and speculation in an unusually explicit manner. The prominence of multipurpose banks is not surprising in economies that have large foreign-exchange surpluses but weak capital markets and infrastructures. The overdevelopment of financial institutions might compensate for the underdevelopment of business associations in general, but it creates some peculiar organizational hybrids. Depending on its particular mix of projects and customers, an Islamic bank can combine the roles of an investors' syndicate and a stock market, a mutual fund and a credit union, a commodities exchange and a casino.

The Islamic banks are also distinguished by their mammoth international transactions and their well-publicized political connections. The banks are popular conduits for workers' remittances, pilgrimage expenses, and petrodollars. They are instrumental in recycling capital from oil-producing states to poorer countries with large surpluses of land and labor. Most Islamic banks are openly allied with government agencies, political parties, royal families, social movements, and liberation struggles. These coalitions frequently cut across national borders, projecting a common set of political and ideological conflicts throughout the Muslim world.

Malaysian peasants making installment payments to the Pilgrims' Investment Fund are also subsidizing the ruling party's affirmative-action program for Muslim entrepreneurs. Foreign pilgrims and guest workers in Saudi Arabia use Islamic banks to support families and shops all over Asia and Africa. Oil revenues from banks in the Persian Gulf countries are paying unemployed Egyptians to reclaim Sudanese farmland, financing Turkey's governing alliance of Islamic politicians and business people, arming Muslim fighters in Bosnia, Afghanistan, and the Philippines. The Russian Federation is asking Islamic banks to combat Iranian influence in the newly independent republics of Central Asia with loans to import prayer leaders from Egypt, Qur'ans from Pakistan, and teachers from Turkey.

The practice of Islamic economics is more advanced that the theory; its resources and organizations are more crystallized than its goals. Although its proponents insist that Islamic economics is a clear alternative to existing systems, it looks more like a financially driven variety of capitalism with a keen aptitude for building transnational political ties to offset its continued weakness in both local and global markets. Some of the more unconventional Islamic investment companies have suffered mismanagement and corruption generating sensational stories about bankruptcies, kickbacks, and secret arms deals. In general, however, their impact is conservative and antirevolutionary.

Domestically, the Islamic firms support moderate, right-of-center democrats and modernizing authoritarians against religious radicals and leftists. In the balance of power among Muslim states, they are firmly identified with the mainstream leaders of the Organization of the Islamic Conference. They help to strengthen alliances between Saudi Arabia, Egypt, Turkey, Pakistan, Indonesia, Malaysia, and Nigeria while countering the influence of Iran, Libya, and Iraq. In the global economy, they use their leverage in financial markets to press the advanced industrial countries for concessions in trade, investment, and technology transfer. Nevertheless, they demand not a new world economic order but merely higher standing in a more flexible hierarchy of nations.

Chapter 8

The Battle for the Soul of Islamic Finance—If It Has One

The rapid accumulation of wealth and power in Islamic enterprises highlights the urgency of assessing its wider implications, moral, social and political. What are the core ideals and guiding principles of Islamic finance? Which interests and constituencies should it serve? What political alliances and strategies is it pursuing regionally and globally?

These issues are a far cry from the expert-driven discussions that have dominated the field in recent years: the nuts-and-bolts efforts to devise new products and transactions that could comply simultaneously with the Shariah and with tightening international banking standards. Debates over Islamic finance are becoming less technical and more social, less legal and more political. Above all, they are refocusing on basic ethical choices that no world religion can or should avoid—choices that concern not simply individual conscience, but also social justice, community identity and planetary survival.

Today more than ever, the fate of Islamic finance is too important to leave to closed circles of technocrats and lawyers, accountants and 'ulama. In the coming decades, most of the industry's core choices will be collective decisions requiring mass participation, open debate and frequent disagreement. The struggles of Islamic finance will inevitably interact with broader struggles to liberalize religious sentiments, economic systems and political regimes, and this in turn could transform relations between Muslims and non-Muslims for generations to come.

In business, religion and politics, the common threads are growing pressures for disclosure, tolerance and democratization. These pressures will force Islamic finance toward constant self-evaluation and reinvention. Indeed, the metamorphosis is already underway, spurred by a host of hybrid projects and experimental alliances with mass consumers, micro-lenders and ethical investors.

Islamic finance is coming out of its cocoon, sporting a novel appetite for eclecticism and cross-fertilization, as well as for partnership and convergence. Instead of rehashing the old debate about whether "Islamic economics" will replace world capitalism or reduplicate it, we are beginning to explore how Muslim and non-Muslim reformers can collaborate in fashioning a more humane global economy that offers greater justice and opportunity for everyone.

Moving to the Middle

The most sweeping changes stem from efforts to reach out to the vast middle classes in the Islamic world and to the Muslim diasporas of Western Europe and North America. After decades of "financial engineering" and new product development, Islamic bankers are poised to provide integrated financial services that cover the entire lifespan. Their repertoire includes educational loans, credit cards, auto finance, mortgages, commercial lending, insurance, individual investing and retirement planning.

Penetrating mass retail markets will force Islamic finance to tailor its services to the special needs of local cultures and jurisdictions. As Islamic bankers learn to listen more to their customers and regulators, they will loosen the grip of the religious and academic authorities that have guided the industry in the past. Self-conscious strategies of market segmentation will promote more diverse practices and standards. The futile quest for a unitary pan-Islamic model will give way to mutual recognition of alternate approaches and "full faith and credit" for contracts embodying either majority or minority rules. The genius of the shari'a has always been its common-law knack for adapting to different cultures and changing times. That flexibility and pluralism will be even more indispensable as the geographic and social scope of Islamic finance becomes more truly universal.

Good Things Come in Small Packages

The growing interest in micro-lending is a welcome antidote to Islamic finance's long predilection for multimillionaire clients and big-ticket projects in energy and infrastructure. When Muhammad Yunus won the Nobel Prize, hardly anyone saw the Grameen Bank as a faith-based enterprise or as the brainchild of an Islamic modernizer. The chasm between the populist origins of Islamic economics and the high-roller image of contemporary Islamic bankers could not have been more glaring. Lingering skepticism about the short-term profitability of micro-lending obscures the greater value of the political and moral support that Islamic finance must earn from ordinary people throughout Asia and Africa if it is to survive in its own heartland.

Islamic micro-lending will have to be much more than a sound business plan; it must also be a broad political initiative that anchors the industry in the lives of the masses. Business people and technocrats can never accomplish such a mission by themselves. They will have to cultivate a wide network of allies in international organizations, governments, political parties, social movements and community groups. Most Islamic banks already have such networks, but they need to become much more formal, inclusive and transparent. Islamic finance is determined to integrate with new regulatory regimes of the global economy, but it must devote equal efforts to integrate with all levels of its own societies.

The Ethical Edge

Compared to the vast potential of retail banking to the middle class and micro-lending to the poor, the field of ethical investing offers both lower risks and lower returns. In theory, Islamic banking is ethical investing par excellence. It has clear commonalities with the leading types of socially conscious investing in the West, especially in valuing the environment, social justice, public health, corporate governance and world peace. These are modest niche markets where synergies are easy to identify and exploit, but their likely political rewards, transcending nations and cultures, are tantalizing in a world that is weary from fear-mongering about the supposedly inevitable "clash of civilizations."

Ethical investors—Muslim and non-Muslim—make up a latent transnational community that is waiting to be mobilized. Of course, the beauty is that both Muslim and non-Muslim partners are already linked to important social networks in their own countries and abroad. Typically they represent the most cosmopolitan, talented and idealistic social forces whose influence far exceeds their numbers and wealth. These "Investors without Borders" are blessed with a ready-made agenda and an experienced cadre of activists; they simply need a catalyst and a steering committee to become an organized reality.

Working Together

The most exciting frontier of Islamic finance arises from a new set of proposals for "mutuality" that aims at nothing less than re-conceiving the ummah and its relations with the rest of humanity. Proponents of mutuality offer the best hope for returning Islamic finance to its original quest for of community, solidarity and equality. For them, Islamic finance is part of a larger experiment to build local cultures of trust that can rekindle the ummah's historical identity and purpose. Mutuality comes in countless forms: trusts, cooperatives, endowments, worker-owned enterprises, barter agreements, publicly held funds and transparent corporations. The common denominator is a dispersion of wealth and power that undermines dominant monopolies and elites.

Islamic visions of mutuality are a natural evolution of the inherent idealism of Islamic economics. However, mutuality's relations with contemporary Islamic banking are filled with tension and suspicion. Today's industry leaders still see mutuality as either a rebellious vanguard or a romantic throwback, but not as a serious partner or rival. Nonetheless, the mutuality movement is bound to grow as Islamic finance reinvents itself in the coming years and current leaders are swept away. Mutuality is a powerful rallying point for critics who think that Islamic banking is indistinguishable from conventional capitalism, and it will become a constant prod demanding that the industry transform itself as well as its social environments.

The Permanent Revolution in Islamic Finance

As the core constituencies of Islamic finance expand, basic changes will also follow in who decides what is Islamic and in the criteria they use in making those judgments. The special authority of the financially literate 'ulama will gradually give way to the standardized knowledge of technocrats, business professionals and lawyers. All experts, religious and secular, will eventually lose influence as power shifts to transnational regulators, organized interest groups and impersonal markets. Educated Muslims in divergent cultural and political settings will make up their own minds about the Islamic credentials of alternative products, heeding their consciences and pocket-books ahead of the self-interested religious and business leaders that are competing for their savings.

The dispersion of decision-making will also erode the authority of traditional texts and historical practice. The future of Islamic finance will rely less on reinterpreting medieval jurisprudence and more on the bargaining of self-conscious social groups and their political representatives. Their compacts will rest on common understandings of Islam's eternal principles, not on hidebound rules and arcane categorizations whose rationales were forgotten centuries ago. In view of the rapidly changing balance of forces in most Muslim societies, those compacts will have to be renegotiated periodically, insuring that no version of Islamic finance will endure beyond a single generation.

The speedy rise of new classes and generations means that Islamic banking cannot pretend that it is a self-sufficient universe. Simultaneous revolutions in the global economy and the ummah are forcing Islamic finance to engage mass audiences of Muslims and non-Muslims with ever more creative and interactive strategies. Some of the most promising strategies have already gained traction in an impressive set of parallel movements: integrated financial services for the middle class, micro-lending to the poor, ethical investing and mutuality. The key question for the near future is not whether these forces will gain acceptance, but how much of the existing industry will be demolished by their wake.

Chapter 9

The Revolution in Islamic Finance

The development of Islamic banking simultaneously represents an expansion of the global financial system, a revival and re-adaptation of shari'a principles along a spectrum of cultures and polities, and a potential bridge across gaps that increasingly divide Muslims from one another and from other great civilizations. Islamic finance is a natural magnet for interdisciplinary and cross-cultural researchers. It stands at the intersections of law and economics and of religion and politics, both globally and nationally. In the fields of international and comparative law, it provides a particularly exciting laboratory for students of international regimes, legal and religious pluralism, and the cross-fertilization of Western and non-Western legal traditions.

Students of international law and politics will recognize the new regulatory architecture of Islamic finance as an international regime-in-the-making that is accepting direction from a more established yet still evolving global regime of banking regulators dominated by the industrialized nations of Europe and North America.[1] As these two regulatory systems interact, it will be intriguing to see how they influence one another. Islamic bankers are keen to win greater recognition and legitimacy in global financial circles, and they seem resigned to complying with the prevailing movements toward standardization, disclosure, and corporate governance. However, they also want to preserve distinctive religious values and identities, sparking constant debate over when convergence and harmonization might go too

[1] For comparative discussions of international regimes, see Underdal, Arild and Oran R. Young, eds. (2004). *Regime Consequences: Methodological Challenges and Research Strategies*, Dordrecht: Kluwer; Rosenau, James N. and Ernst-Otto Czempiel, eds. (1992). *Governance without Government: Order and Change in World Politics*, Cambridge: Cambridge University Press.

far. Non-Muslim bankers and regulators are increasingly attentive to such concerns, especially as "shari'a-compliant" arms of Western banks become powerful and innovative players in Islamic financial markets around the world. Both the global and the Islamic regulatory regimes have strong reasons to accommodate the other's sensitivities; compliance is becoming a two-way street, and each side has a vital stake in the other's rule-making processes.

If the crux of successful international regimes is institutionalizing trust and learning, then hopefully global finance and Islamic finance can strengthen their mutual regard and use it as an ongoing basis for solving common problems. Because many of those problems are ethical and human rather than merely technical and professional, the shared values of monotheism might help to support a productive dialogue. Western bankers are well aware that their industry leaders have shifted strategies from deregulation to re-regulation due to a wave of ethical and leadership failures that threatened the stability and integrity of the global financial system. Some leaders of the financial services industry are calling for broad reforms that would promote a more just and humane variety of world capitalism.[2] Similarly, Islamic banking is still recovering from its own crises, stemming from past scandals and from new fears of manipulation by terrorist groups. Its quest for transparency and uniform standards is also an effort to reset the moral compass that was supposed to guide Islamic finance all along.[3]

For students of legal and religious pluralism, Islamic finance exemplifies the Muslim world's continuing talent for mixing disparate traditions in an eclectic and dynamic synthesis. The theory and practice of Islamic economics supports more ambitious efforts to turn the shari'a into a living law that can help to shape social change for many

---

[2] For a recent example of capitalist auto-criticism see Bogle, John C. (2005). *The Battle for the Soul of Capitalism*, New Haven: Yale University Press.

[3] For critical overviews of the history of the Islamic financial services industry see Kuran, Timur (2004). *Islam and Mammon: The Economic Predicaments of Islamism*, Princeton: Princeton University Press; and Warde, Ibrahim (2010). *Islamic Finance in the Global Economy*, Edinburgh: Edinburgh University Press.

generations. Today, as in the past, the shari'a blends holy scripture and oral traditions with multiple styles of human interpretation. It constantly interacts with non-religious law from several sources, particularly local custom, state legislation, and a wide array of Western imports.[4] The rise of modern international law adds yet another factor to the equation, creating opportunities for a reinvigorated shari'a to influence developments far beyond Islam's historical heartlands.

Continued openness and flexibility in Islamic law are especially important as scholarly interest focuses on the problems of globalization and legal transplants. All cultures harbor suspicions that international law is the work of foreigners and that it clashes with some of their fundamental indigenous values. Adapting to international norms forces every society to re-examine its legal traditions in a critical manner, leading to the frequent assertion that most "systems" of law are hybrids that constantly struggle to reconcile multiple inheritances and borrowings.[5] From this perspective, the supposed incoherence of law in the Islamic world is a nearly universal reality that echoes the histories and contemporary predicaments of all societies. Seeing the shari'a and its tribulations not as an aberration of the "other," but as a variation on our own condition nudges us a bit closer to constructive conversation between civilizations.[6] This should be good news for liberal and

---

[4] On the composite and dynamic nature of Islamic law see Masud, Muhammad Khalid, Brinkley Messick, and David S. Powers, eds. (1996). *Islamic Legal Interpretation: Muftis and Their Fatwas*, Harvard: Harvard University Press; and Coulson, Noel J. (1969) *Conflicts and Tensions in Islamic Jurisprudence*, Chicago: University of Chicago Press.

[5] See, for example, Glenn, H. Patrick (2004). *Legal Traditions of the World: Sustainable Diversity in Law*, New York: Oxford University Press; and Snyder, Francis (1999). *Global Economic Networks and Global Legal Pluralism*, Florence: European University Institute.

[6] For examples of the comparative study of legal pluralism in the Islamic world see Yilmaz, Ihsan (2005). *Muslim Laws, Politics and Society in Modern Nation-States: Dynamic Legal Pluralisms in England, Turkey and Pakistan*, Aldershot: Ashgate; Dupret, Baudouin, Maurits Berger, and Laila al-Zwaini, eds. (1999). *Legal Pluralism in the Arab World*, Dordrecht: Kluwer.

cosmopolitan forces in every culture that refuse to allow fanatics and fundamentalists to dictate the global agenda.

Commercial interests from all religious backgrounds have a vested interest in holding the world together, and it is no surprise that global banking is emerging as an arena for cooperation between Muslim and Western business leaders even as their politicians and citizens seem to drift further apart. Western nations have many good reasons for encouraging the success of Islamic banking and smoothing its integration into a more stable global economy. Progress toward financial harmonization could pave the way for cooperation on other issues, including the far more contentious fields of politics and security.

Islamic finance will need all of the international assistance it can solicit because it is at a crossroads that will force the entire movement to reinvent itself. Five years from now, its landscape will be unrecognizable to the cluster of institutions and personalities that view themselves as today's unassailable industry leaders. This article examines mounting pressures that are driving the current revolution in Islamic finance. Islamic bankers must now adapt to simultaneous challenges on three fronts: integration with the global financial system; coordination with the leading international organizations of the Islamic world; and penetration of mass markets in dozens of countries with conflicting cultural, political, and economic conditions. To complicate matters, all of these audiences are moving targets, experiencing upheavals at least as profound as the metamorphosis of Islamic finance itself.

Integration with the Global Financial Order

The most urgent pressure on Islamic banks is the need to comply with the tighter regulatory provisions adopted by the Basel Committee on Banking Supervision of the Bank for International Settlements. The Basel Committee, created in 1974 by central bank governors of the Group of Ten nations, formulates broad supervisory standards and statements of best practice encouraging governments around the world to converge toward common approaches in banking regulation.[7] The new

[7] The Basel Committee now includes central banks from the G-10 countries (Belgium,

Basel Capital Accord ("Basel II") contains a package of tougher guidelines for assessing and controlling financial risk by 2008. Basel II's "three pillars" require larger capital reserves, tighter central bank supervision, and greater public disclosure of risk factors to financial markets.[8] Islamic banks have joined smaller Western financial institutions both in criticizing the new standards as favoring dominant mega-banks and in trying to negotiate special terms and later deadlines for implementation.

Islamic bankers realize that they have very little leverage in these negotiations because global regulators are determined to impose a measure of discipline on volatile markets in the wake of earlier scandals and failures. Several Western governments are also insisting that Islamic banks prove they have no connection with terrorists.[9] Under these

---

Canada, France, Germany, Italy, Japan, the Netherlands, Sweden, Switzerland, the United Kingdom and the United States), and representatives from Luxembourg and Spain. It meets four times a year, usually at the Bank for International Settlements in Basel, where its twelve member permanent Secretariat is located. It is an informal policy forum with no founding treaty and no power to issue binding regulations, but it has developed into the global standard-setting agency for bank supervision. For an overview of the history and operations of the Basel Committee see Bank for International Settlements, *About BIS*, available online at http://www.bis.org/about/index.htm (accessed 14 January 2013).

[8] See Bank for International Settlements, Basel Committee on Banking Supervision (2004). *Basel II: International Convergence of Capital Measurement and Capital Standards: A Revised Framework*, 4, available online at http://www.bis.org/publ/bcbs107.htm (accessed 14 January 2013); and Keefe, David (2004). Bringing Shariah and Basel into accord, *Global Risk Regulator Newsletter*, Jan., 2d Sec, 10, available online at http://www.globalriskregulator.com/archive/January2004-16.html (accessed 14 January 2013).

[9] See, for example, Kassem, Mahmoud and Anita Greil (2001). Islamic banking reputation suffers in wake of Sept. 11, *Dow Jones International News*, 5 November; and Taylor, John B. (2002). Introductory Remarks by John B. Taylor, Undersecretary for Intl Affairs, US Treasury, at the Islamic Finance 101 Seminar, US Treasury Dept, Washington, DC, April 26. Available online http://www.docstoc.com/docs/63576787/Introductory-Remarks-at-The-Islamic-Finance-101-Seminar-_26-April-02_ (accessed 14 January 2013).

conditions, Islamic banks have no choice but to comply with Basel II. Such compliance is certain to encourage greater consolidation nationally and regionally as more innovative institutions swallow up competitors, particularly those lacking local political protection.

Many in the Islamic financial community view higher international banking standards not as a threat, but as an opportunity to strengthen the moral and ethical principles that inspired their movement in the first place. The founders of Islamic economics always insisted that they were creating a more just alternative to modern capitalism, not a mere imitation with religious window dressing.[10] Their heirs are increasingly critical of would-be Islamic bankers who seem eager to play by Western rules and who claim to observe the shari'a's ban on lending money at interest while employing countless legal fictions and multiparty transactions that violate it in practice and spirit.[11]

The most powerful Muslim indictment of today's Islamic banking is that it has become addicted to legal formalism and contractual subterfuge while losing sight of the higher goals and intentions ("maqasid") that law and economics should promote.[12] They argue that

[10] Chapra, M. Umer (2004). Mawlana Mawdudi's contribution to Islamic economics, *Muslim World*, 93, pp. 163–180; and Ahmad, Khurshid and Zafar Ishaq Ansari, eds. (1979). *Islamic Perspectives: Studies in Honour of Mawlana Sayyid Abul A'la Mawdudi*, Markfield, Leicestershire: Islamic Foundation.

[11] See Siddiqi, Mohammad Nejatullah (2006). Shariah, economics and the progress of Islamic finance: The role of Shariah experts, *Seventh Harvard University Forum on Islamic Finance*, Harvard Law School, 21 April, available online at http://www.siddiqi.com/mns/Role_of_Shariah_Experts.htm (accesssed 14 January); and El-Gamal, Mahmoud A. (2004). "Interest" and the paradox of contemporary Islamic law and finance, *Fordham International Law Journal*, 27, 108–09.

[12] For an excellent critique of legal formalism in Islamic finance, see El-Gamal, Mahmoud A. (2005). Mutuality as an antidote to rent-seeking shari'a-arbitrage in Islamic finance, April, available online at http://ilovetheuae.com/2012/11/17/mutuality-as-an-antidote-to-rent-seeking-shariah-arbitrage-in-islamic-finance/ (accessed 14 January 2013).

Islam's core values abhor exploitation and extreme inequalities in wealth.[13] Muslim banks should not merely fall in line with global capitalism, they should help to humanize it. When international regulators demand greater honesty and disclosure genuine Islamic bankers should not just comply, they should *over-comply* because their religion holds them to a higher standard.[14]

Many commentators urge those in Islamic finance to add their voices to the chorus of Western reformers trying to build a new type of world capitalism that values social solidarity and egalitarianism. Several writers—Muslim and non-Muslim—have noted the common themes between Islamic economics and finance and certain well-established Western movements, including cooperative societies, credit unions, socially-conscious investment funds, green parties, educational endowments, and progressive Christianity.[15] In this vision, integrating Islamic banks into the global financial system can "Islamize" world capitalism at least as much as it Westernizes Muslim economic behavior.

---

[13] On the centrality of social justice in Islam, see Rahman, Fazlur (2009). *Major Themes of the Qur'an*, Chicago: University of Chicago Press; and Rahman, Fazlur (1970). Islam and social justice, *Pakistan Forum*, October–November 1970, available online at http://www.jstor.org/discover/10.2307/2568964?uid=3738992&uid=2129&uid=2&uid=70&uid=4&sid=21101529256813 (accessed 14 January 2013).

[14] For a critique of the "malfunction" of shari'a financial advising that fails to interpret Islamic "maqasid" in light of current circumstances, see Siddiqi (2006). Shariah, economics and the progress of Islamic finance: The role of Shariah experts (cited in note 11).

[15] Maurer, Bill (2005). *Mutual Life, Limited: Islamic Banking, Alternative Currencies, Lateral Reason*, Princeton: Princeton University Press; MacDonald, G. Jeffrey (2005). For investors with a conscience, options grow, *Christian Science Monitor*, 19 September; Shakespeare, Rodney (2006). An Islamic money supply as the means to integration, *Seventh Harvard University Forum on Islamic Finance*, Harvard Law School, 23 April. Available online at http://www.globaljusticemovement.net/articles/7HUF-IslamicFinance-rs-0603.htm (accessed 14 January 2013).

Coordinating with Islamic International Organizations

The Organization of Islamic Cooperation ("OIC," formerly named the Organization of the Islamic Conference) is the preeminent international organization in the Muslim world—the so-called United Nations of Islam. The OIC and its specialized agencies are responsible for setting and monitoring industry-wide standards for Islamic financial institutions. The Islamic Financial Services Board ("IFSB"), established in 2002, and the Accounting and Auditing Organization for Islamic Financial Institutions ("AAOIFI"), founded in 1991, are the key forums where central bankers, religious scholars, and Islamic banks negotiate uniform regulations and guidelines for Islamic finance in all of the OIC's fifty-seven member states. Both the IFSB and the AAOIFI were established with the assistance of the Islamic Development Bank, the OIC's principle financial organ.[16]

Their task is daunting. They must not only ensure compliance with the new global regime of Basel II, they must also coax religious advisors from divergent backgrounds to approve uniform rules and procedures that are compatible with the shari'a. "Basel compliance" is relatively straightforward compared to "shari'a compliance" because central bankers and national governments have the power and motivation to phase-in global regulations, but they seldom have either the religious authority or the political support needed to interpret and harmonize specialized and hotly contested matters of Islamic law.

Filling this power vacuum has created a bonanza for the "financial 'ulama"—a narrow class of Islamic scholars with a credible claim to knowledge of both classical shari'a and modern business practices. All institutions that provide or regulate Islamic financial services have a shari'a advisory board that reviews products and policies to ensure that they do not violate religious norms. Each institution is free

[16] See Organization of Islamic Cooperation website available online at http://www.oic-oci.org/ (accessed 14 January); Islamic Financial Services Board website available online at http://www.ifsb.org/ (accessed 14 January 2013); Accounting and Auditing Organization for Islamic Financial Institutions website available online at http://www.aaoifi.com/aaoifi/ (accessed 14 January 2013); Islamic Development Bank website available online at http://www.isdb.org/irj/portal/anonymous (accessed 14 January 2013).

to choose its own religious advisors and they, in turn, may refer to any sources and principles they regard as appropriate. Many 'ulama serve on multiple boards simultaneously. The same religious scholars frequently advise competing businesses, government regulators, private entrepreneurs, Muslim-run companies in their own regions, and non-Muslim-owned multinational corporations headquartered in Europe, North America, and the Far East.[17] The financial 'ulama often serve their clients not only as outside auditors, but also as permanent consultants or even as regular employees. These inherent conflicts of interest and temptations for self-dealing compromise advisors and clients alike. The OIC is racing to develop common ethical standards for shari'a advisory boards and to set up training programs that can staff these boards with certified experts in Islamic finance.[18] In time, these initiatives should mitigate the chaos and cynicism surrounding advisory boards by improving competence and honesty, but they will not stem the widening divergence of scholarly and public opinion on basic questions of doctrine and policy.

The OIC faces a dilemma in trying to promote uniform practices in Islamic financial centers that now span every continent and culture—the same regional rivalries that divide the Islamic business world also drive the struggle for power within the OIC itself. Doctrinal disputes over the suitability of new financial products frequently reflect economic competition between geographic and ethnic groups, particularly between Arabs and non-Arabs, between the Persian Gulf and Southeast Asia, and between majority-Muslim nations and the burgeoning Muslim diasporas in Europe and the Americas.

The OIC is no longer a preserve of the Arabian oil monarchies that created and funded it during the 1970s. Today it more accurately

---

[17] Concerning the financial and political connections of the 'ulama in several countries, see generally Henry, Clement M. and Rodney Wilson, eds. (2004). *The Politics of Islamic Finance*, Edinburgh: University of Edinburgh Press.

[18] See Abdel Karim, Rifaat Ahmed (2006). Address at *Islamic Financial Services Board 3d Summit on Aligning the Architecture of Islamic Finance to the Evolving Industry Needs*, Beirut, 17–18 May.

represents the Islamic world as a whole, where about 80 percent of the population is non-Arab. Three regional factions have worked out an explicit power-sharing formula in which OIC leadership rotates among Arab, Asian, and African blocks, and each faction presents separate reports and recommendations at plenary sessions.[19]

Similarly, the world of Islamic finance is becoming more pluralistic every day. Older centers such as Kuwait and Bahrain face innovative rivals in Kuala Lumpur and Singapore, Istanbul and Karachi, London and Geneva, and Los Angeles and Toronto. OIC regulators can go only so far in pressing for financial harmonization and uniformity before dissident groups decide to go their own way. Every nascent international regime has to be aware of its own limits,[20] and the OIC's Islamic finance agencies are no exception. Insisting on compliance with controversial standards could destroy the Islamic finance regime while aggravating the broader power struggle that is straining the OIC as a whole.

Penetrating Mass Markets

While the global expansion of Islamic finance presents many specific challenges, the most important challenge for Islamic bankers is to win wide acceptance in their own societies. Islamic finance is far more successful in spreading laterally across borders and cultures than in deepening its roots to serve the daily needs of ordinary savers and consumers. Although the genesis of Islamic banking was recycling petrodollars for conservative Arabian monarchies and millionaires, its future lies in more cosmopolitan societies where rising middle classes are

---

[19] Bianchi, Robert R. (2004). *Guests of God: Pilgrimage and Politics in the Islamic World*, New York: Oxford University Press, pp. 46–47.

[20] Concerning the compliance and enforcement dilemmas of international regimes, see Hasenclever, Andreas, Peter Mayer, and Volker Rittberger (1997). *Theories of International Regimes*, Cambridge, U.K.: Cambridge University Press; and Chayes, Abram and Antonia Handler Chayes (1995). *The New Sovereignty: Compliance with International Regulatory Agreements*, Cambridge, Massachusetts: Harvard University Press.

creating mass markets for home and auto loans, small business financing, educational and retirement savings, and individual investing.

New demand for Islamic financial services is springing from thousands of local communities worldwide, forcing bankers, regulators, and religious leaders to improvise solutions that best suit their unique circumstances.[21] Islamic finance has always been a fluid blend of business, politics, and religion, adapting to cultural differences and changing tastes. This tradition of flexibility and ingenuity will become increasingly indispensable as Islamic finance grows to reflect the diversity and vitality of Muslims around the globe.

If Islamic finance succeeds in tapping mass markets, its transformation will be both profound and unpredictable. Most of its potential customers have never seen a survey questionnaire or focus group. Many are willing to heed the advice of local 'ulama about the Islamic credentials of specific products and institutions, but younger, educated Muslims often prefer to make their own judgments, particularly when they think that scholarly opinion is divided, poorly informed, and tainted by self-interest.

The revolution in Islamic finance will be even more dramatic if the industry makes good on its hopes of appealing to non-Muslims. Islamic bankers who are spearheading the drive toward consumer finance are explicitly marketing their services to non-Muslims in pluralistic regions such as South and Southeast Asia, Africa, Europe, and America. Inevitably, the already porous lines between Islamic and conventional banking will be redrawn countless times in many different environments.[22]

Given this pervasive uncertainty, Islamic bankers have many opportunities to shape evolving norms and practices instead of merely

---

[21] See Chiu, Shirley, Robin Newberger, and Anna Paulson (2005). Islamic finance in the United States: A small but growing industry, *Chicago Fed Letter*, May; and Jaffer, Sohail, ed. (2005). *Islamic Retail Banking and Finance: Global Challenges and Opportunities*, London: Euromoney Books.

[22] Matthews, Owen (2005). How the west came to run Islamic banks, *Newsweek*, 31 October.

conforming to conditions imposed by regulators, politicians, and clients. The very youth and fragmentation of Islamic finance could become assets if the Islamic finance community encourages industry flexibility while negotiating new international regimes and alliances with both Muslims and non-Muslims.

Islamic Finance and the Democratization of Religious Thought

Muslims today are thinking for themselves in all matters of religion, particularly when they intersect with novel questions of economics, politics, and ethics. The world of Islamic finance is one of several laboratories where independent-minded Muslims are redefining the social implications of their faith, heeding their own consciences more than old-fashioned preachers and authoritarian governments. Most people are highly skeptical of efforts to discover which modern contracts are permitted and prohibited simply by looking to tradition. 'Ulama and self-anointed experts who claim such skills strain credulity.

Sacred texts and classical authorities can provide initial principles and helpful analogies, but they are silent on most of the critical choices of public policy and personal behavior facing contemporary world citizens. The shari'a has always been a predominantly human construction—multiple layers of interpretation and inconsistent applications that defy codification and monism. Educated Muslims in every walk of life are critically re-examining traditional teachings in light of modern science and local conditions, demolishing what little remains of the 'ulama's supposed monopoly on interpretive authority.[23]

The rapid democratization of Muslim thought will probably frustrate the OIC's campaign for uniformity and standardization in Islamic finance. The common law roots of the shari'a have made pluralism and change inevitable under any conditions, and those qualities will become even more valued as Islam achieves a truly universal

[23] Arkoun, Mohammed (2002). *The Unthought in Contemporary Islamic Thought*, London: Saqi; see, for example, Ajijola, Alhaji Adeleke Dirisu (1998). The problem of *'ulama*, in Charles Kurzman, ed, *Liberal Islam: A Sourcebook*, New York: Oxford University Press.

personality. OIC technocrats would be wise to wait and watch as a series of regional mass markets develop varying techniques for balancing the special mix of ethical and economic risks that permeate every aspect of Islamic finance. For harmonization to be successful it will have to be negotiated by regional market leaders and central banks, not imposed by a fledgling international agency.

The most difficult decisions for potential clients of Islamic banks are personal and subjective calculations of their level of comfort with uncertainty, both spiritual and financial. Each person is responsible for making a good-faith judgment in the face of divided authority and imperfect information. Every conscience must weigh the likelihood of error and its consequences for worldly fortunes as well as immortal souls.

The current range of religious opinion on Islamic finance provides many alternatives for people with varying tolerance for spiritual risk. The general consensus upholds the formal ban on interest despite frequent assertions that the Qur'an prohibits usury and exploitation rather than interest per se. There is also widespread agreement that simple loans are disfavored transactions that should be restructured as sales, leases, partnerships, or some combination of all three.[24]

All things being equal, partnerships are preferred because they are seen as promoting reciprocity and solidarity as well as entrepreneurship. Indeed, many regard Islamic profit-and loss-sharing agreements as precursors of modern venture capitalism. Sales are least preferred because historically they were used to disguise interest-bearing loans as markups and installment payments. Sales are still the most common type of Islamic financing, but shari'a advisory boards are increasingly adopting stricter rules to guard against sham transactions.[25]

---

[24] See generally El-Gamal, *Fordham International Law Journal*, 27 (cited in note 11); Thomas, Abdulkader, Stella El-Gamal (2005). *Fordham International Law Journal*, 27 (cited in note 11); Archer, Simon, Rifaat Ahmed Cox, and Bryan Kraty, eds. (2005). *Structuring Islamic Finance Transactions*, London: Euromoney (emphasis on chapters 3–5 on *mudaraba* and *musharaka*, on *murabaha*, and on *ijarah*).

[25] Abdel Karim, Rifaat Ahmed and Simon Archer (2002). *Islamic Finance: Innovation and Growth*, London: Euromoney.

Leases are usually seen as better than sales but not as meritorious as partnerships. Muslim and Western financial engineers have created a flock of leasing contracts that mimic nearly every product of conventional banking. Multinational banking consortia use leases as the keystones of many government-sponsored infrastructure projects, especially when their revenue streams and underlying assets can be securitized and sold in secondary markets.[26]

For a time, it appeared that disagreements over the more complex leasing projects would divide conservative Arabian and innovative Asian countries into irreconcilable factions of Islamic banking. The core difference between their views concerned the propriety of selling debt instruments at discounts—a practice that traditionalist ‘ulama view as disguised interest and that most financial professionals regard as a precondition for creating secondary markets and liquidity. In the last few years, however, there has been a remarkable rapprochement between these camps, and commentators on each side have adopted intermediate positions that once seemed inconceivable. For example, Malaysian writers acknowledge the need to defer to Persian Gulf sensibilities in order to attract more foreign investment while Saudi scholars are openly advocating the creation of futures and derivatives markets that would be shari‘a-compliant.[27]

---

[26] For examples of complex leasing arrangements that have been deemed shari‘a-compliant see Obaidullah, Mohammed (2005). *Islamic Financial Services*, Abdulaziz University, pp. 79–88; and Esty, Benjamin C. (2000). The Equate project: An introduction to Islamic project finance, *Journal of Structured Finance*, 5:4, 7–20, available online at http://www.iijournals.com/doi/abs/10.3905/jsf.2000.320197 (accessed 14 January 2013).

[27] Al-Saati, Abdul Rahim (2002). Shar’ia compatible futures, *Journal of King Abdulaziz University: Islamic Economics*, 15: 3; and Rosly, Saiful Azhar and Mahmood M. Sanusi (1999). The application of bay’ al-‘inah and bay’ al-dayn, in Malaysian Islamic bonds: An Islamic analysis, *International Journal of Islamic Financial Services*, 1:1, July–September.

This cross-fertilization and mutual learning suggests that the current pressure for OIC standardization of shari'a norms is premature. Islamic bankers and national regulators are doing precisely what they need to do—listening to their markets and to one another, and altering their repertoire of services accordingly. The future of Islamic finance rests not with an international technocracy or a central committee of handpicked religious advisors, but with millions of Muslim and non-Muslim clients who will examine their consciences and pocketbooks in voting for a range of competing approaches to their constantly changing needs and identities.

Increasing competition will force the new Islamic finance to become more consolidated, but also more diversified to suit regional and cultural tastes. The spread of the Internet and electronic banking will empower clients to mix and match services from many institutions regardless of location and investment style. Rising middle classes in Muslim societies, overseas workers, and diaspora communities will create global financial networks criss-crossing nations, sects, and languages. The growing participation of non-Muslims as managers, partners, and clients will spark recurrent debates about the core meaning and purpose of Islamic finance and its contributions to humanity. And these debates will bring Muslims back to the same questions they have been pondering since the birth of Islam: How do they forge a universal identity inspired by eternal ideals while adapting to new realities and ancient divisions?

Chapter 10

Islamic Finance and the International System: Integration without Colonialism

As Islamic financial institutions develop in strength and scope, they interact more frequently with governments and conventional financial structures as well as multinational enterprises and international organizations. The emerging Islamic network and the international system are reshaping one another at the same time that together they are transforming the world economy. Because both Islamic and conventional institutions are struggling to reinvent themselves in an uncertain global environment, the most likely future is not the simple "domestication" of burgeoning Islamic practices by Western-dominated structures, but an improvised series of reciprocal influences and mutual adaptations that could evolve into an intentional process of collective learning and cooperation. This essay will explore the possibilities for integrating Islamic finance into a more open network of multicultural structures capable of promoting global growth and equity, highlighting what international lawyers and international relations theorists have described as the emergence of "international regimes" and "transnational civil society."

The Kozlowski-Bin Laden Effect: From the Washington Consensus to Basel II and SOX

Efforts to integrate Islamic finance into the world economy coincide with a time of crisis and soul searching when our most powerful business leaders are wondering if capitalism has lost its way and if they can save it from its own excesses. Regulation has been reborn even if we prefer to call it "self-regulation" and this incarnation promises to be truly universal—embracing nation-states and international organizations as well as global banks and conglomerates and transnational associations of professionals, investors, and consumers on all continents.

The new mindset is a stunning departure from the triumphant liberalism of the Washington consensus that heralded the collapse of the Soviet Union with categorical endorsements of deregulation, privatization, and free trade. Today the same power centers have fashioned an ambitious interventionism around the mantras of "capital adequacy," "risk assessment," "transparency," and "corporate governance." Instead of celebrating "market freedom," they stress "market discipline;" instead of relying on the "invisible hand" they call for compliance with "core principles" and "codes of conduct" reinforced with the threat of sanctions and prosecution.

The burgeoning ethos of re-regulation spearheaded by the Basel Capital Accords and the Sarbanes-Oxley Act follows two decades of financial failures and ethical abuses that have redrawn our cognitive map of global business, exposing the ubiquity of "managers' capitalism," "corporate kleptocracy," and "offshore underworlds." The line between banking and crime seems thinner than ever—not merely in the unfamiliar realms of Islamic finance and "Islamic" terrorism, but at the very heart of the most respectable business circles in Europe and North America.

Business Is Business and a Dollar Isn't What It Used To Be

As conventional banking seeks to integrate Islamic finance into a more centrally regulated global economy, it is also adopting a business model that more closely resembles the ideals if not the practices of Muslim investors. International banks are moving away from their traditional reliance on lending money at interest toward a wide array of fee-based services geared to managing risks and earning returns on assets. The rise of a more integrated financial services industry has lowered the old barriers between providers and consumers of capital, encouraging quasi-partnerships where risks and returns are shared instead of compartmentalized. The greater prominence of investment banking and venture capital alliances brings conventional finance closer to the Islamic view that merchant banking is a higher calling than bankrolling merchants.

In fact, Western bankers and lawyers have proven to be some of the most astute innovators of Islamic finance. By engineering new shari'a-compliant products and orchestrating multinational mega-deals with important Islamic participation, they have spurred a broad interpenetration of Muslim and Western financial networks and set the stage for their eventual integration in a unitary international system. The nodes and building blocks of that system are already well established in close working relationships between technocrats, business people, and professionals that link Europe and North America with the Middle East and Asia. The upper echelons of the modern financial community comprise an increasingly distinct segment of transnational civil society—a universe of its own beyond nation and culture, based on common training and on socialization to professional norms that grow more explicit and binding each year.

Will Westerners Take Over Islamic Finance?

Islamic banking and investment have probably passed the point were the global economy can allow them to fail or to go their separate way. Regulators are on the rise, determined to pull in the reins on ever more unstable world markets, and the Islamic markets are no exception. Yet there is no more certain way to destroy the Islamic financial experiment than to subordinate it to non-Muslims. If foreigners try to control Islamic institutions too much or too directly, the entire sector can be stigmatized in the eyes of its own supporters, particularly those who are already skeptical about overblown marketing that appeals to religion for profit.

Islamic finance can only be brought into a global regulatory net by Muslim regulators—not by anonymous agencies headquartered in Christian countries or by "helal windows" attached to mansions built by riba. The pivotal actors in this process are the Central Banks of the Islamic world. They alone possess the expertise, authority, and connections needed to fashion the alliances—nationally, regionally, and globally—that can pull Islamic finance together and negotiate its future in an increasingly volatile world economy.

The 'ulama are an indispensable if often difficult partner in any coalition that financial technocrats seek to lead. Collectively, the 'ulama act as gatekeepers ever mindful of their power—and their sacred duty—to quicken social innovation, to question it or to kill it altogether.

Regulators and bankers are eager to enlist the ‘ulama’s legitimacy and expertise, but they are equally determined to prevent religious leaders from exercising an effective veto. Thus, most of the Shari‘a Advisory Boards that review new financial products and contracts are ad hoc committees of handpicked ‘ulama who frequently serve alongside academics, entrepreneurs, and politically connected bureaucrats.

The ‘Ulama and the Accounting Firms: Probity Versus Sorcery

The growing—and prospering—cadre of “financial ‘ulama” face the classic predicament of the would-be auditor who also tries to serve as an inside consultant. The inherent conflicts of interest are obvious and potentially fatal to client and professional alike. Indeed, it was precisely the implosion of the great accounting houses-turned-consulting firms and the big banks-turned-brokers that helped to launch the current wave of regulatory zeal sweeping both conventional and Islamic finance. Ironically, some of today’s most illustrious financial ‘ulama are building multifunctional professional practices just when the disgraced accounting and banking giants are severing such ties and trying to reclaim their shattered niches.

Although the ‘ulama are under mounting criticism for their inconsistent rulings on several controversial issues, their decentralized case-by-case approach gives Islamic finance remarkable flexibility in developing multiple markets in widely separated regions and cultures. It is much too soon to restrict the spirited debate over proper forms of financial innovation, particularly when the conversation is sparking borrowing and cross-fertilization among Muslims worldwide. Islamic finance is still germinating in many countries and fields. Its institutions are constantly reinventing themselves and most of its future client base has never seen a survey questionnaire or a focus group.

One of the most insightful commentators on Islamic finance opines that the ‘ulama opportunistically engage in “shari‘a arbitrage.” Mahmoud A. El-Gamal identifies the paradox of contemporary Islamic law and finance in the ‘ulama’s willingness to denounce the interest-based operations of conventional banks while simultaneously blessing Muslim-run institutions that mimic their services in all but name.

Professor El-Gamal correctly notes that the 'ulama are very similar to arbitragers because they take advantage of disparities between separate markets—in this case legal as well as economic markets—that do not share common rules and information. Criticizing the inconsistency and hypocrisy that threaten the credibility of the entire field, he urges that Islamic finance must achieve greater coherence and uniformity before it can expect broad support from Muslims let alone acceptance under international standards.

On the same evidence, however, I would suggest the opposite conclusion—instead of eliminating shari'a arbitrage, let it proceed until it does its job. Let the 'ulama continue to endorse an array of practices with variable claims to shari'a compliance, encourage entrepreneurs to offer competing baskets of services, and give citizens in the emerging markets a voice in the outcome. Instead of insisting that conformity with the shari'a is an all or nothing proposition, view it as a probability—and a risk—of being "more or less Islamic." Let the 'ulama lead the way in assessing those risks initially, but invite the entire umma to participate in an admittedly imperfect and open-ended process that is bound to change over time and adapt to local circumstances.

Shari'a arbitrage helps to segment the market for Islamic financial services by permitting individuals to choose among alternative practices depending on their preferences in balancing moral virtue and economic utility. Decision-makers can assess the probabilities and degrees of shari'a compliance for various solutions and choose according to their tolerance of the recognized risks—both spiritual and material. No one will expect consensus on the propriety of specific decisions, but everyone can appreciate the need to respect personal differences in matters of conscience where sincere intention may be our only guide.

This sort of market segmentation is already quite advanced concerning the basic building blocks of Islamic financial practice. A common way to avoid the appearance of charging interest is to structure a loan as though it were another type of transaction—a sale (murabaha), a lease (ijara), or a partnership (mudaraba). However, there is widespread agreement that these three approaches are not equally satisfactory. Many authorities and practitioners believe that a sale is often a loan in disguise, that a partnership is distinct in form and superior in purpose, and that a lease is somewhere in between a sale and a partnership. Legally and morally, all three arrangements are permissible, yet the pecking order is clear—a lease is better than a sale and partnership is the best of the lot.

This is essential information for Muslim rational actors. It gives them the freedom to mix and match an assortment of pre-approved contracts according to their self-defined preferences. It also allows businesses and consumers to "vote for" the competing Islamic approaches that best suit their changing needs so that markets arise from popular demand instead of legal fiat.

This sort of market segmentation will inevitably erode the power of the 'ulama as their limited knowledge becomes just one of many factors influencing collective decisions. Globalization and the information revolution are probably diluting the authority of all experts and it is hard to imagine how religious scholars could escape the trend. Many decision-making theorists claim that expert monopolies are already giving way to "smart crowds" and "qualified groups" with free access to current research and informed opinion on nearly every aspect of daily life. In fact, the emerging orthodoxy assures us that a modern mass usually makes more accurate judgments than an old-fashioned specialist. If so, then today's shari'a arbitragers may be digging their own graves by nurturing Islamic markets and electorates that can act as rival sources of consensus in the future.

When Is There Too Much Convergence and Harmonization?

These ruminations lead me to conclude that the current campaign to standardize Islamic finance is premature. The current patchwork of law and practice might seem chaotic at times, but is it any worse than the incoherence of the common law before the advent of the Uniform Commercial Code? Perhaps we should disaggregate our regulatory thinking about Islamic finance, focusing more on the "financial" than the "Islamic." It is far more important for the industry to adopt internationally accepted standards of good business than to pursue a phantom of religious perfection. Islamic institutions that toe the universal ethical line today will have ample opportunity to agree on more specialized and idealistic norms tomorrow.

Building an international regime to manage Islamic finance will require a step-by-step strategy that puts global compliance ahead of shari‘a compliance. Regulators should firmly push the industry toward adopting evolving rules of capital adequacy, disclosure, and corporate governance. However, they should also provide a neutral venue where industry leaders can continue their contentious debates over sensitive questions of religious law with no immediate pressure to produce binding decisions. Delay in adopting new world standards would make the regime irrelevant, but any effort to homogenize a pluralistic legal tradition would blow the regime apart. In shari‘a matters, international regulators need to enmesh industry representatives from all countries and branches in an ongoing bargaining process that they can gradually embrace as a home of their own making and a symbol of their common fate.

International Regimes and Transnational Civil Societies

The core of the new Islamic financial regime is already up and running. The Organization of the Islamic Conference—the so-called United Nations of the Islamic world—launched the Islamic Financial Services Board in 2002 and the Accounting and Auditing Organization for Islamic Financial Institutions in 1991. These standard setting bodies inherit both the authority and the political problems of the entire OIC framework. Like all successful regimes, this one will need to juggle multiple functions simultaneously—mediator and arbitrator, monitor and enforcer, information broker and debate umpire. Above all, it must earn recognition from both members and global interlocutors as the interest aggregator extraordinaire for a sprawling and poorly understood economic powerhouse.

The vigorous beginning of the IFSB is encouraging, but we should be realistic in assessing the pervasive power struggles that will shape its agenda and hamper its effectiveness. Two examples, one national and the other international, are particularly worrisome—political infighting in the Central Bank of Malaysia and regional rivalries shaking the OIC edifice as a whole.

The Shari'a Advisory Board of Malaysia's Central Bank is a classic study in balance of power politics that descended into factional infighting and sudden purge. In its early years, the board reflected a professional and partisan coalition assembling 'ulama, academics, and bureaucrats connected to rival wings of the ruling party that were led by former Prime Minister Mohammad Mahathir his one-time lieutenant Anwar Ibrahim. Mahathir's campaign to disgrace and imprison Anwar influenced every corner of public life in Malaysia and the shari'a board was no exception. Pro-Anwar members were dropped and a rump assembly of Mahathir loyalists ran matters for several years until Abdullah Badawi became Prime Minister and filled the vacancies with his own nominees.

Simultaneous scandals at Tabung Haji—a world pioneer in both Islamic banking and pilgrimage management—further tarnished the industry's reputation. If Malaysia expects to remain a pacesetter in Islamic finance instead of becoming a mere outlier, it can hardly afford exposing official shari'a bodies to political cronyism, especially when the "Islamic" opposition party is systematically shut out of the discussion. The Malaysian drama is far from unique; shari'a boards in all countries and institutions are susceptible to similar pressures and they need to adopt more convincing safeguards of their independence and integrity.

The OIC reflects even deeper conflicts on a far grander scale. Mounting demands for OIC reform show that the uneasy balance between Arab, Asian, and African blocks is giving way to an open battle for control pitting the once dominant Gulf kingdoms against the most dynamic and ambitious non-Arab members led by Turkey, Pakistan, Malaysia, and Indonesia. This is a far-reaching power struggle likely to continue for decades. It is impossible to predict the implications for Islamic finance, but the smart money will probably wager on growing influence for the eclectic experiments of Asia and Europe at the expense of the lingering attachment to formalism in the Gulf.

Most of the OIC reform proposals circulating these days strive for a stronger Islamic voice in the United Nations system. If adopted, they could also bolster the Islamic finance regime in negotiating with members and non-members alike. Nonetheless, one proposal stands out as a terrible idea—establishing a shari'a super court to issue final and binding decisions in the name of Islam. Similar plans have been floated in the OIC for years and each time they have failed. There is no place for an Islamic Sanhedrin. We already have a World Court—the International Court of Justice associated with the United Nations. We should all be strengthening that tribunal instead of tinkering with knock-offs that have no future.

III: Democracy and Islamic Modernism

Chapter 11

Egypt's Revolutionary Elections

Egypt's parliamentary elections of 2011 and 2012 were revolutionary in several ways. They followed a historic mass uprising that broke the back of the military regime that had ruled the country for 60 years. In that sense, they were post-revolutionary events that helped a still shaken society to settle down and regain its footing. However, as we grasp the extraordinary scope of voter participation and the dramatic power shifts it unleashed, we realize that the elections continued and deepened the revolution—indeed, that they came to embody the revolution and reveal more fully its profound implications for social as well as political change. And if we consider the uprisings and the elections together, it is even more evident that Egypt's revolution has just begun. The closer we examine the voting patterns as well as the partisan alliances and counter-alliances, the more we understand that in district after district—in city, town, and countryside—Egypt's divisions and dreams were everywhere on display with a poignancy and desperation that we have never before seen so clearly and that we will learn to expect as commonplace in the near future and for many years to come.

Voters and candidates from all regions and persuasions showed enormous sophistication and pragmatism in using their new freedom and power. Through multiple rounds of choosing between shifting combinations of programs and personalities, they decided how best to reward friends and punish enemies even when the final alternatives seemed unappealing or downright loathsome. In constantly weighing and re-weighing second-best and third-best choices, they often had to compromise and share power with rival groups both locally and nationally. Adversaries in one district frequently became allies in other races in which they faced stronger enemies that could only be defeated with common efforts. Even when no formal nationwide coalitions existed, candidates brokered tacit pacts district-by-district, contest-by-contest, and round-by-round throughout the three month election marathon.

The pluralism and fluidity of electoral competition exposed all of Egypt's worst cleavages—class, religious, and regional animosities that authoritarian rulers had smothered and manipulated for three generations with little opportunity for genuine representation or independent negotiation. At the same time, however, the elections also revealed some striking and encouraging resources among Egypt's new political elite, particularly a talent for compromise and an appetite for cooperation that could be indispensible in its efforts to draft a new constitution and to manage a contentious era of coalition government.

Nationwide Alignments of the Major Parties

A handful of parties dominated the elections (see Appendix A). The top six parties won 93 percent of the total vote and the top four won 88 percent (see Appendix C). Only the Muslim Brotherhood's Freedom and Justice Party (FJP) demonstrated anything approaching nationwide coverage. The Salafist Nur Party, the Wafd, and the newly formed Egyptian Block enjoyed strong support in regional bastions, but not beyond. The Wasat Party of "centrist" Muslims and The Revolution Continues Party of Tahrir Square youth leaders turned in disappointing performances even by their own accounts (see Appendix D).

The deepest partisan cleavages by far were the common antipathy to Nur and to the remnants of the National Democratic Party (see Table 11.1). Everyone ran against the old regime, but their ancient hatred for Mubarak was soon exceeded by their growing fear of the Islamic radicals. And as Nur became the universal adversary, the Ikhwan became the preferred firewall for liberals, both secular and religious, who sought to protect Egypt's democratic experiment against twin authoritarian threats—from the plots of disgraced elites eager for revenge and from the smoldering fury of the poor who were no longer invisible. Overall Ikhwan support had no strong negative correlation to vote for either the Wafd or the Egyptian Block; all three parties were more opposed to Nur than to one another.

Table 11.1. Intercorrelations between votes for major parties in party list districts (Pearson's r's, N = 46).

	Wafd	FJP	EB	NDPs	Seculars
Nur	**-.3346**	**-.3969**	**-.4499**	**-.4786**	**-.8447**
Wafd		-.0569	**-.2879**	.1664	**.3270**
FJP			.0781	-.1767	-.1560
EB				-.0824	**.4412**
NDPs					**.6181**

Note: The correlation coefficient is a measure of the degree to which two variable's movements are associated statistically but not necessarily causally. The Pearson product-moment coefficient (r) ranges in value from a minimum of -1.000 (signifying a perfect negative relationship) to a maximum of 1.000 (signifying a perfect positive relationship). A coefficient of 0.000 indicates no statistical relationship. N signifies the number of cases in the calculation.[1]
Source: Author.

The Ikhwan used their pivotal position to maximum advantage in playing off Nur against secular rivals. Where FJP candidates were strong, they went head-to-head against Nur and everyone else. Where they were weak and Nur was strong, they joined forces with secular parties to undercut Nur. And when both Muslim parties were weak, they worked out a division of labor by running in separate districts so that they could pool pro-Muslim voters in tight races.

The conflicts between liberal and radical Muslims were matched by equally sharp divisions among secular parties with rival social and economic interests (see Figure 11.1). The Egyptian Block's more urban and Christian supporters were worlds apart from the Wafd's more rural and Muslim followers. Wafd leaders could not make up their minds about which alliances they wanted to pursue. They flirted with the Ikhwan and then abandoned them. They resented the new money and quick success of the Egyptian Block while fuming over the Coptic Church's open appeal for Christians to support their own party instead of falling in line behind the well-worn Wafdist slogans of sectarian harmony and national unity. In the end, Wafdist candidates cut deals in

[1] For more complete descriptions and illustrations, see Hubert M. Blalock, *Social Statistics* (New York: McGraw-Hill, 1965); Hayward Alker, *Mathematics and Politics* (New York: Macmillan, 1979); and R. Mark Sirkin, *Statistics for the Social Sciences* (Thousand Oaks, CA: Sage, 2005).

all directions depending on their needs in each district. Their penchant for teaming up with former Mubarak loyalists usually backfired, leaving the Wafd's already squabbling factions even more reasons to blame one another for their collective failures.[2]

Map 11.1. Egypt.

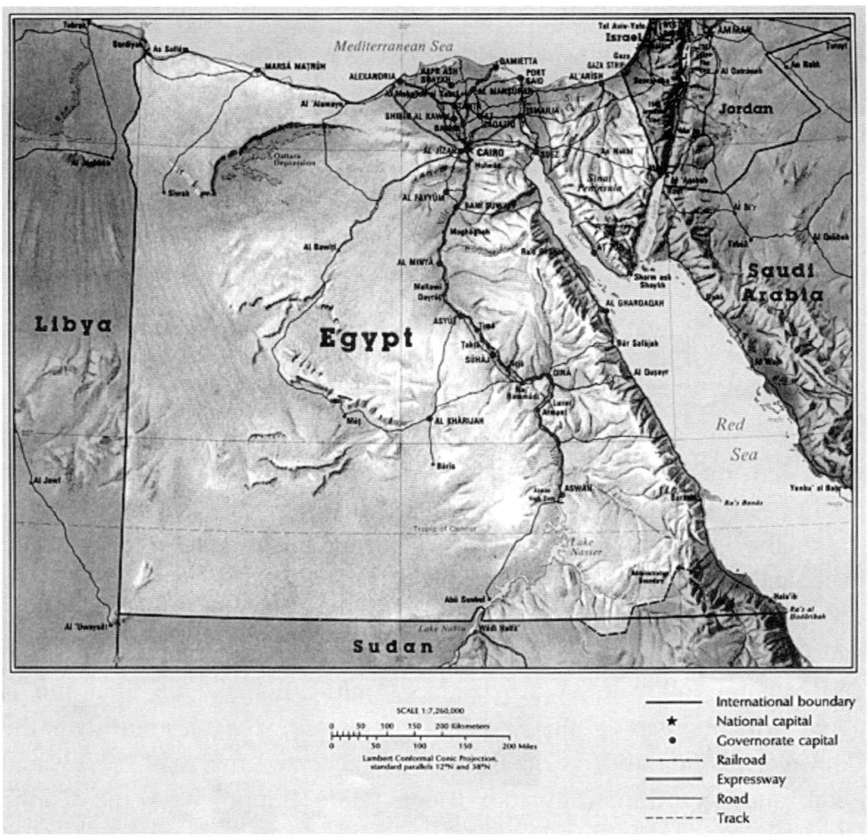

Source: University of Texas Libraries.

[2] Hussein, Abdel-Rahman (2011). After Crushing Defeat, Wafd Wonders What's Next, *Al-Masry Al-Youm*, 8 December; *Al Masry Al Youm*, Al-Wafd yurad 'ala al-Kutla: Hasalna 'ala 15 muqa'da wa haqaqtum 8 faqat (The Wafd Responds to the Egyptian Block: We Won Fifteen Seats and You Got Only Eight), 19 December.

Figure 11.1. Tacit alliance of Islamic and secular liberals versus Salafis and NDP remnants.

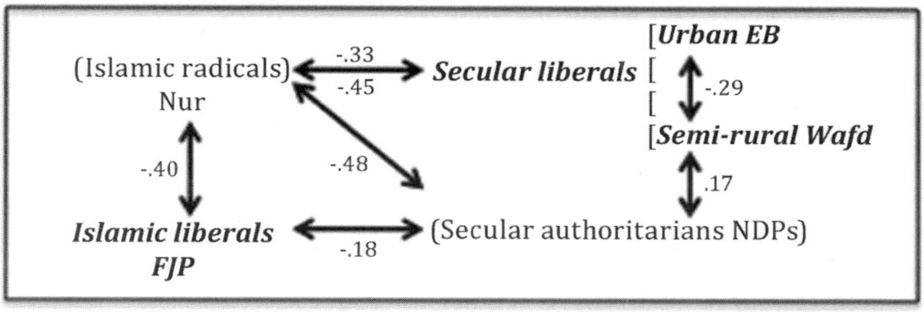

Key: Arrows indicate the most important correlations between votes for the major parties. Numbers indicate the strength of relationships measured by Pearson's r.
Source: Author.

Key Match-ups between Parties in Local Districts

A third of parliament—166 members—was elected from small local districts where candidates needed to win a majority of all votes cast. In all but a handful of cases, this required two rounds of polling in which the two largest vote getters from the first round faced one another in a decisive run-off election. Sore losers had ample opportunity to get even by ganging up against front-runners and rival insurgents frequently joined forces to defeat local big wigs. Many run-offs were decided by razor-thin margins and turnout rates were always lower than in the first round of voting. Under these conditions, party leaders could trade support in several contests at once, particularly in the same district and governorate. Party loyalists quickly got the message and responded by shifting their second round votes to tip the balance in the preferred direction.

Three groups dominated these winner-take-all races (see Figure 11.2). More than 40 percent of the contests pitted the FJP against Nur and another 19 percent paired the FJP with NDP successors. The remaining battles involved the FJP or Nur and a secular party. Only four percent of the elections were decided between finalists who were neither FJP nor Nur candidates.

Figure 11.2. Party match-ups in contests for individual seats.

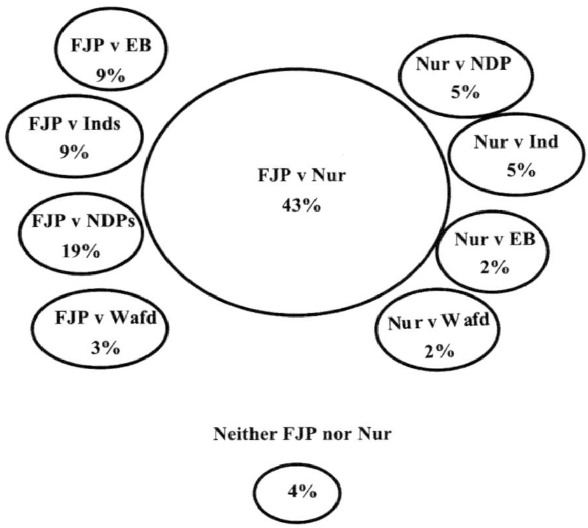

Source: Author.

The Ikhwan feasted on these races. They won 80 percent of the individual seat elections that they contested, divided evenly between victories over Nur and over the secular parties (see Figure 11.3). FJP candidates defeated Nur rivals in three-fourths of their confrontations and they were even more successful against opponents from the Egyptian Block and the NDP successor groups. The Ikhwan was the only group that performed more effectively in single-district races that required absolute majorities than in the party-list contests in which seats were shared according to proportional representation. In the new Egyptian Parliament, the FJP accounts for about 47 percent of all elected members, but it controls 66 percent of the winner-take-all seats compared to less than 40 percent of the party-list seats.

Nur also had reason to celebrate after its stunning successes in local races in every part of the country. Nur won over two-thirds of the contests it entered against all of the secular parties. Even when the Ikhwan defeated Nur, it was often in a photo finish in which all other parties ganged up to push back a first-round surge by the Salafis (see Figure 11.4). Nearly one half of the FJP-Nur battles were decided by margins of ten percent or less—an extraordinary achievement in view of the clear mismatch between the two parties' organizational resources and political experience (see Figure 11.5). Nur leaders came away from the district elections knowing that they had connected with marginalized voters everywhere and confident that they were breathing down the Ikhwan's neck.

Figure 11.3. FJP and Nur success rates in contests for individual district seats.

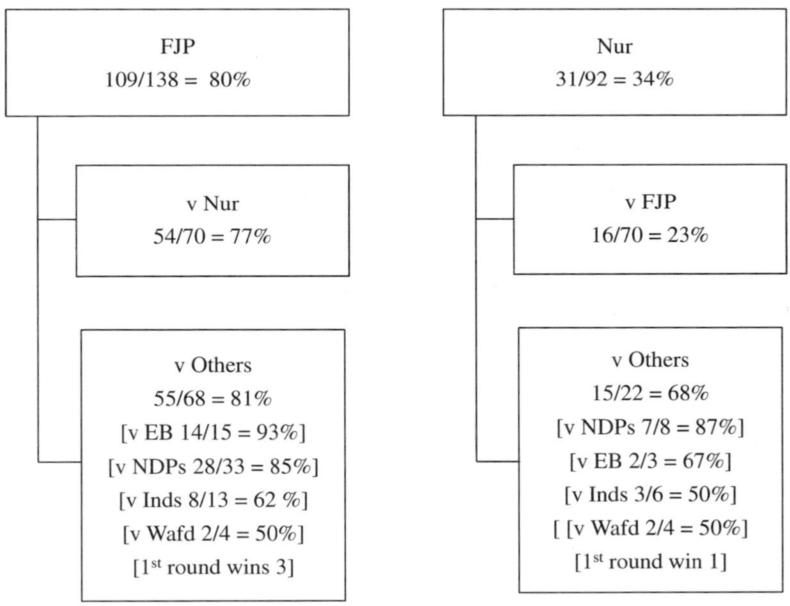

Source: Author.

Figure 11.4. FJP margins of victory in face-offs with Nur for 70 individual district seats.

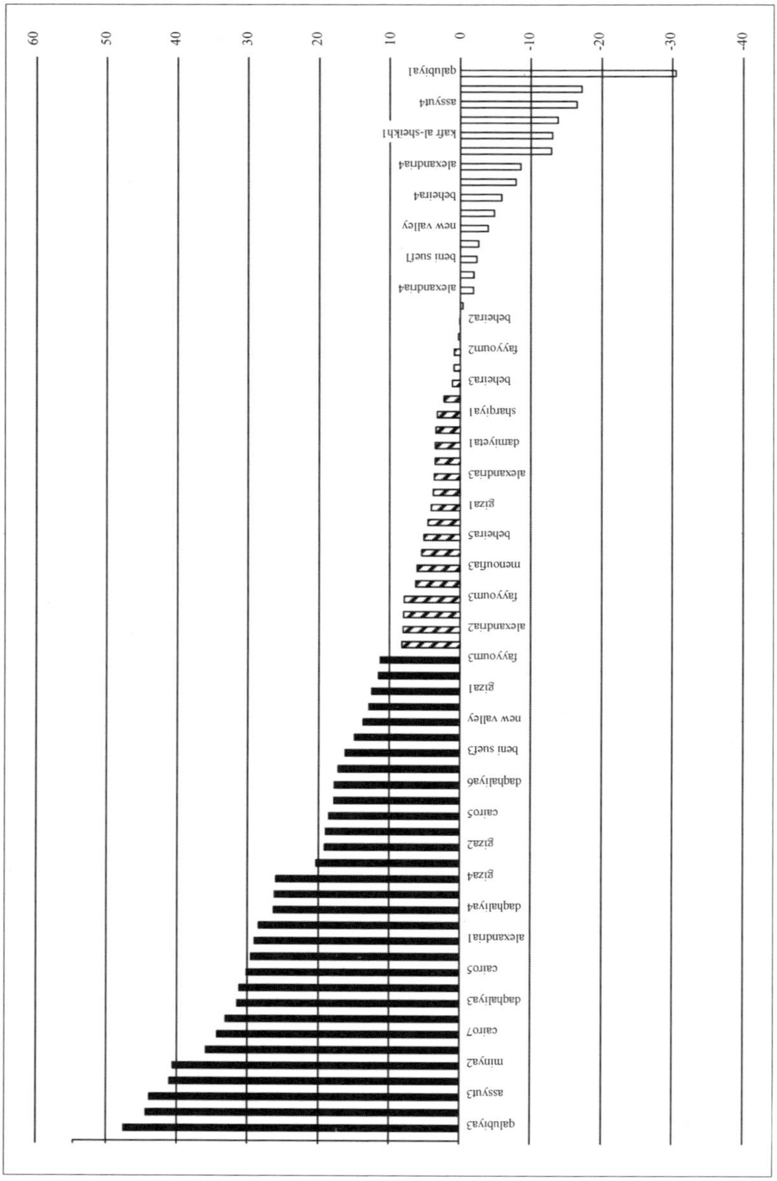

Source: Author.

Figure 11.5. Margins of victory in FJP and Nur competition for 70 individual district seats.

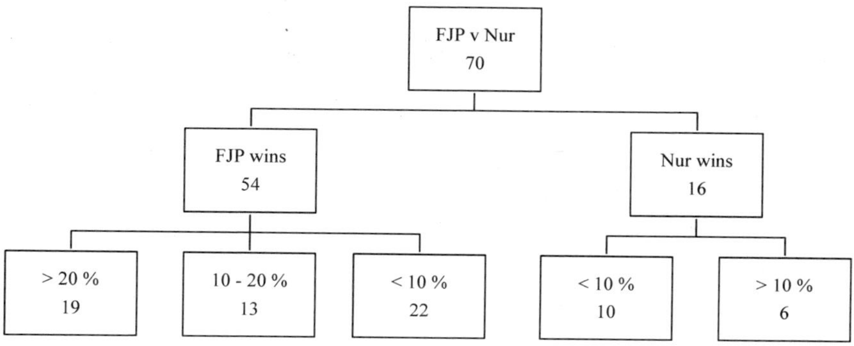

Source: Author.

Four Arenas of Social Struggle—Class and Religious Conflicts in Urban and Rural Districts

While the Ikhwan and Nur competed for pro-Muslim support, the Wafd and the Egyptian Block battled for third place by appealing to more secular-minded voters. The Ikhwan-Nur rivalry and the Wafd-Egyptian Block quarrels were the two most dominant partisan cleavages in the nation as a whole. Viewing voter alignments along these two overriding dimensions, we can see the relative strength of each party in different regions and among various demographic groups. Figure 11.6 plots margins of victory in FJP versus Nur contests against margins of victory in Wafd versus Egyptian Block races in the 46 party list districts, classifying districts into four regional groupings—the big cities (Cairo, Giza, and Alexandria), the Nile Delta, Upper Egypt, and the Canal Zone and border areas.

The Ikhwan and Nur competed in rallying Muslim farmers and wage-earners against the provincial elites (*'ayan*) led by the Wafd and its NDP allies.[3] Nur focused on poorer farmers and agricultural workers

[3] Binder, Leonard (1978). *In a Moment of Enthusiasm: Political Power and the Second Stratum in Egypt*, Chicago: University of Chicago Press.

while the Ikhwan appealed to small farmers who worked their own lands and to the struggling middle classes in the provincial towns and capitals. At the same time, the Ikhwan and Nur also coordinated battles against Egyptian Block efforts to mobilize Christian voters. In these races, the Ikhwan keyed on the big cities while Nur concentrated on rural and small town districts.

Figure 11.6. Class and religious conflicts in urban and rural districts (Margins of victory in FJP v Nur contests and in Wafd v Egyptian Block contests).

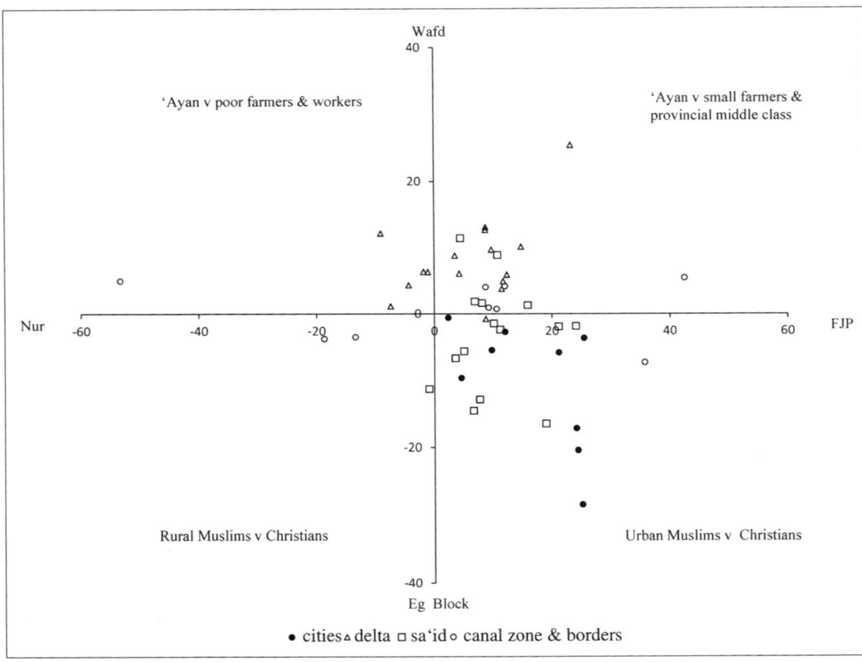

Source: Author.

For example, in the party list contests of the Nile Delta (triangles), the districts cluster in two zones of conflict—struggles between local notables and middle income townsfolk (the top right quadrant) and battles between local notables and lower class rural groups (the top left quadrant). The FJP led the challenge against the *'ayan* in the more urban districts of the Delta whereas Nur carried the battle in the more rural areas. In contrast, districts in the big cities (filled circles) cluster in zones of conflict between Muslims and Christians (the lower right quadrant). The FJP surpassed Nur in all of these districts, but Nur performed much better in Giza and Alexandria than in Cairo.

Class tensions and religious tensions encouraged different patterns of partisan conflict. When economic and class divisions were salient, the Ikhwan and Nur mobilized separate sources of social discontent—with more urban and middle income groups favoring the Ikhwan and with rural and marginalized voters supporting Nur. When Christian-Muslim tensions were salient, Nur spearheaded pro-Muslim sentiments in the countryside whereas the Ikhwan took the lead in the big cities and provincial capitals. On the class front, the main targets of the Ikhwan and Nur were fellow Muslims who benefited most from the old regime—Wafdist landlords and their NDP partners. On the religious front, the chief opponent was the nexus of Coptic churchmen and Egyptian Block entrepreneurs that sought to represent Christians of all classes in both the cities and the countryside.

Muslim voters were deeply divided by class and economic interests whereas Christians were more inclined to rally around the banner of religious solidarity. Muslims split between three parties that represented not only rival religious views but also competing class coalitions—the privileged notables of the Wafd, the middle class moderates of the Ikhwan, and the fire-eating Salafis who claimed to speak for the voiceless. Christian voters, on the other hand, were more receptive to religious appeals, sensing a unique opportunity to establish a separate political base and facing stronger pressures from radical Muslim candidates. By supporting a single new party despite their profound social and regional differences, Christian voters were effectively declaring political independence from the Muslim-dominated parties—

both liberal and authoritarian—that had claimed to speak on their behalf for over a century.[4]

Nur Rocks the World

Although the Ikhwan won the elections, it was Nur that stole the spotlight. Nur's achievement was impressive not merely because of the sheer number of votes and seats it amassed, but because more than any party it tapped the power of the poor and the hopeless. Before the elections, the conventional wisdom portrayed Nur as little more than a cult of religious fanatics who were out of touch with the modern world.[5] After the elections, it was clear that Nur had spearheaded a movement of social protest that no other party dared to embrace.

The social and geographic profile of Nur's support reflects inequality and injustice far more than religion. The party's power is firmly anchored in the poorest backwaters of the Nile Delta and the slums of Alexandria. When we follow the trails of Nur's appeal, we discover the bitter tastes and smells of misery in a thousand wretched neighborhoods and villages. Tropical fever, polluted drinking water, infected livestock, salinized land, radioactive irrigation canals, downstream farms of rock and sand, migrant slums, and farm workers on reclaimed desert land—these are the hallmarks of Nur bastions all along the Mediterranean coast from Alexandria's western suburbs to Port Sa'id. In Baheira, Kafr al-Sheikh, Damietta, Daqhaliya, Sharqiya, and Qalubiya, Nur followers were consistently concentrated in the poorest

---

[4] Michael, Maggie (2011). Christians Under Siege in Post-revolution Egypt, *Associated Press*, 11 October.

[5] el-Sherif, Ashraf (2011). Islamism after the Arab Spring, *Current History*, December.

lands, the driest irrigation sites, the most diseased households, and the biggest pools of agricultural wage labor.[6]

Partitioning Kafr al-Sheikh

Nur's early breakthroughs jolted the other parties into action. Within a matter of days, they were forming alliances and counter alliances to push back the surprising surges of populism that sprang up in one district after another. In the lower Delta province of Kafr al-Sheikh, they closed ranks to draw the lines against Nur both politically and geographically. In the first round of polling, Nur and the Ikhwan had won eight of the twelve seats (four each) in Kafr al-Sheikh's party-list districts. At the same time, Nur candidates finished first in four of the six races for individual seats and, heading into the runoff elections, they seemed poised to form the biggest block in Kafr al-Sheikh's 18-member parliamentary delegation. At the eleventh hour, local Wafd leaders stepped in to broker a multiparty power-sharing agreement that blocked the looming Nur majority with a three-way partition of the entire province.

The Wafdist pact amounted to a social-political armistice that tried to hand each party a separate demographic and geographic constituency. Nur kept only two of the four seats it won in the first round—both in the poorest and most disease-ridden southern villages surrounding the town of Kafr al-Sheikh. The Wafd and former NDP

---

[6] Kotb, Tarek H.S. *et al.* (2000). Soil Salinization in the Nile Delta and Related Policy Issues in Egypt, *Agricultural Water Management*, 43: 239–261; Geriesh, Mohamed H. *et al.* (2008). Problems of Drinking Water Treatment Along Ismailia Canal Province, Egypt, *Journal of Zhejiang University Science*, 9:3, 232–242; Malik, W.E.Y. Abdel *et al.* (2010). Radiological Review Studies on Ismailiya Canal Ecology, Tenth Radiation Physics and Protection Conference, Nasr City-Cairo, Egypt, 27–30 November, 211–230; Hegazy, Yamen M. *et al.* (2011). Ruminant Brucellosis in the Kafr El Sheikh Governorate of the Nile Delta, Egypt: Prevalence of a Neglected Zoonosis, *Public Library of Science: Neglected Tropical Diseases*, January.

candidates controlled the city of Dasuq and its fertile hinterland along the Rosetta branch of the Nile—the original homeland of Sa'ad Zaghlul, the founder of the Wafd and the iconic leader of Egypt's first nationalist revolution in 1919.

The FJP was both a beneficiary and a target of this arrangement. The FJP picked up the two seats that Nur was expected to win in Hamul district, a mixed region of villages and small towns in the northern and eastern parts of the province. In exchange, the FJP lost a seat in the city of Dasuq where their candidate had enjoyed a comfortable lead in the first round. The Wafdist landlord, Muhammad 'Abd al-'Alim Dawud, won easily, piling up the largest margin in the governorate with 70 percent of the vote. Dawud's coattails helped his urban ally and NDP successor, Yusuf al-Badri 'Abd al-Fattah, to squeak past the Ikhwan's Muhammad 'Ali al-Hilisi, who had won nearly twice as many votes as 'Abd al-Fattah just two weeks earlier.

Map 11.2. Kafr al-Sheikh.

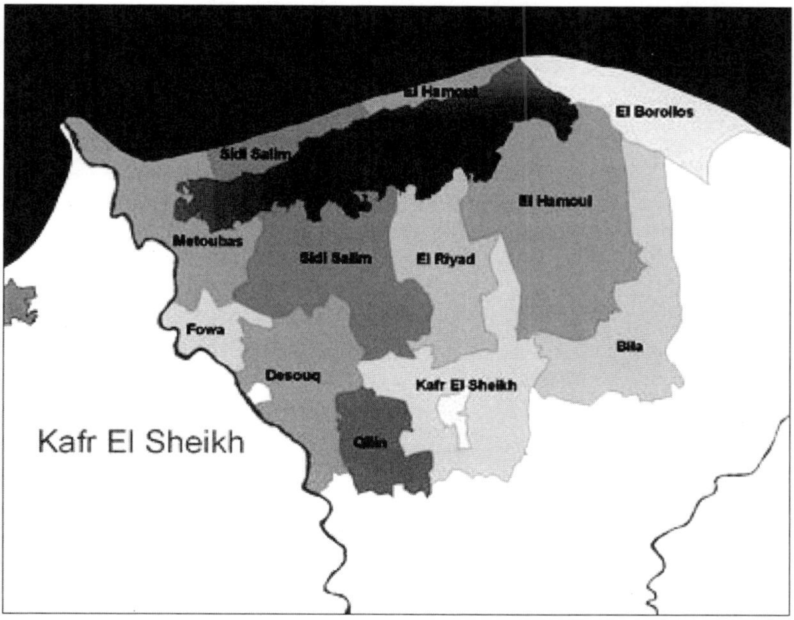

Source: Egypt Travel Search.

When the dust cleared, the final tally was: Nur 2, Ikhwan 2, Wafd-NDP successors 2, with each block entrenched in neighboring districts and separate social strata. The Wafd helped the NDP remnants drive the Ikhwan from Dasuq, and all three parties joined to push Nur out of Hamul. The Wafd orchestrated the bargaining and the Ikhwan was the pivot, agreeing to concede the city to the old guard in exchange for help in rolling back Nur's gains in the countryside (see Figure 11.7 and Table 11.2).

Figure 11.7. Power-sharing and partition in Kafr al-Sheikh.

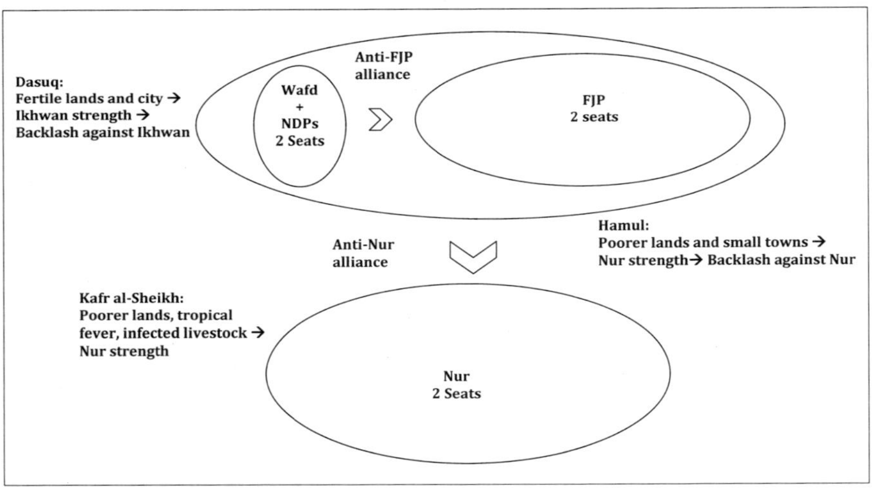

Source: Author.

Table 11.2. Kafr al-Sheikh—Votes for professional and worker-farmer seats (Number of votes and percent of total votes cast).

	Round One				Runoffs			
District–seat	Nur	FJP	Wafd	NDPs	Nur	FJP	Wafd	NDPs
KSheikh								
pro	140,447	49,844			**186,126**	143,613		
w-f	103,664	54,634			**215,126**	114,613		
Hamul								
pro	67,739	49,079			92,619	***116,220***		
w-f	54,136	31,237			100,581	***108,258***		
Dasuq								
pro		65,792		39,885		108,866		***110,368***
w-f		44,387	128,448			65,662	**153,572**	
KSheikh								
pro	34.43	12.22			**56.45**	43.55		
w-f	25.41	13.39			**64.24**	34.76		
Hamul								
pro	17.02	10.83			44.35	***55.65***		
w-f	23.49	18.77			48.16	***51.84***		
Dasuq								
pro		22.38		13.57		49.66		***50.34***
w-f		15.10	43.70			29.95	**70.05**	
pro seats	(2)	(1)	(0)	(0)	**1**	**1**	**0**	**1**
w-f seats	(2)	(0)	(1)	(0)	**1**	**1**	**1**	**0**

Note: **Bold** = Runoff winners; ***Italics*** = Runoff winners who finished in second place in round one.
Source: Author.

In the nearby province of Damietta, the Wafd-Ikhwan backlash against Nur was even more effective. During the first round, Nur had won the party-list vote while seizing the lead in three of the four individual district contests. In the end, Nur came away with no individual seats at all because its rivals pooled forces to defeat it by the slimmest of margins—no more than one or two percentage points—in every race (see Table 11.3). The same pattern appeared throughout the Nile Delta governorates, with the Ikhwan and Wafd teaming up to snatch away one or two seats at a time from Nur front-runners in Alexandria, Baheira, Gharbiya, Minufiya, and Sharqiya.

Table 11.3. Damietta—Votes for professional and worker-farmer seats (Number of votes and percent of total votes cast).

	Round One			Runoffs		
District–seat	Nur	FJP	Wafd	Nur	FJP	Wafd
Damietta						
pro	50,796	**125,734**		57,275	**135,587**	
w-f	**89,947**	84,062		93,010	***99,852***	
Kafr Sa'd						
pro	**65,694**	49,437		101,689	***104,052***	
w-f	**65,165**		51,018	99,734		***106,007***
Damietta						
pro	19.38	47.97		29.70	**70.30**	
w-f	34.32	32.07		48.23	***51.77***	
Kafr Sa'd						
pro	23.20	17.46		49.43	***50.57***	
w-f	23.02		18.02	48.48		***51.52***
pro seats	(1)	(1)	(0)	**0**	**2**	**0**
w-f seats	(2)	(0)	(0)	**0**	**1**	**1**

Note: **Bold** = Runoff winners; ***Italics*** = Runoff winners who finished in second place in round one.
Source: Author.

Crushing the Landlords

On the farmlands at the edges of the Nile Delta, the Ikhwan and Nur were unstoppable. In Baheira, west of the Rosetta branch, Nur finished first in both party-list districts. In the runoff round, the Ikhwan regrouped and joined Nur in sweeping the contests for individual seats—seven going to the FJP and three to Nur. In Sharqiya, east of the Damietta branch, the Ikhwan won all ten district seats against a list of Mubarak-era holdovers cobbled together by Wafdist landlords. Wafdist power brokers in Sharqiya made a colossal blunder by insisting on going head-to-head against both of the Muslim parties. Their humiliation helped to spark a long series of postelection revolts against the Wafd's aged and stumbling national leaders.[7]

The Baheira contest looked like a replay of Kafr al-Sheikh except that, this time, the landlords were too weak and disorganized to

[7] Afify, Heba (2011). "In Sharqiya, Islamists are Poised to Sweep Seats," *Al-Masry Al-Youm*, 14 December.

act as spoilers. In each of Baheira's districts, Ikhwan and Nur strength followed familiar demographic fault lines. The FJP won the city of Damanhur in the north and the middle-sized farms along the Nile to the east. Nur carried the poorer farmers of the interior and the agricultural workers on reclaimed semi-desert lands in the west and south. The intermediate zones—the secondary city of Kafr al-Dawar and the surrounding countryside—swayed back and forth between the first round and the runoffs, with neither party winning by more than three or four percentage points.

In Sharqiya, Nur was a bit player in the showdown between the Ikhwan and the landlords, but the contest's political geography was typical of the Delta as a whole. The FJP dominated the city of Zagazig and the small farmers on fertile lands to the north. Nur did best in the south, around the big estates of Bilbeis and in the struggling downstream villages that depend on the contaminated waters of the Isma'iliya irrigation canal. Ironically, it was precisely in this location—on the Bilbeis estate of the head of the Wafd's "southern faction" in Sharqiya—that the landlords had caucused to endorse the Mubarak era holdovers that the Ikhwan mowed down just two weeks later.[8]

Fayyum and its Multiple Discontents

In Fayyum, the Ikhwan and Nur quickly mobilized a complex set of social grievances and local rivalries that seemed tailor-made for their strategies. At first, it appeared that the Ikhwan had simply scored another grand slam in Fayyum by winning the party-list votes and then sweeping all six of the individual seats. In fact, Nur found deep pockets of support, putting it in striking distance of victory in several races and carving out a firm niche for the future.

Fayyum's politics revolve around the unequal distribution of water and voting power. Recurring drought has put enormous pressure on its compact population and delicate ecology. The city has always been

[8] *Al-Masry al-Youm*, "Ba'd sa'at min 'ilan da'ma lil-Musilhi: al-Wafd yutifiq ma' 3 min murashshai al-'iada" (Hours After Announcing Support for al-Musilhi, the Wafd Allies with Three Run-off Candidates), 19 December 2011b.

underrepresented and outvoted by farmers whose livelihood depends on diverting the Nile tributary for irrigation. As those waters dwindle, the persistent cleavage between town and country is overshadowed by still fiercer battles between competing groups of farmers, particularly the richer southern growers versus the poorer northerners near the polluted lake that collects most of the drainage from the rest of the province (see Map 11.3).[9] Even the luckier landholders closer to the headwaters are feuding more than ever because upstream farmers are stealing water more frequently from their downstream neighbors.[10] The result is an increasingly fractured and desperate electorate in which political entrepreneurs enjoy multiple avenues of entry.

As usual, Ikhwan candidates tapped into the frustration of the urban middle class while Nur thrived in the backward rural areas where land and water quality were poorest and deteriorating most rapidly (see Figure 11.8). The distinctive feature of Fayyum's politics was the sharp polarization within the ranks of the prosperous southern farmers who had traditionally ruled the roost and who differed little from one another except in terms of who was better positioned to jerry-rig the irrigation canals in their favor. Nur polled almost as well in these wealthy but parched southern districts as it did in the down-and-out northern villages—a departure from its usual lower class roots and a clear contradiction of the assumption that its appeal stems from religious extremism instead of economic interest.

---

[9] Amin, Shahira (2010). Egypt's Farmers Desperate for Clean Water, CNN, 10 November.

[10] Wolters, W. *et al.* (1987). Division of Irrigation Water in the Fayoum, Egypt, *Irrigation and Drainage Systems*, 1: 159–172; Wolters, W. *et al.* (1989). Managing the Water Balance of the Fayoum Depression, Egypt, *Irrigation and Drainage Systems*, 3: 103–123; Natter, Katharina (2010). The Failures of Egyptian Agricultural Policy, *Daily News* (Egypt), 20 June.

Map 11.3. Fayyum.

Source: Egypt Program Support Unit, Canadian International Development Agency.

Figure 11.8. The ecological and social bases of political conflict in Fayyum.

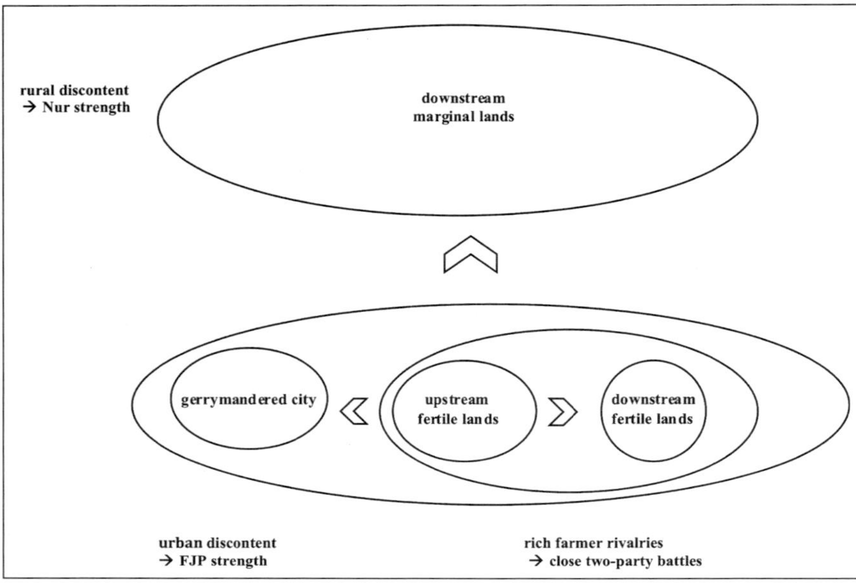

Source: Author.

Religious Clashes in Town and Country

Whereas class cleavages dominated the Delta, religious tensions were rawest in the big cities and in the southern districts of Upper Egypt. When pro-Christian candidates entered the field, the Ikhwan and Nur generally ran in separate races instead of competing against one another. This tactic was devastating for the Egyptian Block, which held its own in the party-list battles only to lose 16 of the 18 individual seat races when they faced a pro-Muslim party.

In Cairo, the Ikhwan's home turf was never in doubt. Its strongholds are centered in the historic neighborhoods of "Islamic Cairo"—Gamaliya, Khalifa, and Hadayiq al-Quba—and stretch northward to include Zeitun, 'Ain Shams, and Shubra and southward through Abdin and Sayida Zeynab. The Ikhwan nucleus is the heart of pre-colonial Cairo—solid residential quarters dominated by mixed income households surrounding the busy market and mosque-filled passages that every foreign tourist remembers no matter how brief the visit. The adjacent quarters feature mainly British-era construction where Christians and migrants comprise sizeable minorities.[11] In these parts of central Cairo, the Egyptian Block made it to the runoffs in seven contests and then lost by large margins in all but one—a seat in Qasr al-Nil's commercial district in which it won with a bare majority. In Cairo, the Ikhwan's stiffest competition appeared in the newer and more distant semi-suburban areas of Misr al-Gadida, Madinat Nasr, and Ma'adi, where educated middle-class voters shied away from all of the parties and chose four independent candidates instead.

In Giza and Alexandria, Nur's strength rose dramatically at the expense of both the Ikhwan and the Egyptian Block, especially in neighborhoods with high proportions of rural migrants (see Table 11.4). Ikhwan leaders later admitted that they had been complacent in Alexandria because of their party's strong showings there during Mubarak's rule. In Giza as well, the Ikhwan were caught off guard by Nur's obvious preparation and popularity.

[11] Sims, David (2003). "Urban Slums Report: The Case of Cairo, Egypt," *UN-Habitat Global Report on Human Settlements*, pp. 195–228, Malta: Gutenberg Press.

Map 11.4. The city of Cairo.

Source: EDAR.

Table 11.4. Percent party list votes by district – Cities.

District–seats	FJP	Nur	Eg. Block	Wafd	Wasat	Thawra	Top 6 parties
*Cairo1–10	39.45	15.36	23.50	6.23	3.37	2.66	90.57
Cairo1–10 revote	40.49	15.41	28.47	0.00	2.38	0.00	86.75
Cairo2–8	35.65	11.31	26.22	5.76	7.22	4.18	90.34
Cairo3–8	39.94	14.52	18.33	14.67	2.93	3.45	93.83
Cairo4–10	40.48	19.35	13.14	7.32	3.39	3.62	87.30
Giza1–10	41.09	29.10	10.52	7.80	5.75	0.00	94.25
Giza2–10	37.83	28.12	10.05	4.60	6.04	2.77	89.43
Alex.1–10	34.41	29.85	16.02	6.40	3.27	4.11	94.06
Alex.2–10	35.32	32.96	6.15	5.55	1.73	10.04	91.75
Total –76	**37.96**	**24.68**	**14.13**	**6.38**	**4.42**	**3.60**	**91.16**

* Annulled
Source: Author.

Battles for the individual seats in Alexandria and Giza were among the closest and most bitter in the nation. Nur won no individual seats in Giza, but it ran well in the outlying districts of Waraq to the north and around the Pyramids to the west. Nur also pressed Ikhwan candidates along the Nile bank in southern Giza where Christian-Muslim violence has flared up many times in recent years. In Alexandria, the Ikhwan barely held the central districts of Muharram Beg and Raml, while Nur took the poor southern suburbs of Mina al-Basal by similarly narrow margins. In the northern neighborhood of Montaza, the Ikhwan allied with liberals and Christians to defeat Nur's front-runner from the first round—a particularly menacing shaykh, Abdel Monem al-Shahat, who was calling democracy a form of atheism and claiming that the works of Naghib Mahfuz spread debauchery and prostitution.[12] At the same time, however, Nur joined all of the liberal parties in unseating a long-time NDP leader with an Ikhwan-backed judge, Mahmud

[12] Elyan, Tamim and Tom Heneghan (2011). "Egyptian Voters Reject Salafi Hardliner in Run-off," *Reuters*, 7 December; Tarek, Sherif (2011). "Liberals and Democrats Revel in Salafist Electoral Defeats," *Ahramonline*, 7 December.

al-Khudairi, who advocated a "Turkish-style" coalition government of moderate Muslims and secular democrats.[13]

In Upper Egypt, Ikhwan-Nur competition gradually gave way to an explicit division of labor as they confronted the growing strength of Christians and of local landlords and tribal leaders who had been part of the NDP. Collaboration took two forms. Sometimes they divided an entire governorate into geographic spheres of influence. Even when the Ikhwan and Nur faced off against each other, the towns usually favored the Ikhwan whereas the villages supported Nur, so that the voters sorted themselves out along clear geographic lines. In other cases, the Ikhwan and Nur leaders took matters into their own hands. Instead of partitioning a whole province, they divided up the local districts by contesting only one seat in each constituency and conceding the second seat to the other pro-Muslim party. In this manner, they took turns in rallying Muslim majorities against pro-Christian candidates of the Egyptian Block and against the feudal notables left over from Mubarak's days.

This division of labor strategy gained momentum as the two parties carried their campaigns southward to the Upper Nile Valley. Direct competition was greatest in Fayyum—as chronicled above—and Beni Sueif, and much more muted in Minya and Assyut. Minya split neatly into equal northern and southern zones—the Ikhwan winning the more urban districts of Minya and Beni Mazar and Nur taking the more rural and Christian ones of Markaz Minya, Abu Qirqas, and Malawi (see Table 11.5).[14] In Assyut, they blended competition and cooperation district by district. In the provincial capital, the Ikhwan stood aside so that Nur could defeat the NDP holdover while the Ikhwan's own candidate trounced the Egyptian Block. In the outlying areas of Assyut,

---

[13] Maher, Hatem and Sherif Tarek (2011). Reformist Judge, New MP Mahmoud El-Khodeiry on Islamist Ascendancy, Palestine, *Ahramonline*, 15 December.

[14] Youssef, Abdel Rahman (2012). Copts, Islamists Face Off in Minya Run-offs, *Daily News* (Egypt), 11 January; Ashraf Kamal (2012). I'lan nata'ij al-frmaq'aid al-fardiya bil-Minya (Announcement of the Results for Individual Seats in Minya), *Al-Wafd*, 11 January; al-Husaini, Hujaj (2012). Al-Hurriya wa al-'Adala wa al-Nur yiqtisaman 8 muqa'd lil-fardi bil-Minya (Freedom and Justice and Nur Divide Eight Individual Seats in Minya), *Al-Ahram*, 14 January.

Nur and Ikhwan leaders clashed over just one seat per district, leaving the Ikhwan free to dispatch pro-Christian and NDP opponents in races for the second seats.[15]

Table 11.5. Minya—Votes for professional and worker-farmer seats (percent of total votes cast).

	Round One				Runoffs			
District–seat	FJP	Nur	Eg. Block	NDPs	FJP	Nur	Eg. Block	NDPs
Minya								
pro	15.33			9.39	**63.71**			36.29
w-f	9.19			4.48	**57.47**			42.53
Beni Mazar								
pro	17.06	5.09			**71.95**	28.05		
w-f	13.11	6.24			**70.51**	29.49		
Mkz Minya, Abu Qirqas								
pro	5.75	9.69			43.48	**56.52**		
w-f		7.15	6.04			**76.67**	23.33	
Malawi								
pro		9.56		8.24		**58.50**		41.50
w-f		11.60		9.67		**63.09**		36.91
pro seats	(2)	(2)	(0)	(0)	**2**	**2**	**0**	**0**
w-f seats	(2)	(2)	(0)	(0)	**2**	**2**	**0**	**0**

Note: **Bold** = Runoff winners; ***Italics*** = Runoff winners who finished in second place in round one.
Source: Author.

In Sohag and Qena, district level collaboration reached its peak. Ikhwan and Nur candidates did not run against one another in a single race in these governorates. Together they won 13 out of 16 seats—seven for the Ikhwan and six for Nur—leaving rival *'ayan* and independents to fight for the rest (see Tables 11.6 and 11.7). Voters in Qena were so

[15] Radwan, Islam (2011). "Copts and the Salafis in Asyut: 'One Hand'?" *Egyptvotes.org*, 19 December; Radwan, Islam (2012a). "Bakr wa 'Abd ul-Jawad wa Musa wa Qarshi fil-i'ada bil-da'ira al-thalatha fi Assyut" (Bakr, 'Abd al-Jawad, Musa, and Qarshi in the Run-offs in Assyut's Third District), *Al-Ahram*, 14 January and Radwan, Islam (2012b). "Fawz Khalaf bil-fi'at wa i'ada bayn Sadiq wa 'Abd al-Nasr 'ala al-'umal fil-da'ira Assyut" (Victory of Khalaf in the Professional Seat and Run-off of Sadiq and Abd al-Nasr for the Worker Seat in Assyut District), *Al-Ahram*, 14 January.

furious over *'ayan* manipulation of the elections in Naga Hamadi that they blocked the railroad connections to Cairo for several days until the courts agreed to order a new round of polling that barred the previous front-runner.[16] In both governorates, pro-Muslim candidates benefited from growing divisions among Christians who debated the wisdom of politicizing the churches and from an upsurge in village revolts against old tribal leaders who had continued to oppose the revolution right up to the election.[17]

In Sohag, Nur placed first in both party-list districts. In the runoff elections, the FJP and Nur won eight of the ten individual seats even though Egyptian Block and NDP candidates had led the first round polling in all but one of the races. Such upsets occurred in several governorates, but usually in just a few races out of many. Only in Sohag and Damietta were second round reversals the rule instead of the exception.

---

[16] Mahmud al-Dasuqi, 'Iada bayn al-Ghul wa Qandil bi Qena wa al-Jama'a al-Islamiya wa al-Hurriya wa al-'Adala yu'aradan (Run-off between al-Ghul and Qandil in Qena; the Islamic Society and Freedom and Justice Object), *Al-Ahram*, 11 January 2012a and Baltajiya yamn'aun ahali qariya Abu Shusha bi Qena min al-khuruj lil-taswit (Thugs Prevent the Villagers of Abu Susha in Qena from Going Out to Vote), *Al-Ahram*, 15 January 2012b and Amin al-Hurriya wa al-'Adala bi Naga Hamadi: al-Salafiyun ankaru tahalafhum ma'a 'Abdalrahim al-Ghul (The Leader of Freedom and Justice in Naga Hamadi: The Salafis Deny Allying with Abdalrahim al-Ghul), *Al-Ahram*, 15 January 2012c.

[17] Serageldin, Samia (2012). The Dead Pope Rises: Coptic Conundrum in Egypt, *Salon.com*, 20 March; el-Gergawi, Sherry (2012). Egyptian Copts Call for 'Brotherhood' of Their Own, *Ahram Weekly*, 31 March.

Table 11.6. Sohag—Votes for professional and worker-farmer seats (percent of total votes cast).

District–seat	Round One					Runoffs				
	FJP	Nur	EB	NDPs	Ind	FJP	Nur	EB	NDPs	Ind
Sohag, Akhmim										
pro	13.2			15.9		***66.4***			33.6	
w-f		12.1	15.5				***69.0***	31.0		
Maghagha										
pro	11.4				11.8	***55.6***				44.4
w-f		12.5		14.5			***53.3***		46.7	
Tahta, Tama										
pro	20.7		20.8			*60.0*		40.0		
w-f		19.5					60.9			39.1
Girga, Mansha										
pro		24.8		19.8			61.1		38.9	
w-f				24.9					45.6	*54.4*
Balyana										
pro	16.6			23.5		*53.0*			47.0	
w-f				31.8					52.9	47.1
pro seats	(0)	(1)	(1)	(2)	1	***4***	**1**	0	0	0
w-f seats	(0)	(1)	(1)	(3)	0	0	***3***	0	**1**	**1**

Note: **Bold** = Runoff winners; ***Italics*** = Runoff winners who finished in second place in round one.

Source: Author.

Table 11.7. Qena—Votes for professional and worker-farmer seats (percent of total votes cast).

	Round One			Runoffs		
District–seat	FJP	Nur	NDPs	FJP	Nur	NDPs
Qena, Qaft						
pro	21.44		3.20	**76.97**		23.03
w-f		6.70	3.90		**68.88**	31.12
Naga Hamadi, Qus, Naqada						
pro		3.31	3.14		**41.45**	***58.55***
w-f	18.85		5.28	**70.50**		29.50
Abu Tisht, Dashna, Farshawt						
pro			7.21	**58.57**		41.43
w-f		7.93	[4.13/6.75]		**62.42**	37.58
pro seats	(1)	(2)	(0)	**2**	**0**	**1**
w-f seats	(1)	(1)	(1)	**1**	**2**	**0**

Note: [Brackets] = Annulled. **Bold** = runoff winners; ***Italics*** = runoff winners who finished in second place in round one.
Source: Author.

In Luxor and Aswan—the most urbanized regions of Upper Egypt—semi-competitiveness remerged. In each case, Ikhwan candidates had to battle Nur for one seat and a secular party for the other—this time the Wafd instead of the Egyptian Block and NDP successors. In the end, the Ikhwan took both seats in Luxor and lost both seats in Aswan.

Ikhwan and Nur leaders showed great pragmatism and flexibility in adapting to the variegated landscape of religious animosity and feudal power in Upper Egypt. Neither party was at home in this territory—not the urban middle-class Ikhwan and certainly not the northern-based Salafis who thrived along the salty rim of the Mediterranean coast and in the big city slums. Precisely because both parties were aware of their weakness in the Sa'id, they used greater caution and modesty in planning their campaigns and making the most of meager resources.

The FJP's edge in the southern towns was largely due to the Ikhwan's tireless work in organizing provincial-level professional syndicates and student groups throughout Egypt since the later years of the Sadat era.[18] Nur had to rely more on local intermediaries, particularly the militant Islamic groups that were beginning to resurface after years of skirmishing with police forces all along the upper Nile and across the surrounding deserts. Although these were valuable bridgeheads, they were not yet the sort of reliable bases that national party organizations require. Those who believe that the Ikhwan and Nur enjoyed an unfair advantage in these elections because Mubarak tolerated them more than other opponents and because Persian Gulf Arabs fattened them with funds might reconsider their views if they look more closely at the planning and compromise these parties displayed in nearly every race and district that they contested.[19]

The elections were a learning experience for all of the parties and their supporters in deciding when to compromise and when to fight and in choosing the most appropriate allies in rapidly changing circumstances. These are the same skills that Egypt's new democratic leaders will have to sharpen on a daily basis as they tackle the endless backlog of problems that have accumulated for at least a generation. Whether drafting a constitution or forming coalition governments or haggling over economic and social policy, no party will be able to impose its preferences and every group will have to live with compromises they deplore. Mindful of the military's consuming ambition and the old regime's thirst for revenge, Egypt's democrats have good reason to fear their common enemies far more than they fear one another. That awareness—along with the bargaining skills developed in three months of electoral battle—can help the democratic revolution survive the certain storms ahead, but only if both the winning and losing sides have the wisdom to keep trading votes and sharing power.

The Muslim Brothers are forced by circumstance to embrace the thankless task of straddling the chasm between Nur and the secular parties. This will create a dizzying parade of ad hoc alliances and ugly

---

18 Bianchi, Robert R. (1989). *Unruly Corporatism: Associational Life in Twentieth-Century Egypt*, New York: Oxford University Press.

19 Ibrahim, Saad Eddin (2011). Ikhwan wa Qatariyun...wa Salafiyun wa Sa‘udiyun (The Ikhwan and the Qataris; the Salafis and the Saudis), *Al-Masry Al-Youm*, 17 December.

compromises on critical issues that Egyptians are likely to be debating for at least a decade—presidential contests, civilian control of the military, the separation of powers, the role of the private sector and foreign investment, relations with the United States and Israel, and countless efforts to expand and roll back the rights of women and Christians.

The Ikhwan has no choice but to be democratic because it is a pluralist coalition trying to lead a tumultuous and cosmopolitan society. The Ikhwan is too small to monopolize power and too big to suppress its inner conflicts. Knowing it cannot rule alone, it seeks a new set of allies for every issue, and every alliance with outsiders heightens disagreements between its own factions over the proper course of the party, the movement, and the country. Extremism of any sort will tear the Ikhwan apart long before it can tear Egypt apart. Its leaders will have to govern the same way that they campaigned—from the center and with hands outstretched in many directions at once.

Appendix 11.A. The Major Political Parties

Freedom and Justice Party
Founded by the Muslim Brotherhood (*Al-Ikhwan Al-Muslimun*) and well-connected to professional and community associations in the provincial capitals and towns.

Nur
Led by Islamic preachers with diverse religious and political views who claim to represent the poorest and most marginalized peasants and urban migrants, particularly in the Nile Delta.

Wafd
The successor of the nationalist movement that led the 1919 Revolution and struggled to build parliamentary democracy in the face of opposition from the monarchy and the British before the 1952 Revolution. Headed by old rural landholders with extensive urban interests in business and the professions.

Egyptian Block
A coalition of small parties funded by big business leaders and supported by many activists in the Coptic community who desire an independent Christian voice to counter Muslim political power.

Wasat
A small group of Muslim modernists who try to create a tolerant religious "center" between the Muslim Brotherhood and the major secular parties, particularly the Wafd and the Egyptian Block.

The Revolution Continues (Al-Thawra Mustamira)
The strongest new party to emerge from the Revolution of 2011 with many supporters in the largest cities and in a handful of provincial capitals.

National Democratic Party successors

Several small parties are popularly known as "remnants" of the Mubarak regime because most of their candidates served in executive or legislative posts under the authoritarian governments. These include the National Party, the Reform and Development Party, the Egyptian Citizen Party, the Freedom Party, and the Union Party, as well as several self-described "independent" groups.

Appendix 11.B. The Timeline and Structure of the Elections

Timeline

The elections occurred in three stages spread out over about two months. Each stage covered nine governorates.

Stage one

Governorates—Cairo, Alexandria, Port Sa'id, Fayyum, Luxor, Damietta, Kafr al-Sheikh, Assyut, and the Red Sea
First round—November 28–29, 2011
Run-offs—December 5–6, 2011
Court-ordered revotes—January 10–11 and January 17–18, 2012

Stage two

Governorates—Giza, Beni Sueif, Minufiya, Sharqiya, Isma'iliya, Suez, Baheira, Sohag, and Aswan
First round—December 14–15, 2011
Run-offs—December 21–22, 2011
Court-ordered revotes—January 14–15 and January 18–19, 2012

Stage three

Governorates—Qalubiya, Gharbiya, Daqhaliya, Minya, Qena, North Sinai, South Sinai, New Valley, and Matruh
First round—January 3–4, 2012
Run-offs—January 10–11, 2012
Court-ordered revotes—January 16–17, 2012 and January 18–19, 2012

Map 11.5. The Governorates of Egypt.

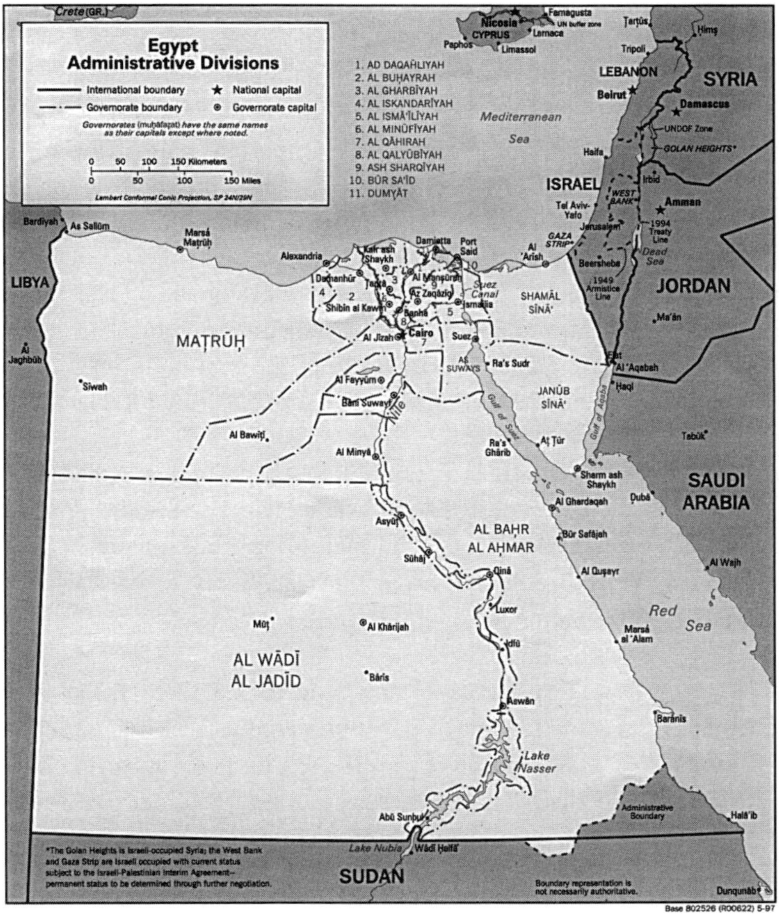

Source: University of Texas Libraries.

Structure

Hybrid representation. Egypt's system of parliamentary representation combines three different methods of allocating seats—proportional representation, majority rule, and functional representation (also described as corporatism).

Proportional representation is the most important part of the formula. It applies for two-thirds of the deputies who are chosen from candidate lists prepared by party leaders. Each party wins a number of seats that corresponds to its share of the total vote.

Majority rule applies in the elections for individual seats at the local level. In each district, victory requires an absolute majority of the vote. Usually, no candidate achieves a majority in the first balloting so the top two vote getters must then compete in a separate run off election at a later date.

Functional representation is a symbolic vestige of the Arab Socialist era. The categories of "professional" and "worker-farmer" originally designated seats reserved for occupational groups, but in current practice these labels have little relevance and they are likely to be abolished in future electoral arrangements.

Party list districts. Two-thirds of the seats (332) were filled through proportional representation. Each party prepared a list of candidates and won a number of seats that closely reflected its percentage of the total vote in each of 46 districts. Every governorate contained between one and four party-list districts depending on its population size.

Individual seat districts. One-third of the seats (166) were filled by first-past-the-post elections in which victory required a majority of all votes cast. If no candidate achieved an absolute majority, then the top two vote getters battled it out in a run-off election about two weeks after the initial voting. Candidates ran in 83 local districts that were usually subdivisions of the larger party-list districts. Every district elected two representatives—one "professional" and one "worker-farmer." Every governorate contained between one and nine individual-seat districts according to the size of its population.

Examples. Voters in Cairo elected a total of 54 deputies—36 deputies from four party list districts and 18 deputies (nine professionals and nine workers-farmers) from nine individual seat districts. In Kafr al-Sheikh, voters elected a total of 18 deputies—12 deputies from two party list districts and six deputies (three professionals and three workers-farmers) from three individual seat districts.

Appendix 11.C. Nationwide Vote for Party Lists

Party	Total votes	Percent votes	Total seats	Percent seats
FJP	10,138,134	36.40	127	38.25
Nur	7,534,266	27.05	96	28.92
Wafd	2,480,391	8.91	36	10.84
Egyptian Block	2,402,238	8.63	33	9.94
Wasat	989,004	3.55	10	3.01
Revolution Continues	745,863	2.68	7	2.11
Reform and Development	604,415	2.17	8	2.41
Freedom	514,029	1.85	4	1.20
National	425,021	1.53	4	1.20
Conservatives	272,910	0.98	0	0.00
Democratic Peace	248,281	0.89	1	0.30
Egyptian Citizen	235,395	0.85	3	0.90
Adl	184,553	0.66	0	0.00
Egyptian Arab Union	149,253	0.54	1	0.30
Union	141,382	0.51	2	0.60
21 other parties	785,935	2.82	0	0.00
Total	**27,851,070**	**100.00**	**332**	**100.00**

Appendix 11.D. Party List Votes

Party List Votes by District – Cities

District–Seats	FJP	Nur	Egyptian Block	Wafd	Wasat	Thawra	Total
*Cairo1–10	426,938	166,195	254,339	67,416	36,429	28,782	1,082,142
Cairo1–10	158,254	60,219	111,288	0	9,303	0	390,838
Cairo2–8	312,229	99,032	229,624	50,437	63,275	36,597	875,785
Cairo3–8	163,235	59,342	74,897	59,942	11,962	14,080	408,692
Cairo4–10	455,623	217,750	147,880	82,399	38,132	40,712	1,125,467
Giza1–10	571,262	404,549	146,217	108,398	79,930	0	1,390,329
Giza2–10	546,974	406,543	145,346	66,528	87,368	40,077	1,445,699
Alex1–10	395,961	343,500	184,407	73,679	37,641	47,325	1,150,865
Alex2–10	357,990	334,051	62,305	56,259	17,579	101,711	1,013,473
Total–76	**2,961,528**	**1,924,986**	**1,101,964**	**497,642**	**345,190**	**280,502**	**7,801,148**

* Annulled

Source: Author.

Percent Party List Votes by District – Cities

District–Seats	FJP	Nur	Egyptian Block	Wafd	Wasat	Thawra	Top 6 Parties
*Cairo1–10	39.45	15.36	23.50	6.23	3.37	2.66	90.57
Cairo1–10	40.49	15.41	28.47	0.00	2.38	0.00	86.75
Cairo2–8	35.65	11.31	26.22	5.76	7.22	4.18	90.34
Cairo3–8	39.94	14.52	18.33	14.67	2.93	3.45	93.83
Cairo4–10	40.48	19.35	13.14	7.32	3.39	3.62	87.30
Giza1–10	41.09	29.10	10.52	7.80	5.75	0.00	94.25
Giza2–10	37.83	28.12	10.05	4.60	6.04	2.77	89.43
Alex1–10	34.41	29.85	16.02	6.40	3.27	4.11	94.06
Alex2–10	35.32	32.96	6.15	5.55	1.73	10.04	91.75
Total–76	**37.96**	**24.68**	**14.13**	**6.38**	**4.42**	**3.60**	**91.16**

*Annulled

Source: Author.

Party List Votes by District – Nile Delta

District–Seats	FJP	Nur	Egyptian Block	Wafd	Wasat	Thawra	Total
Men1–8	210,357	138,121	37,973	68,987	30,434	0	618,621
Men2–8	269,038	109,600	0	174,463	17,287	11,280	686,587
Sha1–10	432,693	302,376	76,067	119,904	25,430	22,948	1,138,924
Sha2–10	425,680	249,119	45,680	167,101	36,045	10,803	1,197,875
Beh1–12	477,121	534,913	58,586	117,417	0	29,023	1,336,877
Beh2–8	198,394	208,743	11,926	48,726	11,172	7,451	572,436
Qalu1–4	188,641	123,497	26,315	57,972	32,828	15,898	528,921
Qalu2–8	461,383	355,908	88,221	78,915	26,020	18,281	1,205,853
*Daq1–8	259,004	229,084	22,325	97,454	12,935	103,888	851,245
Daq1–8	162,025	123,492	6,783	44,205	5,608	74,801	487,581
Daq2–8	241,350	180,795	13,062	73,580	8,598	54,662	623,303
*Daq3–8	252,828	219,348	20,258	68,521	18,735	69,313	784,772
Daq3–8	141,157	115,653	0	27,078	0	49,175	437,704
Gha1–10	255,704	265,216	65,967	122,966	17,187	29,009	891,959
Gha2–10	371,730	285,781	46,339	171,392	21,813	0	988,820
Damie–8	169,253	209,726	18,378	24,630	73,876	3,982	543,594
K Sh1–8	212,064	276,654	0	86,466	11,896	0	710,870
K Sh2–4	94,486	68,007	6,976	46,636	19,919	17,979	303,661
Total–132	**4,519,726**	**3,756,888**	**538,073**	**1,525,130**	**364,175**	**394,517**	**12,984,318**

*Annulled

Source: Author.

Percent Party List Votes by District – Nile Delta

District–Seats	FJP	Nur	Egyptian Block	Wafd	Wasat	Thawra	Top 6 Parties
Menoufia1–8	34.00	22.33	6.14	11.15	4.92	0.00	78.54
Menoufia2–8	39.18	15.96	0.00	25.41	2.52	1.64	84.72
Sharq1–10	37.99	26.55	6.68	10.53	2.23	2.01	86.00
Sharq2–10	35.54	20.80	3.81	13.95	3.01	0.90	78.01
Beheira1–12	35.69	40.01	4.38	8.78	0.00	2.17	91.04
Beheira2–8	34.66	36.47	2.08	8.51	1.95	1.30	84.97
Qalubiya1–4	35.67	23.35	4.98	10.96	6.21	3.01	84.16
Qalubia2–8	38.26	29.52	7.32	6.54	2.16	1.52	85.31
*Daqahliya1–8	30.43	26.91	2.62	11.45	1.52	12.20	85.13
Daq1–8	33.23	25.33	1.39	9.07	1.15	15.34	85.51
Daq2–8	38.72	29.01	2.10	11.80	1.38	8.77	91.78
*Daq3–8	32.22	27.95	2.58	8.73	2.39	8.83	82.70
Daq3–8	32.25	26.42	0.00	6.19	0.00	11.23	76.09
Gharb1–10	28.67	29.73	7.40	13.79	1.93	3.25	84.76
Gharb2–10	37.59	28.90	4.69	17.33	2.21	0.00	90.72
Damietta–8	31.14	38.58	3.38	4.53	13.59	0.73	91.95
K Sheikh1–8	29.83	38.92	0.00	12.16	1.67	0.00	82.59
K Sheikh2–4	31.12	22.40	2.30	15.36	6.56	5.92	83.65
Total–132	34.81	28.93	4.14	11.75	2.80	3.04	85.48

*Annulled

Source: Author.

Party List Votes by District – Upper Egypt

District–Seats	FJP	Nur	Egyptian Block	Wafd	Wasat	Thawra	Total
Fayyum1–8	200,976	130,093	10,108	16,048	17,683	22,445	447,743
Fayyum2–4	131,153	116,534	16,321	0	4,630	0	291,143
BeniSueif1–8	233,938	207,468	0	67,714	18,247	19,420	592,771
BeniSueif2–4	135,073	100,168	31,059	23,599	0	0	312,858
Minya1–8	362,318	174,146	44,392	29,787	49,898	7,563	782,707
Minya2–8	243,346	191,074	133,246	45,435	27,943	0	680,235
Assiyut1–8	261,321	136,920	133,437	24,497	21,881	12,098	657,027
Assiyut2–8	128,072	102,082	71,520	14,027	6,224	0	393,188
Sohag1–12	222,672	229,829	125,081	36,448	21,785	9,660	783,535
*Sohag2–8	76,121	64,173	51,661	29,339	16,143	5,014	335,261
Sohag2–8	37,026	40,686	17,445	8,022	10,168	0	148,875
Qena–4	114,822	77,006	0	31,351	8,460	10,022	352,003
Qena2–8	87,911	64,693	13,831	20,223	11,631	0	337,728
Luxor–4	118,566	50,691	41,726	35,533	10,098	0	321,285
*Aswan–4	148,369	104,079	40,621	34,246	12,369	10,209	439,084
Aswan–4	60,235	48,238	15,992	18,442	0	5,015	171,117
Total–96	**2,337,429**	**1,669,628**	**654,160**	**371,126**	**208,648**	**86,223**	**6,272,215**

*Annulled

Source: Author.

Percent Party List Votes by District – Upper Egypt

District–Seats	FJP	Nur	Egyptian Block	Wafd	Wasat	Thawra	Top 6 Parties
Fayyum1–8	44.89	29.06	2.26	3.58	3.95	5.01	88.75
Fayyum2–4	45.05	40.03	5.61	0.00	1.59	0.00	92.27
Beni Sueif1–8	39.47	35.00	0.00	11.42	3.08	3.28	92.24
Beni Sueif2–4	43.17	32.02	9.93	7.54	0.00	0.00	92.66
Minya1–8	46.29	22.25	5.67	3.81	6.38	0.97	85.36
Minya2–8	35.77	28.09	19.59	6.68	4.11	0.00	94.24
Assiyut1–8	39.77	20.84	20.31	3.73	3.33	1.84	89.82
Assiyut2–8	32.57	25.96	18.19	3.57	1.58	0.00	81.88
Sohag1–12	28.42	29.33	15.96	4.65	2.78	1.23	82.38
*Sohag2–8	22.70	19.14	15.41	8.75	4.82	1.50	72.32
Sohag2–8	24.87	27.33	11.72	5.39	6.83	0	76.14
Qena–4	32.62	21.88	0.00	8.91	2.40	2.85	68.65
Qena2–8	26.03	19.16	4.10	5.99	3.44	0.00	58.71
Luxor–4	36.90	15.78	12.99	11.06	3.14	0.00	79.87
*Aswan–4	33.79	23.70	9.25	7.80	2.82	2.33	79.69
Aswan–4	35.20	28.19	9.35	10.78	0	2.93	86.44
Total–96	**37.27**	**26.62**	**10.43**	**5.92**	**3.33**	**1.37**	**84.93**

*Annulled
Source: Author.

Party List Votes by District – Canal Zone and Border Areas

District–Seats	FJP	Nur	Egyptian Block	Wafd	Wasat	Thawra	Total
P Said–4	96,532	61,136	28,510	41,059	38,080	5,460	295,556
Ismailiya–4	183,859	132,992	31,998	35,637	10,138	5,873	481,384
Suez–4	75,316	127,836	23,488	12,983	14,396	0.00	280,661
N Sinai–4	39,315	29,623	1,828	6,389	7,913	0.00	111,221
S Sinai–4	14,334	0.00	3,766	5,614	840	0.00	33,701
Red Sea–4	40,693	0.00	19,391	11,049	6,285	4,776	114,022
NValley–4	22,792	34,376	6,445	3,449	746	0.00	86,225
MMatruh–4	16,314	76,511	1,977	7,655	3,873	0.00	112,860
Total–32	**489,155**	**462,474**	**117,403**	**123,835**	**82,271**	**16,109**	**1,515,630**

Source: Author.

Percent Party List Votes by District – Canal Zone and Border Areas

District–Seats	FJP	Nur	Egyptian Block	Wafd	Wasat	Thawra	Top 6 Parties
P Said–4	32.66	20.69	9.65	13.89	12.88	1.85	91.62
Ismail–4	38.19	27.63	6.65	7.40	2.11	1.22	83.20
Suez–4	26.84	45.55	8.37	4.63	5.13	0.00	90.51
N Sin–4	35.35	26.63	1.64	5.74	7.11	0.00	76.49
S Sin–4	42.53	0.00	11.17	16.66	2.49	0.00	72.86
RSea–4	35.69	0.00	17.01	9.69	5.51	4.19	72.09
NVal–4	26.43	39.87	7.47	4.00	0.87	0.00	78.64
Matru–4	14.46	67.79	1.75	6.78	3.43	0.00	94.21
Total–32	**32.27**	**30.51**	**7.75**	**8.17**	**5.43**	**1.06**	**85.20**

Source: Author.

Appendix 11.E. Voter Turnout

Turnout rates in the governorates (rank order)

Governorate – Seats	Eligible Voters	Round One	Runoffs	Falloff Rate
Suez – 6	378,917	74.07	43.61	41.12
Isma'iliya – 6	696,362	69.13	41.93	39.35
Port Sa'id – 6	437,134	67.61	47.56	29.66
Qalubiya – 18	2,583,418	67.15	23.89	43.26
Sharqiya – 30	3,483,914	67.07	34.06	49.22
Giza – 30	4,262,232	66.54	38.18	42.62
Alexandria – 24	3,303,916	65.51	36.68	44.01
Gharbiya – 30	2,918,551	64.44	35.41	45.05
Damietta – 12	849,235	64.01	46.94	26.67
Beni Sueif – 18	1,415,226	63.99	41.40	35.30
New Valley – 6	140,527	61.36	44.85	26.91
Daqahliya – 36	3,691,143	61.21	32.85	28.36
Baheira – 30	3,198,626	59.69	48.41	18.90
Minufiya – 24	2,215,544	58.91	48.01	18.50
Matruh – 6	199,607	56.54	35.15	21.39
Cairo – 54	4,597,893	55.99	36.27	39.54
South Sinai – 6	60,496	55.71	34.21	38.59
Minya – 24	2,644,830	55.31	34.88	36.94
North Sinai – 6	203,346	54.70	19.45	64.44
Kafr al-Sheikh – 18	1,863,834	54.43	40.66	25.30
Red Sea – 6	220,193	51.78	47.10	9.04
Aswan – 6	852,567	51.20	27.22	46.84
Assiyut – 24	2,071,879	50.69	27.77	45.22
Luxor – 6	666,254	48.22	26.93	44.15
Sohag – 30	2,323,098	48.16	37.61	21.91
Fayyum – 18	1,545,556	47.81	35.93	24.85
Qena – 18	1,585,191	43.51	24.65	18.86

Source: Author.

Turnout varied widely across regions, but everywhere the most important contrast was between round one and the subsequent run-offs when participation fell by 40 percent or more in several governorates.

Higher turnout in the first round helped the smaller parties increase their shares of seats allotted by proportional representation. Lower turnout in the run-off elections strengthened the hands of all party leaders who wanted to build informal coalitions against common enemies. First round losers could gang up against front-runners more effectively with a shrunken pool of voters in which party organization often outweighed popularity and name recognition.

Appendix 11.F. Disparities in District Apportionment

The unequal weighting of votes across regions and neighborhoods is an enduring problem in Egypt's electoral politics. Even when votes are counted honestly and accurately, many citizens find their power diluted or exaggerated because they live in districts that have been systematically favored or disfavored by ruling elites in both authoritarian and democratic eras.[20]

Malapportionment is far from random. Indeed, it follows consistent patterns designed to empower specific constituencies while marginalizing others. The problem is pervasive, affecting every region and demographic category including many neighboring communities with long histories of social conflict and rivalry over land, water, and other scarce resources.

In pinpointing the most glaring disparities, we see some common tendencies. In the big cities, boundaries are drawn to strengthen Cairo over Giza and Alexandria. Within all of the cities, commercial districts and middle class residences benefit at the expense of poorer neighborhoods with concentrations of Christians and rural migrants.

In the countryside, villages are favored over towns, fertile lands closer to the Nile are privileged over poorer lands relying on downstream irrigation, and Upper Egypt benefits more than the Nile Delta. The most overrepresented voters live in the sparsely populated border regions and

---

[20] Ahmed, Amel (2011). Revolutionary blind-spots: The politics of electoral system choice and the Egyptian transition, *Middle East Law and Governance*, 3: 3–12.

the compact cities of the Canal Zone, but their numbers are too small to affect the national balance of power.

In this election, malapportionment was most helpful to candidates with ties to the NDP and most harmful to the FJP, the new liberal parties, and the Egyptian Block. The Wafd benefited slightly and Nur neither gained nor suffered overall. By skewing results in favor of Mubarak loyalists and against their longtime opponents, the current boundaries accomplished their intended goals—and for that reason alone they should be redrawn.

Disparities in district apportionment – Cities
Eligible voters per deputy

List District–Seats	Voters per Seat	Demographic Character	Individual District	Voters per Seat	Demographic Character
Cairo1–10	183,177	newer colonial	1 sahel, shubra	***547,847***	more Christian
		older colonial	2 hadayiq al-quba, zaitun	368,038	more Muslim
Cairo2–8	***245,852***	new suburban	3 madinat nasr	250,405	middle class
		old suburban	4 misr al-gadida	**190,115**	middle class
		suburban	5 ‘ain shams, matariya	***682,578***	migrant
Cairo3–8	**84,987**	central	6 qasr al-nil, abdin, muski	**127,690**	commercial
		central	7 gamalia	212,257	residential
Cairo4–10	180,686	central	8 khalifa, misr al-qadima	364,122	older commercial
		suburban	9 helwan, ma’di	***539,307***	newer residential
Giza1–10	***211,035***	suburban	1 giza	***634,068***	older center
			2 bulaq dakrur	***421,105***	newer suburb
Giza2–10	***215,189***	suburban	3 imbaba, aguza	***424,099***	newer suburb
		semi-rural	4 al-haram	330,323	far west
			5 waraq, awsim	321,522	far north

Source: Author

(Continued)

(*Continued*)

Alexandria1–6	***277,443***	north suburb central	1 montaza 2 ramla	424,192 408,137	older suburban comm'l-res'l
Alexandria2–10	163,926	central south suburb	3 muharam beg 4 mina al-basal	436,054 383,576	comm'l-res'l newer suburban

Note: **Bold = Overrepresented districts; *Italics = Underrepresented districts.***
Source: Author.

Disparities in district apportionment – Nile Delta

List District–Seats	Voters per Seat	Demographic Character	Individual District	Voters per Seat	Demographic Character
Minufiya1–8	149,005	town-rural	1 shibin al-kum 2 talla, shuhada	320,113 275,906	town rural north
Minufiya2–8	127,939	rural	3 ashmun, bajur 4 minuf, sadat	303,473 **208,281**	rural south rural west
Shariqiya1–10	163,393	city-rural	1 zaqaziq 2 bilbeis	353,257 ***463,707***	city rural south
Sharqiya2–10	184,999	rural	3 derab nigm 4 faqus 5 kafr saqr	346,225 318,652 260,117	rural northwest rural west rural north
Baheira1–12	140,537	urban semi-urban rural	1 damanhur 2 kafr al-dawar 3 abu hummus	334,037 388,139 314,989	main city second city rural central
Baheria2–8	172,861	rural rural	4 kum hamada 5 itai al-barud	304,586 257,563	poor rural west river land
Qalubiya1–4	206,616	city	1 benha	413,232	city
Qalubiya2–8	219,619	town-rural	2 shubra al-khaima 3 khanka	339,036 539,441	suburban rural

(*Continued*)

(*Continued*)

Daqahliya1–8	174,548	urban-rural	1 mansura 2 bilqas, talkha	350,744 347,447	city rural north
Daqahliya2–8	131,368	rural	3 sharbin, dikirnis 4 manzila, minya nasr	248,584 276,890	rural central salted lake lands
Daqahliya3–8	155,477	town-rural	5 mit ghamr, ija 6 sanbalawain	370,660 251,248	rural southwest rural south
Gharbiya1–10	137,103	urban	1 tanta 2 basyun, kafr al-zayat	357,267 328,247	city towns
Gharbiya2–10	154,752	urban-rural	3 mahalla, samanud 4 markaz mahalla 5 zifta, santa	291,650 201,481 280.481	city rural towns & villages
Damietta–8	106,154	semi-urban rural	1 damietta 2 kafr sa'd	195,475 229,143	dumyat city rural
Kafr al-Sheikh1–8	163,278	rural	1 kafr al-sheikh 2 hamul	***371,913*** 281,197	rural rural, semi-urban
Kafr al-Sheikh2–4	**139,404**	semi-urban	3 dasuq	278,807	dasuq city

Source: Author.

Disparities in district apportionment – Upper Egypt

List District–Seats	Voters per Seat	Demographic Character	Individual District	Voters per Seat	Demographic Character
Fayyum1–8	**118,124**	semi-urban rural	1 fayyum 2 fayyum, tamiya villages	***532,939*** **206,028**	fayyum city rural south
Fayyum2–4	150,140	rural	3 sanuris, abshawi	300,281	rural north
Beni Sueif1–8	**112,243**	urban-rural	1 beni sueif 2 wasta, nasr	256,544 **192,428**	center city rural north
Beni Sueif2–4	129,321	rural	3 beba, samasta	258,642	rural south
Minya1–8	174,003	urban-rural	1 minya, samalut 2 beni mazar, maghagha	348,677 347,337	city rural north
Minya2–8	156,601	rural	3 abu qirqas 4 malawi, dir mawas	309,916 316,486	rural far south
Assyut1–8	153,324	urban-rural	1 assyut 2 dayrut, manfalut	249,825 ***363,471***	assyut city rural north
Assyut2–8	**105,661**	rural	3 abnub, fath 4 abu tig, sadfa	263,362 **159,282**	rural east bank rural south
Sohag1–12	**116,095**	urban-rural	1 sohag, akhmim 2 maghagha 3 tahta, tama	287,130 **201,521** **207,920**	city north far north
Sohag2–8	**116,245**	rural	4 girga 5 baliana, dar al-salam	254,682 **210,297**	south far south
Qena1–4	185,433	town-rural	1 qena, qaft 2 qus, naga hamadi	207,113 311,441	town rural-industry
Qena2–8	105,433	rural	3 abu tisht, dashna	274,042	rural north
Luxor–4	166,564	urban	1 luxor	333,127	urban
Aswan–4	***213,142***	urban-rural	1 aswan	***426,284***	urban-rural

Source: Author.

Disparities in district apportionment – Canal Zone and Border Regions

List District–Seats	Voters per Seat	Demographic Character	Individual District	Voters per Seat	Demographic Character
Port Sa'id–4	109,284	urban	port sa'id	218,567	urban
Ismailia–4	***174,088***	urban-rural	ismailia	348,176	urban-rural
Suez–4	**94,729**	urban	suez	**189,459**	urban
North Sinai–4	50,837	towns	al-'arish, rafah	101,673	towns
South Sinai–4	15,124	towns	al-tur, sharm al-sheikh	30,248	towns
Red Sea–4	55,048	coastal towns	hurghada, safaga	110,097	coastal towns
New Valley–4	35,132	oases	kharagiya, wah khar	70,264	oases
Matruh–4	49,902	coastal towns	mersa matruh	99,804	coastal towns

Source: Author.

Note on Data and Methods

All voting data were obtained from open sources and were available online. Official figures from the government electoral commission were checked and supplemented with reports in diverse media, including semi-official, private, and partisan news agencies and websites, predominantly in Arabic and sometimes in English.

In addition to nationwide data sets, files were assembled for each governorate, including maps, tables, demographic data, media coverage, and studies of socioeconomic conditions and ecological problems.

The data analysis follows the lines of my previous studies of electoral politics in Turkey, Pakistan, Indonesia, Malaysia and Nigeria, employing standard methods of cross-tabulation, simple correlation, and mapping.[21]

Like most students of regionalism, my investigations are guided by the enduring insights of V. O. Key, particularly his classic study of southern politics in the United States.[22] By imagining that I was exploring Egypt with his eyes, I realized that his theoretical and historical contributions were even more important than his pioneering methods. He argued that after the American Civil War, southern elites skillfully used one-party and no-party systems to fight off populist protest and central government interventions for nearly a century. His explanation of those control systems—their variety, inner logic, and ultimate futility—are essential reading for anyone trying to understand Egypt's current revolutions—both national and local—in historical perspective.

Note on the Canal Zone and Border Regions

The governorates of the Canal Zone and border regions are a scattered set of settlements that still have weak ties to the Nile Valley and to one another. Each is a special collection of segmented communities juxtaposing military bases, government installations, carpetbagging land developers, and tribal societies carrying on a brisk smuggling trade over vast and poorly guarded borders. Because their most distinctive common features are incoherence and detachment, these areas are a non-region. What happens in one governorate often has little influence on the others—indeed, what happens today might not even influence future developments in the same location.

---

[21] Bianchi, Robert R. (2004). *Guests of God: Pilgrimage and Politics in the Islamic World*, New York: Oxford University Press.

[22] Key, Jr., V.O. (1984) *Southern Politics in State and Nation*, Knoxville, TN: University of Tennessee Press.

Politically, these outliers are overrepresented and under-organized. Parties with nationwide aspirations have few incentives to invest scarce resources here and usually rely on local elites to marshal supporters in an ad hoc manner. Consequently, electoral alliances are weak and shifting as evidenced by Nur's sudden breakthroughs in Suez and Mersah Matruh and by the precarious position of NDP loyalists, who hung on in the Red Sea while being swept away elsewhere.

Chapter 12

The Social and Economic Bases of Ennahdha Power: Khaldunian and Tocquevillian Reflections on the Tunisian Elections

Tunisia is a small land at the center of the world where the spirit of freedom knows no fear and no borders. But it was the last place anyone expected to ignite transcontinental revolution—not in Egypt and Syria and certainly not in Spain, Wisconsin and Tibet. Tunisia was best known not for activism and innovation, but for its exhausted economy, its fractured society, and its corrupt and dispirited polity. If history and social science have taught us anything it is that revolution requires minimal conditions and clearly Tunisia possessed none of them.

Tunisians understood this dismal reality better than anyone because of their special synthesis of Islamic and European learning. Ibn Khaldun explained that the cycles of history flow within the limits that nature imposes on social relations. The lifeblood of the polis is *esprit de corps* (*'asabiyya* in Arabic). Yet all *esprit* is fragile and transient—it must be recreated in every era and nurtured to a ripe old age before succumbing to more vigorous challengers. Khaldunian cycles can be prolonged through skillful statecraft until the day when religion creates a universal identity transcending tribe and empire.[1] But Tunisia enjoyed none of these assets—neither social solidarity nor wise leadership nor religious idealism.

Alexis de Tocqueville taught that collective action stems from the "art of association" which requires cultivation in hospitable climates and lengthy learning by free and attentive publics. As for revolution, we should expect it when conditions have improved to the point where the oppressed have more hope than despair. By Tocqueville's account, even

[1] Mahdi, Muhsin (1964). *Ibn Khaldûn's Philosophy of History: A Study in the Philosophic Foundation of the Science of Culture*, Chicago: University of Chicago Press.

the fall of an old regime would not summon forth citizens' power because political freedoms merely enable but do not spontaneously create effective associations, and without that weapon formal freedom remains meaningless.[2] Both before and after the revolution, Tunisia had the same shortcomings and the same unpromising fate. Ibn Khaldun and Tocqueville had thought of everything—except for the unthinkable.

Suicide is Painless

When Mohammed Bouazizi self-immolated, he destroyed far more than his body—he threw away his soul. All Muslims know that suicide is an unpardonable sin. Worse than breaking taboo or blasphemy, it is sheer ingratitude for all that the universe holds. It is spitting in God's face—the madness of chaos set loose against all creation, divine and human. What then can remain of mere mortal authority in any form—political, paternal, religious or military?

Bouazizi turned the Abrahamic parable upside down. Abraham was prepared to sacrifice his son to proclaim God's omnipotence. The Tunisian fruit peddler destroyed himself to denounce God's injustice. And if hellfire is the inevitable result, then why wait for the afterlife? Let the burning begin now for all to see and tremble. Force a nation of so-called Muslims to witness a wretch sending himself to hell in advance and make them confront their own worthlessness in the bargain. This was not just an act of rebellion—it was a collective insult against a people who thought they had already hit bottom and could sink no further.

No society recovers from such wounds. Just as the body cannot withstand hell on earth, Tunisia's scars are eternal and healing is no more than papering over the inner sores that no one wants to keep in full view. How then do Tunisians endure? How do they revolt and govern themselves in model fashion when all the world knows that to be

---

[2] de Tocqueville, Alexis (orig. pub. 1835) (2011). *Democracy in America*, translated by Harvey C. Mansfield and Delba Winthrop, Chicago: University of Chicago Press; and de Tocqueville, Alexis (orig. pub. 1856) (1998). *The Old Regime and the Revolution, Volume I*, translated by Alan S. Kahan, Chicago: University of Chicago Press.

impossible? They can only do it by rejecting Bouazizi's act as soundly as they glorify his courage. Having followed him in overturning all earthy authority, they must restore the supreme force he scorned. Only by reaffirming unseen power can they regain respect for themselves and reassemble society amid the chaos. This is a psychological imperative as well as a social and political mission. It is the work of re-integration at many levels simultaneously, struggling to put back together what generations of Muslim, Arab, Mediterraneans began tearing apart as soon as they drove the colonial masters from their shores.

The Tunisian people used the elections of October 2011 to begin this integrative work, choosing Ennahdha as the vehicle—and temporary embodiment—of their quest. In exploring the patterns of their votes, we have a rare opportunity to view the depth and multiplicity of their divisions as well as the first steps toward treating them instead of suppressing them.

From the Grand Mosaic to the Seven Tunisias

Unlike Herodotus who called Egypt "the gift of the Nile," Ibn Khaldun saw North Africa as an eternal captive of its dual shorelines along the sea and the desert. A land of limited possibilities—where hardships outweighed endowments—demanded constant adaptation and mutual interchange if even a small population were to move beyond subsistence and flourish next to more fortunate and powerful neighbors. And the human landscape encircling these elongated shores was as rich and variegated as the climate and topography. Three different social universes—city folk, farmers and nomads—crammed together sharing meager resources yet nourished by close ties to vastly different civilizations in Asia, Africa and Europe.[3]

For a people both sustained and imprisoned by such natural forces, everything depended on social relations. History for Ibn Khaldun is not the succession of class struggles over ever-growing surplus. Rather it is the constant tying and loosening of human bonds between

---

[3] Harris, Caroline and Ray Harris (2008). Tunisia: Geography on the Edge, *Geography Review*, September.

communities that depend on one another precisely because their special adaptations allow them to cohabit the same sparse commons where surplus can grow only so much before destroying its surroundings.

Ibn Khaldun had a heightened appreciation of the many ways that nature influences political outcomes, but he was no ecological determinist. He scrupulously explores a host of intervening variables that throw history in one direction or another, including migration, land tenure, trade networks, inheritance, social pacts, ideological formulas, elite socialization, distributive coalitions, the international system and much more. It's all there just as surely as if Montesquieu and Gramsci had been looking over his shoulder while he penned the Prolegomenon.[4]

Nonetheless, Ibn Khaldun's portrayals of North African civilization as generally adaptive and symbiotic are worlds apart from Tunisia's recent descent into environmental degradation, social apartheid and regional colonialism. Such a collapse of public mindedness and disregard for natural patrimony would have seemed suicidal in his day—much as Bouazizi's self-ignition appears to us now. However much he focused on the constituent elements and their mutual struggles, Ibn Khaldun always envisioned a single community moving through endless time and learning from its vicissitudes. Today that social mosaic is shattered and strewn about as Tunisians try to invent a new adhesive to piece themselves back together.

The Tunisia that chose Ennahdha to lead its first democratically elected government was a deeply divided and highly stratified conglomeration of at least seven separate regions. Following Juan Linz's classic study of "the eight Spains," I call them the seven Tunisias (see Figure 12.1).[5] Linz marshaled an array of economic, social and cultural

[4] Ibn Khaldun (orig. pub. 1377) (1989). *The Muqaddimah: An Introduction to History*, translated by Franz Rosenthal, Princeton: Princeton University Press.

[5] Linz, Juan J. and Armando de Miguel (1966). Within-nation differences and comparisons: The eight Spains, in Richard L. Merritt and Stein Rokkan, eds., *Comparing Nations: The Use of Quantitative Data in Cross-National Research*, New Haven: Yale University Press.

data on the provinces of Spain to demonstrate the depth of within-country differences and to explain their enduring impairment of national integration. His insights and methods have been transferred to many other countries and they are indispensable for understanding Tunisia as well.

Figure 12.1. The Seven Tunisias as Juan Linz might see them: North-south and east-west cleavages. *(Ennahdha stongholds in italics)*

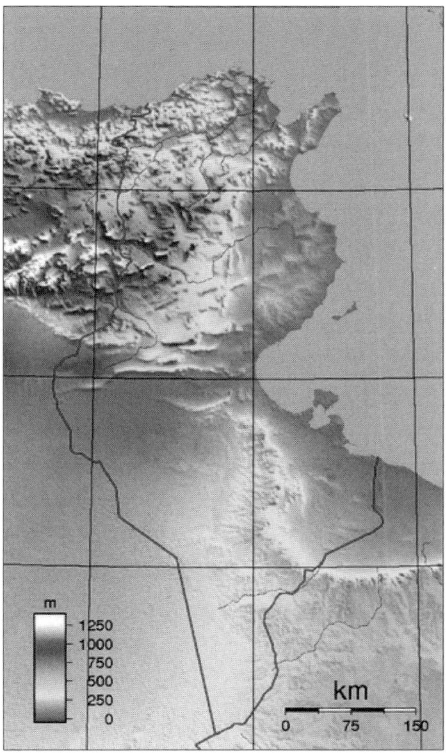

Source: commons.wikimedia.org.

Tunisia has published a wealth of detailed social and ecological statistics broken down by governorates and local districts—physical geography, rainfall and climate, economic activity and employment, consumption patterns, education and literacy, housing, migration, transportation and infrastructure, access to potable drinking water, crop production, livestock—even measures of basic human well-being such as low birth weight, stunted growth, caloric intake, and varieties of animal protein in daily diets.[6] All of the evidence points in the same direction. In recent years, official publications go so far as to label the seven regions and present summary figures for each one even though they have no administrative or scientific status. It is as though the official record keepers concluded that the data had arranged itself into self-evident clusters, which reflect reality more faithfully than the boundaries of governorates and municipalities.[7]

Voting behavior followed the same pattern. Every major party had a specific regional base and social constituency with weak or no support beyond. Ennahdha was the only nationwide political movement covering every district and class, yet even its strength rose and fell in line with the familiar spatial and social cleavages. All of Tunisia's worst divisions—environmental, socioeconomic and political—seemed to coincide and reinforce one another, leaving little room for cross-cutting loyalties and split-the-difference bargaining.

---

[6] Institut National de la Statistique (2010). *Annuaire Statistique de la Tunisie 2005-2009*, Tunis: République Tunisienne Ministère du Développement et de la Coopération Internationale; and Institut National de la Statistique (2010). *La Tunisie en Chiffres 2007-2009*, Tunis: République Tunisienne Ministère du Développement et de la Coopération Internationale.

[7] Belhedi, Amor (2006). Territoires, appartenance et identification: Quelques réflexions à partir du cas Tunisien, *L'Espace géographique*, 4:35, pp. 310–316; and Belhedi, Amor (1999). Les disparités spatiales en Tunisie, état des lieux et enjeux, *Méditerranée*, 91, pp. 63–72.

Identifying and Explaining Ennahdha Power

Ennahdha's success was most impressive at opposite ends of the country—in the vast southern zones bordering the Sahara and the Mediterranean and in the metropolitan complex of greater Tunis (see Figure 12.2). The secular middle-class parties—the Congrès pour la République (CPR) and Ettakatol (the Block for Labor and Freedom)—did best in suburban Tunis and along the fertile eastern coastal plain between Tunis and Sfax. The two best-known leftist parties—the Progressive Democratic Party (PDP) and the Pôle Démocratique Moderniste (PDM)—attracted nearly all of their support in the big cities and even that was from wealthier districts rather than working-class areas. The biggest surprise was the new Aridha Chaabia (People's Petition) Party, which caught fire in the depressed agricultural interior of the northwest and the western mountains. The new coalition government led by Ennahdha, the CPR, and Ettakatol shaped up as an alliance of southern and eastern business interests that left western farmers out in the cold (see Appendix B, The Major Political Parties).

There is much to debate about the contours of Ennahdha's support. One can question its depth, motives and staying power, but there is no doubt concerning its breadth and commanding superiority over all rivals (see Table 12.1). Ennahdha won 37 percent of the total vote compared to a mere 9 percent and 7 percent for the second and third place finishers. It was the leading vote-getter in every district in Tunisia and abroad with only one exception—the destitute backwater of Sidi Bouzid where Mohammad Bouazizi's spectacular protest had ignited the revolution nearly a year earlier (see Figure 12.3).

Ennahdha's demographic profile is a classic example of a cross-class coalition rooted in the middle sectors of Tunisian society. Its popularity is greatest not among the richest or the poorest voters, but everywhere in between—particularly the educated and struggling salary earners and businesses in the provincial towns and the older urban quarters. Ennahdha support correlates most with employment in the tertiary sector, including trade, transport and communications, and administration and education. In the industrial branches, there is a weak

Table 12.1. Major party vote by district (percent).

District	Ennahdha	CPR	Ettakatol	Aridha	PDP	PDM	Others
Bizerte	40.99	7.93	6.70	5.08	5.23	2.79	31.27
Ariana	36.13	9.03	14.00	2.20	5.01	6.96	26.67
Manouba	40.68	9.35	7.94	4.04	3.21	2.19	32.60
Tunis 1	46.31	8.49	13.26	2.16	3.40	2.44	23.94
Tunis 2	30.31	10.81	19.20	0.98	6.08	8.32	24.30
BenArous	42.34	11.07	12.86	1.93	4.80	2.67	24.33
Nabeul 1	31.26	12.32	9.68	7.78	3.73	2.86	32.38
Nabeul 2	29.58	14.19	7.93	5.63	4.45	5.63	32.58
Zaghouan	34.60	5.04	3.60	9.04	6.02	1.26	40.43
Béja	31.08	6.89	6.89	8.34	7.59	1.99	37.23
Jenduba	31.28	5.30	7.80	11.74	6.03	3.19	34.66
Kef	26.72	6.21	5.17	8.07	3.93	2.01	47.89
Siliana	28.46	4.89	3.55	8.81	4.97	1.64	47.68
Kairouan	42.97	4.62	2.28	18.42	1.46	0.84	29.40
Sousse	35.85	5.35	4.16	5.03	3.11	1.88	44.61
Monastir	32.48	4.36	3.88	3.33	2.25	2.08	51.62
Mahdia	31.08	6.37	3.27	7.41	3.86	2.45	45.56
Kasserine	35.21	7.04	2.80	6.02	4.80	2.04	42.09
SidiBouzid	15.46	1.69	1.05	38.20	1.18	0.89	41.52
Sfax 1	47.60	10.25	4.93	8.49	2.84	1.22	24.66
Sfax 2	37.94	13.04	6.04	8.66	1.81	1.32	31.18
Tozeur	43.16	5.05	2.50	3.97	3.54	3.27	38.52
Gabés	53.06	9.95	1.29	5.31	3.16	0.89	26.34
Kébili	40.48	26.71	0.96	4.11	3.74	1.02	22.98
Médenine	47.71	9.87	2.87	4.11	3.77	1.81	29.86
Tataouine	62.91	3.58	1.82	6.04	4.87	0.52	20.26
TUNISIA	**37.41**	**8.58**	**6.91**	**6.89**	**3.85**	**2.70**	**33.66**
France 1	33.70	12.55	11.25	3.94	7.72	8.26	22.57
France 2	34.35	10.05	8.33	0	8.08	6.58	32.61
Germany	42.95	17.22	13.45	8.19	6.95	0.00	11.25
Italy	49.41	5.23	5.54	11.40	5.51	2.05	20.86
Arabworld	45.80	14.52	11.26	3.34	7.29	5.85	11.93
Americas	35.02	18.54	16.38	1.79	9.36	8.79	10.12
ABROAD	**37.63**	**12.44**	**10.75**	**3.75**	**7.69**	**6.43**	**21.31**
TOTAL	**37.42**	**8.78**	**7.10**	**6.73**	**4.04**	**2.89**	**33.04**

Source: Author.

Figure 12.2. The regional distribution of Ennahdha vote.
(high +, low –)

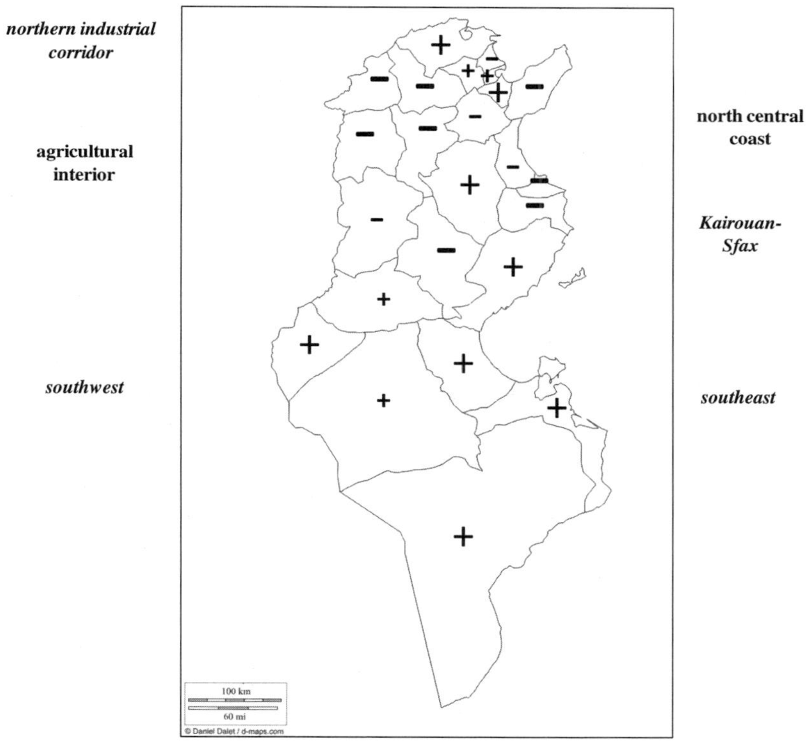

Source: d-maps.com

Figure 12.3. Ennahdha vote by governorate (percent).

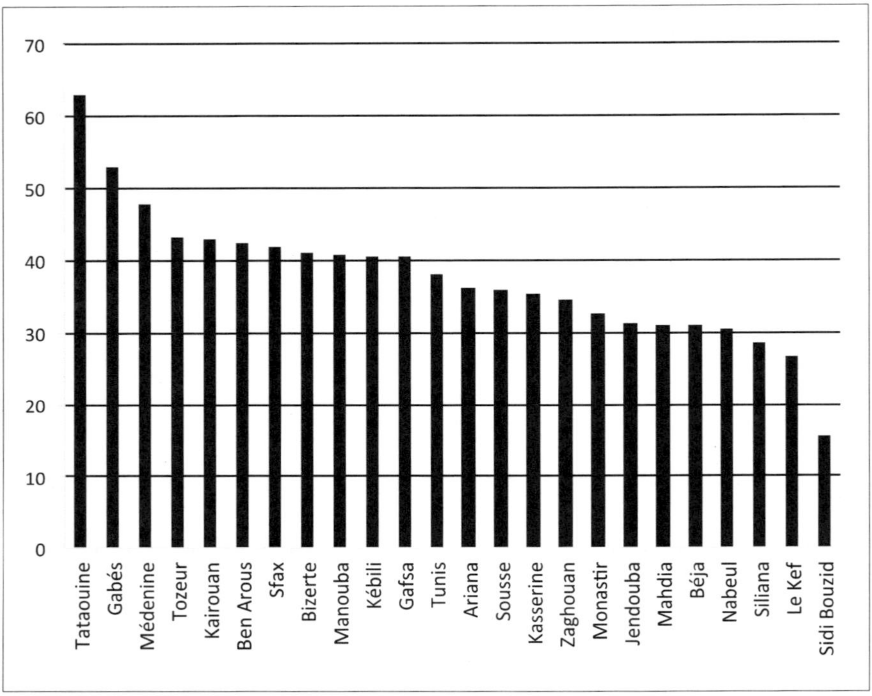

Source: Author.

connection with mining, but not with manufacturing or construction. Tunisian agriculture is by far the least hospitable environment for Ennahdha, supporting instead local notables running as independents or Aridha Chaabia's campaign of rural insurgency (see Table 12.2 and Table 12.3).

Table 12.2. Employment in economic sectors and Ennahdha vote (Pearson's r's).

Agriculture	**-0.4477**
Secondary sectors	0.0781
Tertiary sectors	**0.4290**
Manufacturing	0.0216
Mining	0.2022
Construction	0.0145
Trade	**0.3358**
Transport & Communications	**0.3977**
Administration & Education	**0.2944**
Other services	**0.2896**

Source: Author.

Table 12.3. Agricultural employment and major party vote (Pearson's r's).

Ennahdha	**-0.4477**
CPR	-0.2917
Ettakatol	**-0.4036**
Aridha Chaabia	**0.5639**
PDP	0.2656
PDM	-0.3244
Coalition Government Parties	**-0.6089**

Source: Author.

Ennahdha's following clusters in governorates with mixed and balanced economies rather than in those dominated by a single sector. The most diversified economies also promote the greatest concentration of Ennahdha strongholds. Only in the capital city is a bloated service sector tied to high support for Ennahdha. In general, however, the economic environments where the party did best look very much like Tunisia as a whole (see Figure 12.4).

Figure 12.4. Support for Ennahdha by employment in economic sectors.

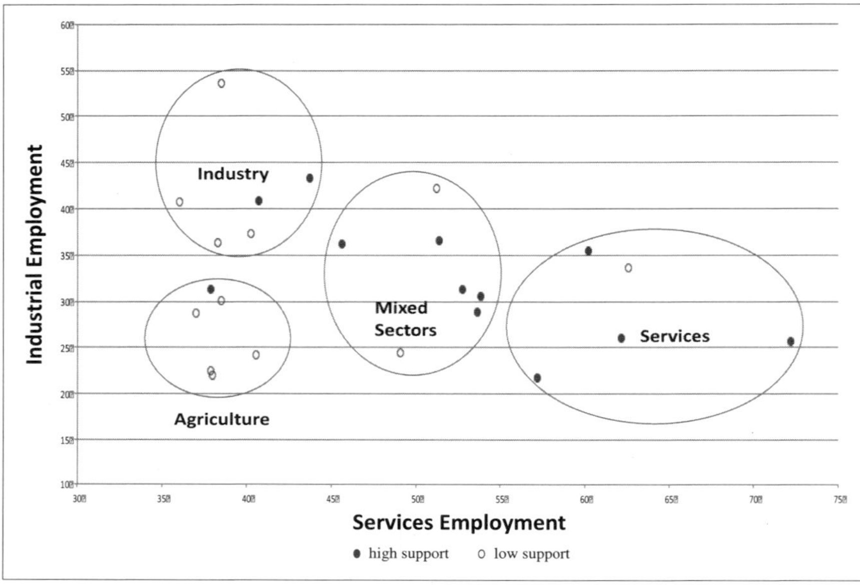

Source: Author.

Ennadha vote correlates very strongly with professional categories, but only for women and not for men. Districts with high proportions of female apprentices and managers were fertile ground for Ennahdha candidates. In contrast, areas where women were still limited to household work preferred other parties (see Table 12.4).

Table 12.4. Professional categories and Ennahdha vote (Pearson's r's).

	Total	Male	Female
Self-employed	-0.0619	-0.1006	-0.1227
Salaried	0.0611	0.0891	0.1426
Manager	0.0195	-0.0627	**0.5700**
Apprentice	0.2655	0.1069	**0.7290**
Home help	-0.0780	-0.0116	-0.2314

Source: Author.

Measures of education and literacy—for both women and men—are strongly linked to Ennahdha vote. Primary and secondary educations are most important and university education is the least important. Illiteracy depresses support for Ennahdha. The relationship is a bit stronger for women than for men and in the countryside more than the cities. There is no evidence that gender biases in school enrollment either encourage or suppress Ennahdha voting (see Table 12.5).

Table 12.5. Education, illiteracy, and Ennahdha vote (Pearson's r's).

Education	
Schooling Rate 6-14 years	**0.4312**
Male Schooling	**0.5014**
Female Schooling	**0.3844**
Male/Female School	-0.1797
Unschooled 10 years+	**-0.4244**
Elementary	**0.3743**
Secondary	**0.3336**
Higher	0.0992
Illiteracy	
Illiteracy 10 yrs+	**-0.4455**
Male Illiteracy	**-0.4190**
Female Illiteracy	**-0.4701**
Female/Male Illiteracy	0.0595
Urban Illiteracy	**-0.4082**
Rural Illiteracy	**-0.4488**

Source: Author.

Nearly every dimension of household consumption per capita correlates with support for Ennahdha. Means of transportation, communication and home appliances are good predictors. Leading examples include basic needs such as land phones as well as more upscale conveniences such as satellite dishes, ovens, cars, mobile phones and refrigerators (see Table 12.6).

Table 12.6. Household consumption and Ennahdha vote (Pearson's r's).

Land Phones	**0.5869**
Satellite Dishes	**0.5000**
Ovens	**0.4200**
Cars	**0.3990**
Mobile Phones	**0.2909**
Refrigerators	**0.2781**
Televisions	0.1867
Tableware	0.1774
Air Conditioners	0.1734
Computers	0.1689
Radios	-0.0363

Source: Author.

The intermediate status of Ennahdha voters is evident in the bulge of support for the party in the middle ranges of consumption compared to the extremes of wealth and poverty. Car ownership typifies the general curvilinear pattern. The most pro-Ennahdha regions—the southeast, the southwest and the northern industrial belt between Tunis and Bizerte—cluster in between the poorer farming areas and the richer metropolis of Greater Tunis. In the same middle band of development, a handful of east coast governorates—Nabeul, Sousse, Monastir and Mahdia—stand out as bastions of Ennahdha's secular opponents and of many independent candidates who were connected to the old regime (see Figure 12.5).[8]

[8] Moudoud, Ezzeddine (1985). L'impossible régionalisation «Jacobine» et le dilemme des disparités régionales en tunisie, *Canadian Journal of Regional Science*, 8:3, 413–438.

Figure 12.5. Ennahdha vote and cars per capita.

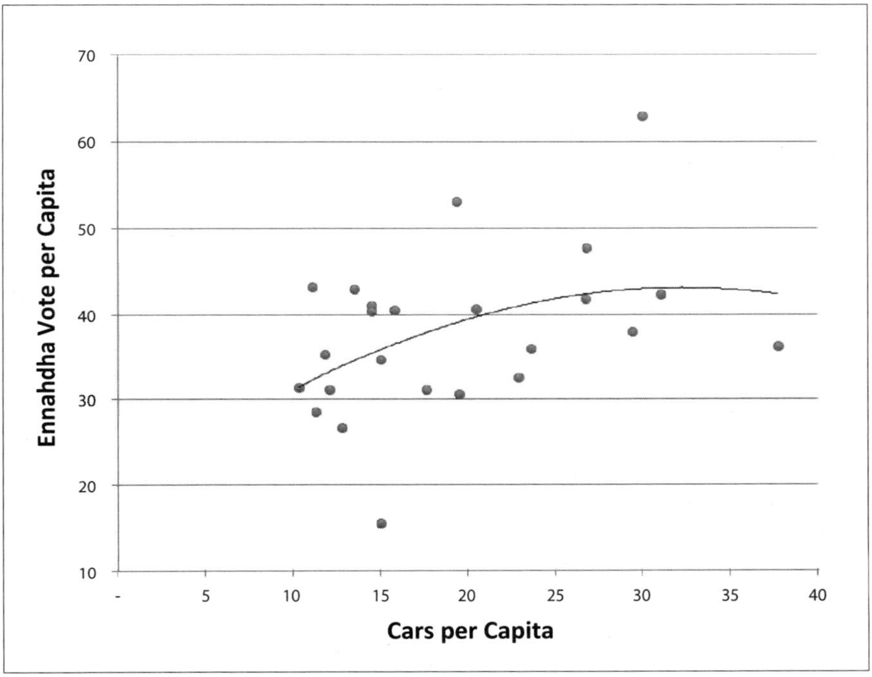

Source: Author.

Many other measures of consumption and personal well-being reveal a strong east-west cleavage running through the geographic center of Tunisia—a contrast that rivals the better-known differences between north and south. In terms of poverty levels, infant health and general nutrition, the middle third of the country is deeply divided between the depressed western plateau and the prosperous coastal plain to the east. These are also the regions where Ennahdha vote was most clearly below the national average, demonstrating once again that the party's hybrid coalition was less appealing at the extremes of the economic spectrum than in the middle (see 'Note on Regional Cleavages' on page 175 and accompanying illustrations).

Aquatic Politics in Tunis—Between the Salt Flats, the Lake, and the Sea

In Tunis, citizens voted according to their social and economic status as reflected by the quality of their neighborhoods. Neighborhood status, in turn, depends on proximity to bodies of water that are relatively clear or foul. Ennahdha's strength was greatest in the poorer districts, particularly in the southwestern quadrant of the city surrounding the vast salt flats (*sébkha*) known as Sebkha Séjumi which flood in the winter and fry in the summer. Ettakatol, the CPR, and the small leftist parties were most successful in the wealthiest neighborhoods, especially the northeastern suburbs on the breezy Mediterranean coast and along the cleaner eastern shores of Lake Tunis. All of the major battleground districts clustered in between these two zones—in the long swath of commercial and residential neighborhoods that form an unbroken line along a 20-kilometer north-south axis with its center near the old Madina (see Table 12.7, Figure 12.6, and Figure 12.7).[9]

---

[9] Chabbi, Morched (2007). L'urbanisation en Tunisie, transformations et tendance d'évolution, *Archi-Mag*, available online at http://www.archi-mag.com/essai_9.php.

Table 12.7. Tunis—Major party vote by neighborhood (percent).

Neighborhood	Ennahdha	Ettakatol	CPR	PDM	PDP	Aridha	Other
Madina	40.69	19.88	8.67	3.64	3.49	0.98	22.65
Bab al-Bahr	34.06	22.48	13.00	5.29	4.32	0.91	19.94
Bab Suwiqa	43.01	19.17	9.89	2.47	2.85	0.90	21.71
al-Sejumi	60.10	7.44	5.01	1.16	2.60	2.23	21.45
al-Zuhur	47.17	13.64	9.23	1.86	2.78	1.48	23.84
al-Hrairia	51.79	9.34	8.11	1.41	2.81	2.02	24.53
Sidi Hassine	51.49	6.33	4.73	1.16	2.52	4.73	29.04
al-Wardiya	45.60	14.75	10.74	2.20	3.86	1.21	21.65
al-Kabariya	48.70	10.82	9.73	1.87	3.49	2.93	22.46
Sidi al-Bashir	44.84	15.91	8.69	3.20	3.29	1.30	22.77
Jabal Jellud	44.36	6.25	6.02	1.32	6.18	3.79	32.08
Total Tunis 1	**46.17**	**13.26**	**8.91**	**2.41**	**3.39**	**2.15**	**23.71**
Qartaj	25.42	21.86	8.71	11.91	6.91	1.08	24.10
al-'Umran	40.05	14.54	8.24	4.25	3.97	1.30	27.65
'Umran al-'Ali	44.11	11.50	13.57	2.54	3.41	1.26	23.62
al-Tahrir	42.67	13.90	14.57	3.17	3.25	0.74	21.70
al-Menzah	12.54	22.62	9.20	21.97	10.27	0.24	23.16
Hay Khadra	30.41	17.72	13.14	8.54	6.47	0.71	23.01
Le Bardo	34.25	19.30	14.13	4.78	4.08	0.78	22.69
Halq al-Wadi	26.86	22.32	11.58	7.22	6.08	0.73	25.21
Le Kram	33.55	17.02	10.44	5.07	5.18	1.28	27.46
al-Marsa	24.07	24.40	7.21	10.64	7.49	1.34	24.86
Total Tunis 2	**30.38**	**19.20**	**10.83**	**8.35**	**5.89**	**0.98**	**24.37**
Total Tunis	**37.93**	**16.36**	**9.91**	**5.51**	**4.70**	**1.54**	**24.06**

Source: Author.

Figure 12.6. Tunis—large zones: Contiguous and overlapping.

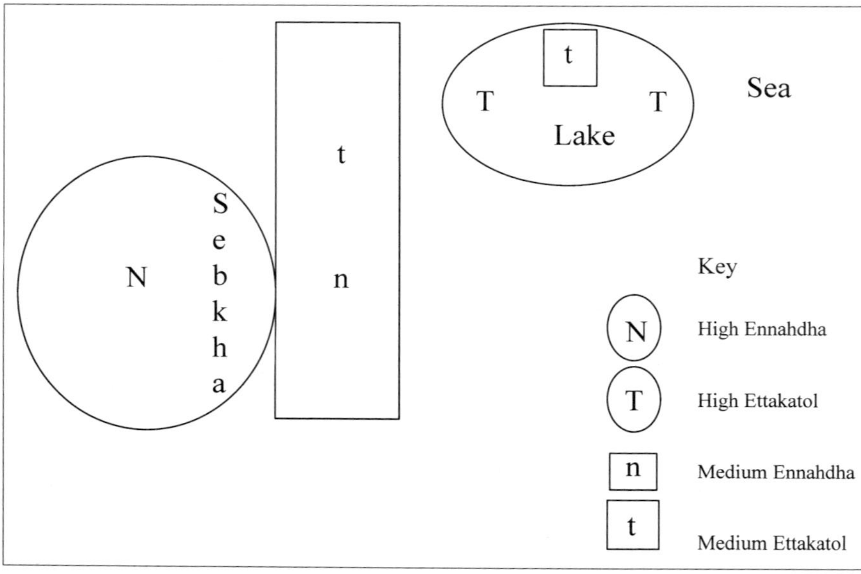

Source: Author.

Figure 12.7. Satellite view of Tunis showing Salt Flats, Lake Tunis, and the sea.

Source: en.wikipedia.org.

This core area is not only densely populated; it is also socially diverse and politically polarized. It includes the historic heart of the city (the Madina) on the central high ground, the early colonial extension slopping eastward to the lake (Bab al-Bahr), and the post-independence concentrations of rural migrants and industrial workers to the south (Séjumi, Sidi al-Béchir, al-Wardiya, al-Kabariya, and Jabal Jellud). Farther north, on the other side of Avenue Habib Bourguiba, are the newer neighborhoods that sprang up after independence to accommodate

Tunisia's burgeoning middle-class–the planned parks and housing projects of 'Umran and the high-end residences of al-Menzah.[10]

This middle ground is where Ennhadha's mobilization skills were at their best and their worst. In the migrant quarter of Séjumi it won 60 percent of the vote, but in upscale al-Menzah it finished in third place with less than 13 percent. Ennahdha's vote was slightly above average in the crowded Madina and slightly below average next door in the more spacious French quarter of Bab al-Bahr. 'Umran was the only centrally located district in which all of the parties performed about as well as they did in the city as a whole. In that sense, 'Umran's voters appeared to be the "most average" citizens in all of Tunis. Nonetheless, even this unremarkable middle-class population was quite polarized. Ennahdha did best among voters in the crowded core area whereas Ettakatol prevailed in the more wooded periphery where parks, water stations, and schools offered relative comfort and convenience (see Tables 12.8–12.10).

Table 12.8. al-Sejumi—Major party vote by school polling station (percent).

School	Ennahdha	Ettakatol	CPR	PDP	Aridha	PDM	Other
March 2	56.90	8.93	6.09	3.07	2.54	1.31	21.16
al-Najah	60.30	6.83	7.48	1.48	2.31	1.20	20.41
Bab Khalid	62.02	4.79	2.98	2.98	2.87	0.85	23.51
Sejumi	62.85	7.09	3.48	2.43	1.60	1.09	21.45
Total	**60.10**	**7.44**	**5.01**	**2.60**	**2.23**	**1.16**	**21.45**

Source: Author.

[10] Chabbi, Morched and Hassen Abid (2008). La mobilité urbaine dans le Grand Tunis: Evolutions et perspectives, *Plan Bleu-Centre d'Activités Régionales*, May, available online at http://www.planbleu.org/publications/mobiliteUrbaine.html.

Table 12.9. al-'Umran—Major party vote by school polling station (percent).

School	Ennahdha	Ettakatol	CPR	PDM	PDP	Aridha	Other
16BisharaKhouri	23.01	26.45	10.54	10.36	6.69	0.48	22.47
Jabal Ahmar1	43.10	9.39	5.42	2.15	3.11	2.20	34.62
Jabal Ahmar2	47.89	7.34	7.89	3.12	5.14	1.83	26.79
Hay al-Ramana	22.72	25.57	11.87	8.65	5.06	0.92	25.21
March Second	44.02	11.73	7.90	3.02	2.21	1.16	29.97
Nahaj Bolonia	28.21	17.90	13.10	7.42	6.55	0.61	26.20
Bir al-Karam	45.66	11.35	6.14	3.04	4.59	1.55	27.67
Ras al-Tabiya	40.81	16.42	10.48	3.83	2.97	1.25	24.24
Bir Atiq	49.45	8.44	6.26	1.55	2.70	0.92	30.67
Fawz 'Umran	38.24	10.88	6.70	2.09	4.40	1.32	36.37
Bir Karam	47.29	13.56	7.28	3.03	2.67	1.64	24.52
Total 'Umran	**40.05**	**14.54**	**8.19**	**4.25**	**3.97**	**1.30**	**27.70**

Source: Author.

Just north of 'Umran, in the wealthy semi-suburb of al-Menzah, Ennahdha suffered its most crushing defeat in all of Tunis. In al-Menzah, the leftist parties swept the field led by Ettakatol and the Pôle Démocratique Moderniste (PDM). Ennahdha barely captured third place by inching past the CPR and the tiny Progressive Democratic Party (PDP). Ennahdha lost all ten polling districts in al-Menzah and never gained more than 19 percent of the vote in any of them. Its most dismal results came along the main road traversing the heart of the neighborhood—Rue Tahar Ben Ammar—particularly around the Mendès France School where Ennahdha's share was under 7 percent. Ennahdha salvaged respectable second place finishes only in two special corners of al-Menzah—in the southwest around the Law and Political Science Faculties of Tunis University and in a far northeastern triangle that hosts a cluster of Islamic schools and charities.

Table 12.10. al-Menzah—Major party vote by school polling station (percent).

School	Ettakatol	PDP	Ennahdha	PDM	CPR	Aridha	Other
Manar1	22.23	18.88	16.17	8.27	11.43	0.41	22.60
Menzah9	21.65	24.70	9.95	12.87	8.15	0.09	22.58
H. Khafsha	21.51	27.00	10.69	10.72	6.44	0.12	23.51
Manar2	22.68	24.97	10.10	11.54	8.74	0.11	21.86
Mutualeville	22.65	28.98	6.51	11.92	4.96	0.06	24.91
Sec Manar1	22.43	14.42	18.69	7.21	16.69	0.53	20.03
Sec Manar2	21.76	16.19	15.98	8.73	13.87	0.34	23.14
MawaqaJamil	26.30	17.09	14.41	10.87	7.80	0.31	23.23
Nahaj Rasas	23.56	15.83	17.47	7.97	10.32	0.88	23.97
ImamMuslim	25.37	13.85	18.11	6.99	11.12	0.13	24.43
Total Menzah	**22.62**	**21.97**	**12.54**	**10.27**	**9.20**	**0.24**	**23.16**

Source: Author.

Although ‘Umran and al-Menzah produced contrasting election results, in both neighborhoods politics followed a common pattern reflecting divided social space. The heart of the district was dominated by one status group aligned with its preferred party whereas a different status group supporting a rival party dominated the outlying areas. The pattern of concentric circles was clear in both neighborhoods. In ‘Umran, a large middle class core outnumbered an upper middle class periphery whereas, in al-Menzah, a more secular core outnumbered a more religious periphery. In both districts, economic and religious issues were closely intertwined. Nonetheless, class divisions were more prominent in socially diverse ‘Umran while religious differences cut more deeply among the generally privileged residents of al-Menzah.

Figure 12.8 summarizes Ennahdha’s strength relative to the combined vote of its four major rivals in these five central city neighborhoods. Each circle represents results from a local polling station coded to allow comparison of all 45 stations district by district. Sejumi and al-Menzah define the extremes of Ennahdha strength and weakness. The Madina and Bab al-Bahar occupy the middle ground but with clear centers of gravity favoring Ennahdha on one hand and the secular parties on the other. ‘Umran is by far the most internally polarized neighborhood of the lot. Its polling stations range widely from high to low support for

Ennahdha. Only one polling place lies near the center of the graph suggesting that partisan competition in 'Umran is closely tied to social and spatial segregation. The very neighborhood in which party strength appeared at first glance to be unusually balanced and "average" turns out on closer examination to be the most deeply divided (non)community in central Tunis.

Figure 12.8. Vote for Ennahdha and the Four Biggest Secular Parties in Sejumi, 'Umran, Madina, Bab al-Bahr, and al-Menzah.

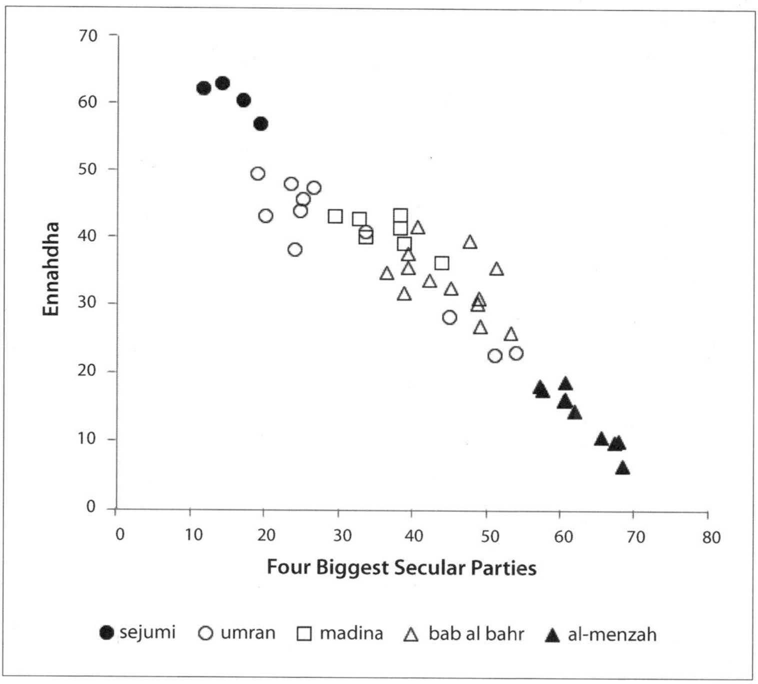

Source: Author.

In the Tunisian capital, the causal connections between ecology and politics are complex but undeniable. The city of Tunis expanded outward from its historic heart in a series of concentric circles. In today's metropolis, the status and quality of neighborhoods generally increases to the north and east and decreases to the south and west. The spatial pattern of residential status closely tracks the underlying continuum of environments ranging from the salt flats and the polluted western lake to the clearer eastern lake and the Mediterranean shore.[11]

Vote for the major parties reflected a similar logic. Voters in wealthier neighborhoods were most likely to support the secular parties of the center and the left—Ettakatol, the CPR, the PDP, and the PMD. Poorer districts preferred Ennahdha and to a lesser degree the Aridha Chaabia. A cluster of socially diverse neighborhoods near the center of the city promoted the most competitive contests, but here as well variations in voters' choices mirrored differences in status and residence.

In Tunis, politics and environment influence one another both directly and indirectly. The geography of good and bad water shapes the spatial distribution of stratified social and economic groups that in turn produces polarized party competition. And as environmental degradation forces ecological issues to the top of the political agenda, governments intervene more directly and more dramatically in restoration, demolition, and grand engineering projects that are supported by conflicting economic and cultural interest groups.

---

[11] Chabbi, Morched and Hassen Abid (2008). La mobilité urbaine dans le Grand Tunis: Evolutions et perspectives, *Plan Bleu-Centre d'Activités Régionales*, May, available online at http://www.planbleu.org/publications/mobiliteUrbaine.html; and Kenzari, Bechir (2004). Lake Tunis, or the Concept of the Third Centre, in Yasser Elsheshtawy, ed., *Planning Middle Eastern Cities: An Urban Kaleidoscope in a Globalizing World*, London: Routledge.

Map 12.1. Tunis neighborhoods.

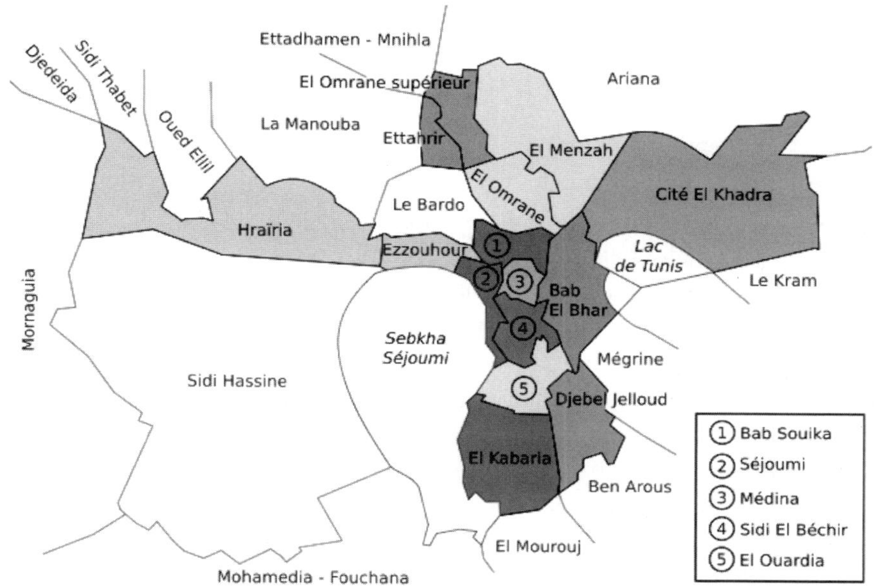

Source: en.wikipedia.org.

Networking the Honeycombs of Sfax

Sfax is Tunisia's second largest city with a population of about 270 thousand compared to the capital's 800 thousand and well ahead of the third largest city of Sousse with about 175 thousand. Sfax is the nation's leading industrial center as well as a hub of foreign trade and a favored destination of migrants from the towns and villages of the interior. It is widely noted for possessing a rich concentration of technical schools and for generating some of the most polluted air and water in the country. Once regarded as the unofficial capital of southern Tunisia, Sfax is making a comeback after years of neglect under Ben 'Ali's misrule. Several of the city's prominent leaders have returned to political life, including Mansour Moalla, a powerful technocrat and minister from the

Bourguiba era who is an old ally of the private sector and Persian Gulf investors.[12]

Yet socially and geographically Sfax hardly seems to be a city at all. In contrast to Tunis' large and overlapping megaregions, Sfax is sliced into more than a dozen scattered neighborhoods that have sprung up independently at different times. Tunis is a prototype of metamorphic metropolitan development where successive power centers have expended enormous effort to refashion urban society as a whole according to their changing visions of empire, colony, and nation. On the other hand, Sfax is a classic example of sedimentary evolution where the major quarters have sneaked up on one another with far less mutual disturbance and interchange.[13]

Sfax's jumbled social landscape made it more difficult for the political parties to coordinate collective action. Election campaigns had to mobilize diverse constituencies that were separated by considerable distances. Nonetheless, party organizations in Sfax still demonstrated impressive talents in the art of association. They produced a respectable turnout rate of 35 percent of the registered voters compared to 42 percent in the lower-class neighborhoods of southern Tunis (Tunis District 1) and 59 percent in the wealthier northern neighborhoods (Tunis District 2).

There was a striking difference between Ennahdha's following and supporters of the other parties. Ennahdha was the only movement with a multi-class base that voted in unison across scattered enclaves of business people, workers, and middle-class salary earners. Geographic separation and economic differences did not prevent effective organizing and coalition building. In this sense, Ennahdha's success in Sfax was a local model of its wider victory in Tunisia as a whole, particularly for the rise of Ennahdha strongholds such as Bizerte, Kairouan, and Gabés—the

---

[12] Moalla, Mansour (2012). Le Bourguisme pêut etre une solution en l'absence d'alternatives sérieuses, *Radioexpressfm.com*, 16 février.

[13] Chabbi, Morched (2007). L'urbanisation en Tunisie, transformations et tendance d'évolution, *Archi-Mag*, available online at http://www.archi-mag.com/essai_9.php.

third tier of widely separated provincial capital cities with populations of about 120 thousand each.

Ennahdha had three rich vote banks in Sfax—the old commercial center of the Madina in the south, the winding streets of Rabadh, the popular quarter in the near north, and the newer middle class residences of Muhammad 'Ali far to the northeast. Together these neighborhoods accounted for nine polling stations in which Ennahdha's vote consistently doubled the combined tally for its two closest rivals—the CPR and Ettakatol (see Table 12.11, Figure 12.9, and Figure 12.10). Ennahdha won in all of the city's 26 voting districts, but these nine neighborhoods yielded the greatest landslides.

The CPR and Ettakatol also had three pockets of strength in which their combined vote equaled Ennahdha's and frequently surpassed it. But these were all upscale neighborhoods with socially privileged voters. The largest pocket was the renovated French Quarter connecting the southern edge of the Madina with the port. The smallest area in which the CPR and Ettakatol ran well was the relatively isolated semi-suburban development of al-Basha in the far north. By far the strongest opposition to Ennahdha was concentrated in between these widely separated regions—in the near northeastern neighborhood of al-Basatin.

Al-Basatin is the oldest and most stable of the European-style residential districts. Socially and culturally, it is the direct counterweight to al-Rabadh. The two neighborhoods sit astride one another in the middle of the city like long diagonal fortresses. Depending on one's perspective, they seem to point both inward and outward. At their southern edges, they slant toward a common center while refusing to converge. Looking northward, they guard divergent routes to vastly different worlds—the inland road that pilgrims and villagers travel to Kairouan and Kasserine versus the coastal highway that beach lovers take to nearby resorts favored by Western tourists.

Table 12.11. Sfax Madina—Major party vote by school polling station (percent).

School	Enna-hdha	CPR	Etta-katol	Voice Ind	Aridha	PDP	PDM	Com	Other
Bab al-Bahr	26.41	15.83	12.36	9.67	3.28	3.99	3.87	2.88	21.71
Anatol France	32.55	18.49	9.29	7.28	4.02	3.10	2.34	2.09	20.84
Ma'had 9 Avril 1938	34.90	10.40	5.76	6.62	2.58	1.72	1.26	1.06	35.71
Muh Ali Hay Khairi	28.68	17.97	13.60	5.97	4.04	3.40	2.16	2.02	22.15
Habib Bourghiba	39.50	11.75	7.30	5.82	3.40	1.47	1.24	1.31	28.21
al-Hadi Shakr	44.81	13.44	7.50	5.27	4.62	2.42	1.08	0.99	19.87
Saha al-Qasba	40.42	11.54	7.15	6.20	4.91	2.15	1.42	1.38	24.84
Majida Bulila	40.17	24.46	6.51	6.01	3.87	1.62	1.21	1.70	14.44
Baghdad1 al-Basatin	29.20	21.84	13.14	6.00	2.27	2.42	3.20	1.52	20.41
Baghdad2 al-Basatin	27.27	23.26	13.49	5.06	2.38	2.79	3.55	2.03	20.17
Muh Ali Hay Khairi	28.68	17.97	13.60	5.97	4.04	3.40	2.16	2.02	22.15
Habib Bourghiba	39.50	11.75	7.30	5.82	3.40	1.47	1.24	1.31	28.21
Jawhar al-Basatin	25.35	16.36	18.50	7.71	1.74	3.48	3.94	1.86	21.06
15 October 1963	42.73	20.14	6.89	5.44	3.93	1.69	1.09	1.01	17.09
Ibn Khaldun 15 November	38.78	17.59	9.51	5.08	3.21	1.56	1.91	1.43	20.93

(*Continued*)

Table 12.11. (*Continued*) Sfax Madina—Major party vote by school polling station (percent).

School	Enna-hdha	CPR	Etta-katol	Voice Ind	Aridha	PDP	PDM	Com	Other
Shaqrun 15 November	39.56	15.79	8.11	5.60	3.80	1.65	2.27	1.06	22.17
Shakib Arslan	39.18	15.90	8.26	5.62	6.28	2.64	1.73	1.49	18.91
Qawmiya al-Rabadh	42.63	12.31	7.30	4.75	4.55	2.00	1.28	1.34	23.84
Ain Sheikh Ruha	43.76	13.24	8.28	6.71	2.84	1.39	1.57	0.88	21.34
Muh al-Jamal	42.15	16.20	9.18	8.35	1.33	3.04	1.58	0.32	17.85
Sidi Abbas Primary	40.58	16.81	9.26	9.39	1.23	1.74	1.45	0.66	18.87
Markaz al-Basha	34.07	16.55	14.19	8.61	0.86	3.16	2.74	0.91	18.91
Sharia Benzart	34.28	12.50	9.20	7.13	3.91	2.68	2.84	1.07	26.38
N al-Jama'a Muh Ali	33.14	10.92	12.28	4.68	5.85	1.36	1.36	1.95	28.46
al-Hadi al-Sa'idi	34.62	15.47	10.95	6.12	3.55	1.96	1.04	1.59	24.71
73 Sh Buqtafa	43.07	15.93	7.94	4.20	3.79	1.76	0.83	1.04	21.43
Rahma Muh Ali	44.28	13.35	5.20	4.56	4.00	1.40	1.04	1.08	25.10
Tariq al-Sultaniya	42.76	9.93	6.32	3.47	7.14	1.29	1.09	1.36	26.65
Sfax Madina	**37.86**	**16.05**	**9.27**	**6.27**	**3.46**	**2.19**	**1.84**	**1.33**	**21.72**

Source: Author.

Figure 12.9. Sfax—small zones: Separated and scattered.

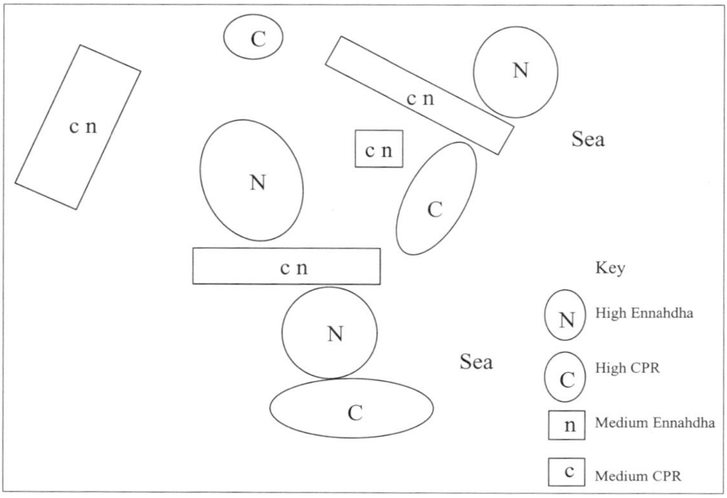

Source: Author.

Figure 12.10. Satellite view of Sfax Showing Madina, Bab al-Bahr, Rabadh, and al-Basatin.

Source: wikimapia.org.

The Tunisian Tigers

Beyond the two largest cities, Ennahdha enjoyed particularly high support in a handful of provincial capitals with rising economies and close links to their hinterlands. The most notable examples were the cities of Gabés on the southern coast, Kairouan in the central interior, and Bizerte in the far north. All three cities share common political, economic, and religious features. They have longstanding personal connections with Ennahdha's leaders, they host vigorous private business communities that resent the extreme centralization of power and resources in Tunis, and they support thriving religious cultures with large investments in Islamic publishing, education, and pilgrimage.[14]

If Ennahdha's victory suggests comparisons with Turkey, the analogies run far deeper than their ruling parties' general commitments to principles of Islamic liberalism that promote democracy and private enterprise. More important in the long-run are the potential similarities in the social and economic profiles of their core constituencies—the voters whose basic material and cultural preferences lead them to provide guaranteed and expanding support for parties that represent them openly and consistently. In Tunisia, we can see such a coalition taking shape much as it did in Turkey over the last sixty years. It will be important to watch which of Tunisia's struggling regional centers might develop into a future Bursa, Konya or Gaziantep. If these provincial cities prosper and continue to identify with politicians who represent a special blend of freedom and piety, then Ennahdha and its possible offshoots are likely to occupy center stage for decades to come.[15]

---

[14] Belhedi, Amor (2007). Le rayonnement spatial des villes tunisiennes à travers la diffusion des entreprises multi-établissements pour l'innovation, *Cybergeo: European Journal of Geography*, 16 April, available online at http://cybergeo.revues.org/5607; and Belhedi, Amor (2006). Territoires, appartenance et identification: Quelques réflexions à partir du cas Tunisien, *L'Espace géographique*, 4:35, 310–316.

[15] Demir, Ömer, Mustafa Acar, and Metin Toprak (2004). Anatolian tigers or Islamic capital: Prospects and challenges, *Middle Eastern Studies*, 40:6, 166–188; and European Stability Initiative (2005). Islamic Calvinists: Change and conservatism in central Anatolia, *esiweb.org*, 19 September.

The Integrative Potential of Conflict in National Reconciliation

The coalition government that Ennahdha formed after its election victory has not achieved anything approaching the national consensus and reconciliation that Tunisians crave. Instead, we see a more vigorous opposition sparking sharper debate on all of the most sensitive issues in the public sphere—basic freedoms, economic policy, women's rights, religious values, regional inequalities, corruption, diplomatic relations with Europe, Turkey, and Arab neighbors, and much more. Tunisia's small parties are reorganizing and rethinking their alliances, the labor unions are resisting wage freezes, and families of the revolutionary martyrs are complaining about mistreatment and ingratitude. Rachid Ghannouchi's vision of a flexible Mediterranean Islam is drawing criticism from defenders of more conservative Arabian-style piety in rival groups and even in his own party. In less than a year, Ennahdha has morphed into the key target of protest after having served as the most potent channel for mobilizing protest. In other words, Tunisia's young democracy is flourishing and Ennahdha is paying the price for its own success.[16]

It may seem counter-intuitive to view conflict as socially beneficial, but social scientists have long appreciated the paradox and today's scholars are spotlighting it more than ever. Conflict can generate debate, and debate can lead to regular interactions that integrate adversaries in networks of bargaining and learning. In time, those networks can diminish violence by calming sentiments and building mutual trust. This is the core teaching of George Simmel, Norbert Elias, and Lewis Coser whose works are enjoying unprecedented attention

[16] Shirayanagi, Kouichi (2011). Tunisian civil society demonstrates in full force in front of Constituent Assembly opening session, *Tunisia-live.com*, 23 November; and Ottaway, David (2012). *Tunisia's Islamists Struggle to Rule*, Washington: Woodrow Wilson International Center for Scholars, April.

among sociologists and scholars in other fields that discuss social change as historical process.[17]

Of course, students of social networking and evolutionary process are deeply indebted to Ibn Khaldun and Tocqueville as well. Many recent insights in social science build upon their classic narratives about the contributions of the "art of association" to the "civilizing process" of restraining and reducing violence. Social scientists and historians who are animated by these questions can find no more fertile ground for inquiry than contemporary Tunisia and other countries that have felt the contagion of the Jasmine Revolution. Nonetheless, something important is missing from this largely European-led discussion—the crucial role of religion in general and Islam in particular.

Bryan Turner has addressed this shortcoming, demonstrating how changes in religious values and practices often made the difference between old customs of "demonizing" and "decivilizing" on one hand and new sentiments of tolerance and integration on the other hand. Turner's admonition implies that Tunisia's most illustrious historian, Ibn Khaldun, was perhaps also the most modern of social theorists because he understood that taming sentiments and affects requires different spiritual and psychological experiences in addition to a rational process of debate and accommodation.[18]

Herein lies the true test for Ennahdha and its rivals—fostering vigorous debate over alternative ways in which Islamic principles can fit into the larger picture of Tunisia as a synthetic society and culture with Mediterranean and Arab foundations. Tunisian quarrels over religion are also quarrels over class and regional inequalities. Indeed, they are all

---

[17] Simmel, Georg (1964). *Conflict and the Web of Group Affiliations*, New York: Simon and Schuster, 1964; Morrow, Raymond A. (2010). Norbert Elias and figurational sociology: The comeback of the century, *Contemporary Sociology*, 38:3, 215–219; and Coser, Lewis A. (1956). *The Functions of Social Conflict*, Glencoe, Illinois: Free Press.

[18] Turner, Bryan S. (2004). Weber and Elias on religion and violence: Warrior charisma and the civilizing process, in *The Sociology of Norbert Elias*, Steven Loyal and Stephen Quilley, eds., Cambridge: Cambridge University Press, pp. 245–264.

merely neighboring corners of the same argument—separable in theory but not in practice.[19]

Power has shifted suddenly and decisively in Tunisia at many levels simultaneously—from the capital to the provinces, from intellectuals and bureaucrats to business people and professionals, from Europeanized nominal Muslims to more Arab-minded and practicing Muslims, and from better educated privileged minorities to ordinary citizens struggling to survive. If Turkey's experience is any guide, it will take a generation or two for Tunisians to adjust to these changes. In the meantime, there will be constant temptations to exaggerate emotion-laden religious differences instead of dealing with more tractable conflicts over sharing power and resources.[20]

Exploring the socioeconomic and regional basis of Tunisian voting behavior allows us to see the decisive role of non-religious factors in current political struggles. Ennahdha's competitors will have to learn to address the perceived needs of common people more candidly and more effectively. Full and open debates over every aspect of Islam in Tunisia are indispensible to any project of national reconciliation. But these debates should not substitute for and distract from the social and regional grievances that have been the root causes of sweeping power shifts in Tunisia and many other countries with similar problems.

---

[19] Shadid, Anthony (2011). Islamists' ideas on democracy and faith face test in Tunisia, *New York Times*, 17 February; and Zelin, Aaron Y. (2011). Ennahda's tight rope act on religion, *Foreign Policy*, 18 November.

[20] Daoudov, Murat (2011). Can Turkey inspire Tunisia? *ArabNews.com*, 24 November; and Couvas, Jacques N. (2011). Turkey admires Tunisia's secular facelift, *Asia Times*, 9 November.

Appendix 12.A. The Major Political Parties

Ennahdha (Renaissance)
Tunisia's strongest Muslim party, led by Rachid Ghannouchi, a businessman from Gabés who lived in Britain before the Jasmine Revolution. The party is best known for its strong nationwide organization, its pragmatic approach to religion, and its appeal to a wide range of social groups in various regions. After winning the election, it led the new coalition government.

Congrès Pour le République (CPR)
A centrist party, led by Moncef Marzouki, a physician from Nabeul who became a well-known human rights activist and opponent of the authoritarian regime. It joined the coalition government and parliament elected Marzouki Tunisia's first post-revolution president.

Ettakatol (The Democratic Forum for Labor and Liberties)
A social democratic party, led by Mustapha Ben Jafar, a radiologist and critic of the Ben Ali regime. It became the third partner in the coalition government and Ben Jafar became Speaker of the Constituent Assembly.

Aridha Chaabia (The People's Petition)
A splinter party of defectors from Ennahdha, led by Hechmi Hamdi, a businessman and media baron based in London. Its strongest roots are in Sidi Bouzid and the western interior where it is viewed as a champion of marginalized rural voters. It is the largest opposition party in the Constituent Assembly.

Progressive Democratic Party (PDP)
A leftist party that appeals mostly to well-educated middle class voters in the cities and to a small segment of workers and migrants. It recently joined several other small groups in forming the Republican Party.

Pôle Démocratique Moderniste (PDM)
A loose coalition of leftist groups with limited support among urban intellectuals and professionals.

Map 12.2. Tunisia electoral districts and number of seats.

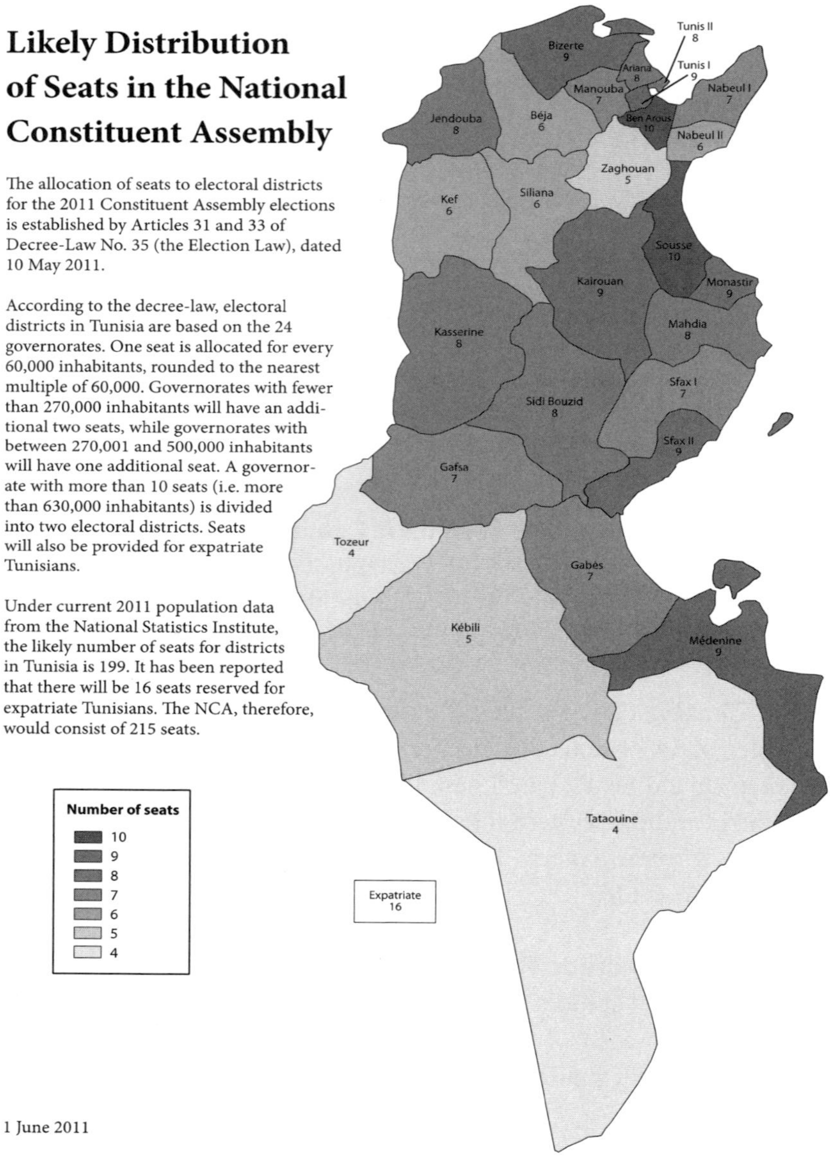

Source: docs.google.com.

Note on Regional Cleavages

Tunisia is divided along two geographic axes—north-south and east-west. Both are the combined products of natural extremes in climate and terrain reinforced by human efforts to dominate resources and power. Particularly in colonial and contemporary Tunisia, human activity has aggravated and exploited natural extremes instead of harmonizing and ameliorating them. This has produced a convergence of multiple inequalities—economic, social and political—that strengthen one another and perpetuates hierarchical relations between regions and within them.[21]

North-south divisions arise from dramatic topographical and climactic shifts over relatively short distances (see Map 12.3 for rainfall levels and see Table 12.12 for rain and livestock statistics). Steep variations in rainfall and terrain create a weak agricultural base confined between mountains and deserts, which is easily ravaged by intense production and overpopulation (see Map 12.4 for interior and coast statistics). Subsistence farming breeds constant migration that cannot be absorbed fully in productive employment elsewhere. This creates bloated construction industries in many provincial towns that are filled with seasonal and part-time farmers who resist moving to the big cities or finding work abroad. They form a transient population of semi-nomads who float between the primary, secondary and tertiary economies without settling down in any of them.

Colonialism and industrialization have encouraged similar and perhaps deeper inequalities between the east and west. Modern transport and communication were planned to strengthen central control over the production and export of local surpluses from agricultural and mineral wealth (see Map 12.5 for highways and railroads). Urban elites in the northern and eastern port cities have pursued a strategy of extraction without reciprocal investment and job creation in the interior. "Semi-colonial" economic and social relations fostered under French rule have become "fully colonial" with the ascendance of Tunisian

---

[21] Attia, Habib (1986). Problématique du developpement du nord-ouest tunisien, *Revue de l'Occident musulman et de la Méditerranée,* 41–42, 264–280.

technocrats and Europeanized commercial elites (see Tables 12.13–12.15 on consumption).[22]

Depending on their circumstances and resources, local peoples have responded to growing marginalization by adapting to, rebelling against or competing with authoritarian rulers and their business partners. Desert and mountain regions have developed a brisk illicit trade over vast and poorly policed borders and coastlines. Miners and unemployed youth have launched more violent strikes and demonstrations both before and after the Jasmine Revolution. And local business groups, including many long-time sympathizers of Ennahdha—invested much of their growing profits in political organizations to counter the dominant party's nexus of power and wealth.

[22] Moudoud, Ezzeddine (1985). L'impossible régionalisation «Jacobine» et le dilemme des disparités régionales en tunisie, *Canadian Journal of Regional Science*, 8:3, 413–438; Belhedi, Amore (1999). Les disparités spatiales en Tunisie, état des lieux et enjeux, *Méditerranée*, 91, 63–72; and Taleb, Rachid (2004). Quelques aspects des relations villes-monde rural en tunisie, *uram-international.com*, 4 October.

Map 12.3. Average annual rainfall (mm).

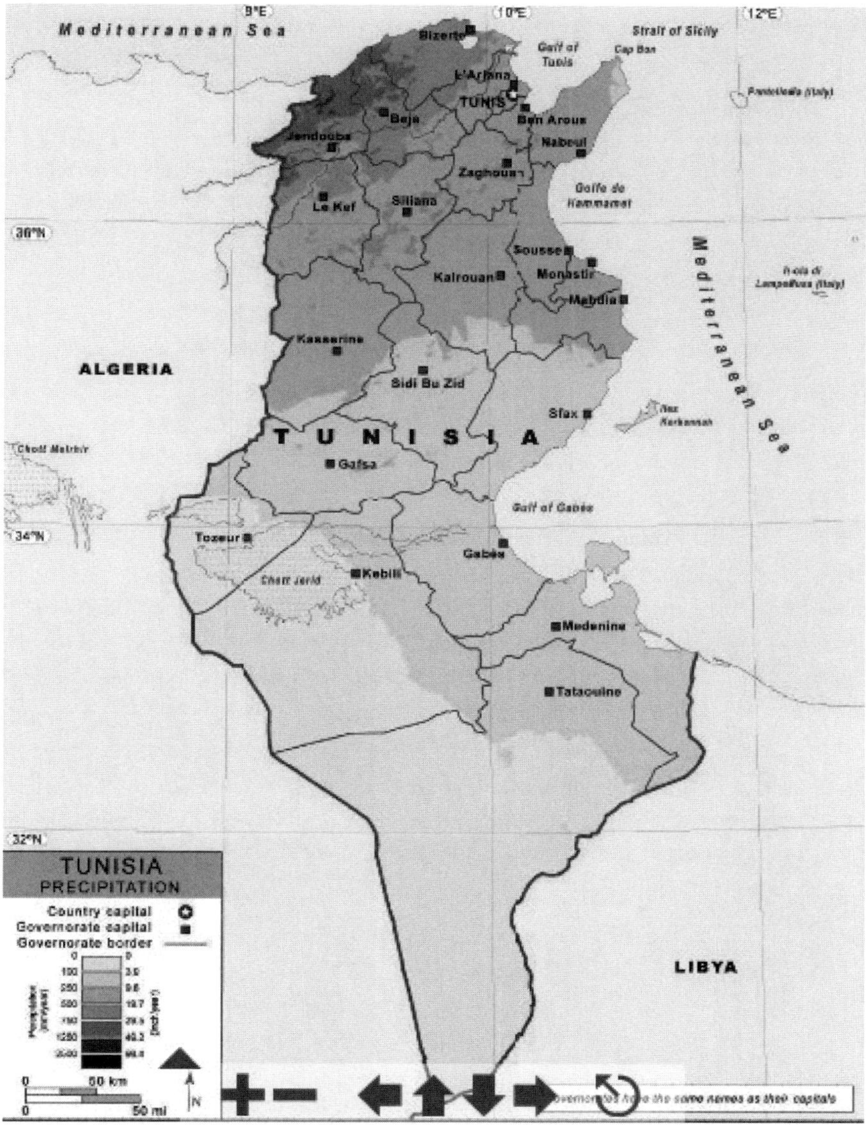

Source: bestcountryreports.com

Map 12.4. Coastal and interior contrasts in northern and central Tunisia
(Ennahdha zones of weaknes in italics).

Medjerda River basin

Tunisian Dorsal

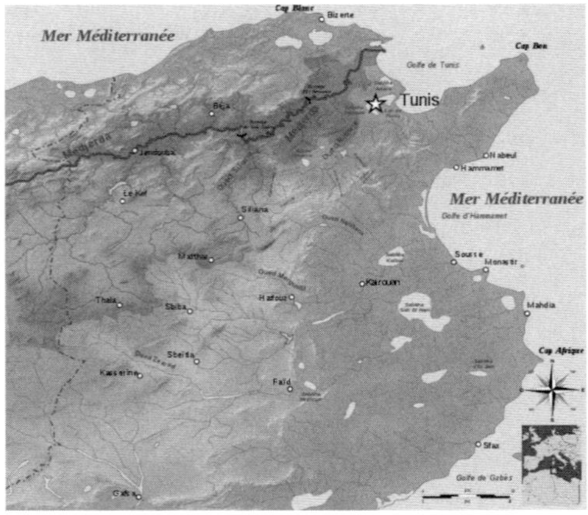

Greater Tunis

Coast & coastal plain

Source: commons.wikimedia.org.

Map 12.5. Transportation networks in Tunisia.

Highways

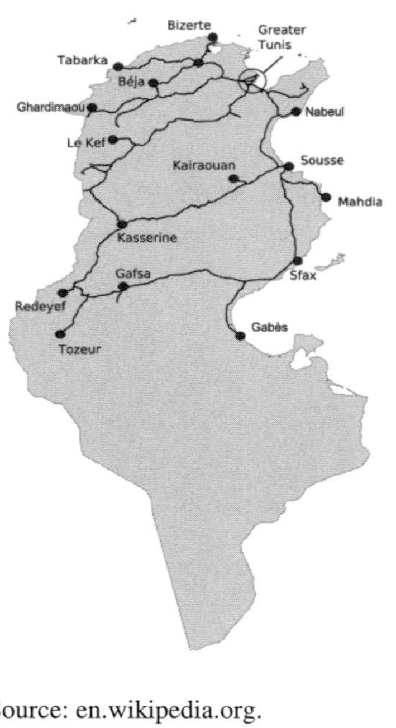

Source: en.wikipedia.org.

Railroads

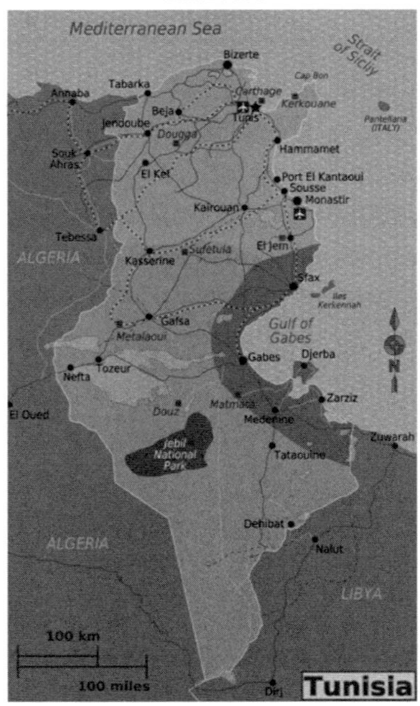

Source: wikitravel.org.

Table 12.12. Rainfall, livestock per capita, and Ennahdha vote (Pearson's r's).

Annual rainfall (mm)	**-0.3784**
Cattle	**-0.4053**
Sheep	0.1240
Goats	0.2530
Camels	**0.6345**

Source: Author.

Table 12.13. Regional disparities in living standards and wellbeing.
Central tendencies: Eastern coast > Western interior; North > South
Most common deviations: Central east +; Central west –

Poverty			
		Greater Tunis	1.4
Northwest	3.1	Northeast	2.7
Central west	*12.8*	Central east	1.2
Southwest	5.5	Southeast	3.8
Low birth weight			
		Greater Tunis	*5.2*
Northwest	3.6	Northeast	3.6
Central west	*7.0*	Central east	3.7
Southwest	6.2	Southeast	5.6
Stunted growth (0–59 months)			
		Greater Tunis	3.7
Northwest	8.6	Northeast	5.7
Central west	8.5	Central east	4.6
Southwest	10.6	Southeast	6.7

Source: Al-Jumhuriya al-Tunsiya Wizara al-Tanmiya, 2007: 142.

Table 12.14. Regional disparities in household expenditures, 2005 (dinars per capita per year).

Consumption Expenditures			
		Greater Tunis	2,390
Northwest	1,416	Northeast	1,613
Central west	*1,138*	Central east	2,084
Southwest	1,466	Southeast	1,826
Food Expenditures			
		Greater Tunis	770
Northwest	577	Northeast	587
Central west	*466*	Central east	695
Southwest	536	Southeast	608

Source: Al-Jumhuriya al-Tunsiya Wizara al-Tanmiya, 2007: 18, 74.

Table 12.15. Regional disparities in the intake of animal products (kilograms per person per year).

Meat & Poultry			
		Greater Tunis	15.3
Northwest	10.0	Northeast	12.4
Central west	*7.5*	Central east	14.1
Southwest	9.6	Southeast	10.4
Fish			
		Greater Tunis	2.9
Northwest	*0.7*	Northeast	2.3
Central west	*0.8*	Central east	5.3
Southwest	1.3	Southeast	2.1
Dairy & Eggs			
		Greater Tunis	11.1
Northwest	8.5	Northeast	9.0
Central west	*5.5*	Central east	8.1
Southwest	7.0	Southeast	7.6

Source: Author.

Note on Ecology, Society, and Politics

Tunisia has inspired a rich body of speculation on the ways in which ecological factors shape society, culture, politics, and history. Muhsin Mahdi's classic exposition of Khaldunian thought is typical of the genre. Its grandiose subtitle—"A Study in the Philosophic Foundation of the Science of Culture"—reminds us that, before universities compartmentalized knowledge, many scholars viewed geography and social science as systematic foundations for the higher pursuits of history and philosophy. The recent revival of environmental awareness rekindles the enduring vein in the sociological imagination that insists everything is related to everything else, including the argument that the rain and terrain helps to predict the rise and fall of empires and civilizations—and vice versa. No wonder then that we are witnessing the simultaneous florescence of global history, Braudellian regional studies and environmentalism.

But there is an important difference in our current thinking about the interconnections of ecology, society, and polity. Instead of viewing nations as self-contained wholes, we are more sensitive to their internal divisions and to their imbedded position in global networks that frequently exacerbate and reproduce those divisions. In today's portrayals, plural societies and dual economies are as commonplace as multi-layered cultures and polycentric governments. Globalism hasn't made the world flat. On the contrary, we see the landscape becoming choppier and more pulverized by the moment (see Figure 12.11 and Figure 12.12).[23]

As a result, it is more difficult than ever to posit a straight line running from ecological conditions to political outcomes. The intermediate territory of economy and society is too fragmented and treacherous to permit effective flow-through from great river systems to Oriental despotisms or from leaky dikes to egalitarian democracies. Instead, we are moving further away from the comfortable security of determinism and into the unpredictable clutches of multivariate and

---

[23] Kremer, Alex *et al.* (2010). *Poor Places, Thriving People: How the Middle East and North Africa Can Rise Above Spatial Disparity*, Washington, DC: World Bank.

multi-level mazes filled with reciprocal causation and infinite feedback. Whether we imagine seven Tunisias or 700—two Americas or 2,000—the spotlight is no longer on ecology's ageless hand in shaping coherent societies, but on globalization's pernicious role in fracturing nations and despoiling environments.

Figure 12.11. Competing explanations of ecological and socioeconomic influences on political behavior.

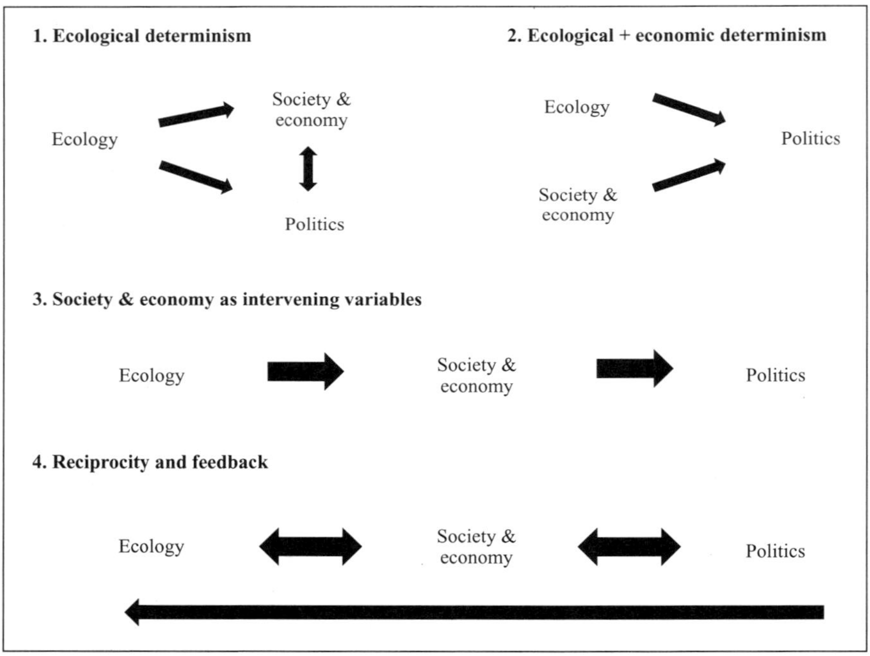

Source: Author.

Figure 12.12. Pluralism, the division of labor, and globalization.

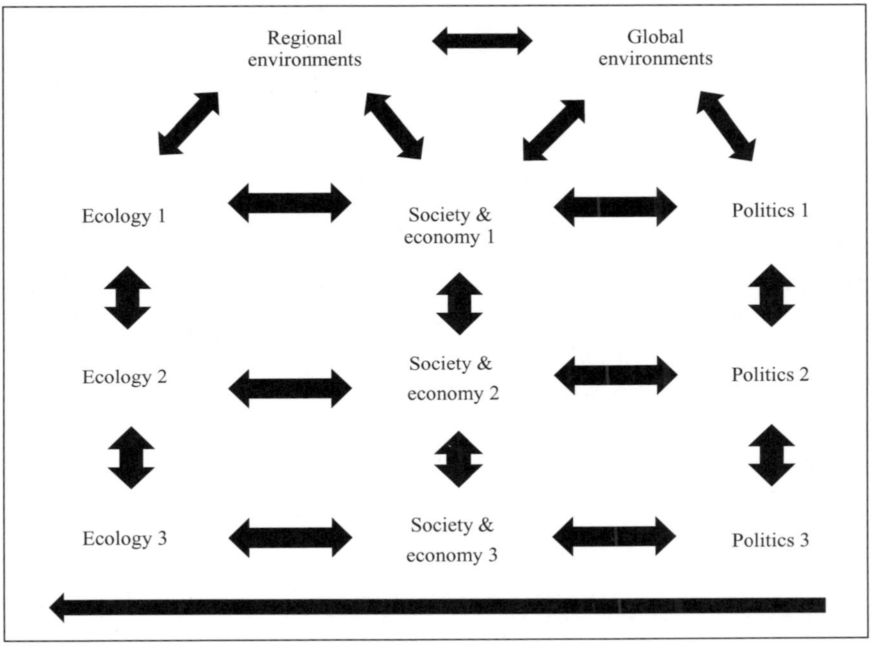

Source: Author.

Chapter 13

On Liberty and Human Interest in the Work of Iliya Harik

Iliya Harik had a skeptical mind and an impatient soul. He loved to probe the paradoxes of politics and philosophy—especially the tension between freedom and justice—but he was never satisfied with his own answers or anyone else's. I liked to tease him by saying that his time at the London School of Economics was as corrupting as a Catholic education would have been, because it branded him with Friedrich von Hayek's worship of free markets. Once exposed to the true faith, I jibed, even the most rebellious spirit was doomed to a lifetime of self-doubt, always measuring new instincts against old dogmas and second-guessing the drive to break free. To make the game more fun, I'd admonish his caution with a quip to the effect that the Phoenicians had probably invented capitalism anyway; and if their Lebanese progeny wanted to create a better political-economic model, they didn't need the permission of British and American neophytes.

The longer I knew Iliya Harik the more he reminded me of John Stuart Mill. And as I began to grasp the long sweep of his intellectual development, I thought of my friend as a modern-day Mill who spent much of his life struggling to understand the nature of liberty, constantly reappraising its meanings and conditions as well as its consequences and limits. Freedom was the common thread in all of Harik's major works, yet he re-imagined the concept and reevaluated it every time he explored a different society or employed a novel theory. Lebanese social history, Egypt's agrarian revolution, the political economies of the Arab nations, and the cross-fertilization of world civilizations—these were the disparate fields where Iliya Harik labored longest and where his contributions remain unsurpassed. Always the keystone was liberty, as Mill understood it—a core human value with a maddening capacity for self-destruction unless it serves a broader vision of social good.

Even though Harik's starting point was a Utilitarian pursuit of the greatest good for the greatest number, he steadily expanded his scope to larger and larger communities, beginning with confessional groups and nation-states, moving to transnational religions and intercontinental civilizations. As the Lebanese political economist grew into a democratic theorist and then a philosopher of culture, there was a double shift in his sensibility. First, Utilitarian rationalism gave way to Fabian egalitarianism, and then to a more dramatic step toward human rights and cultural dialogue that promoted universal human interest in the fashion of Habermas and critical theory. In his final decade, Harik was fusing Mill and Habermas in ways that neither philosopher could have anticipated, asking how freedom could serve the greatest good of all—the common interest of humanity everywhere for generations to come.[1]

It is tempting to speculate whether Iliya Harik was determined to expand his vision precisely because he saw his homeland racing in the opposite direction. What better consolation for the tragedy of Lebanon than to universalize her legendary genius for tolerance and compromise while those virtues struggle to survive the assaults of her own sons and daughters? My own opinion is that Harik's thinking moved forward

[1] Habermas described three types of "human interest"—"technical," "practical," and "emancipatory"—corresponding to different kinds of knowledge and different ways of knowing. "Technical human interest" relies on empirical/analytical ways of knowing through observation and description. "Practical human interest" derives from historical/hermeneutic ways of knowing through the interpretation of texts and social contexts. And "emancipatory human interest" depends on critical/reflective ways of knowing social practices and then changing them through deliberate action (Habermas, Jurgen (1972). *Knowledge and Human Interests*, Boston: Beacon Press). I believe that Iliya Harik stressed each of these links between knowledge and interest at different times in his career. As a political historian of Lebanon, he used social history to document the fate of his native land. As an Arab-American student of international political economy, he relied on cross-cultural insights to interpret relations between rich and poor societies. And as a philosopher of democracy and human rights, he promoted universal values of freedom and dignity that challenged vested interests and prejudices in every culture.

whether Lebanon was rising or sinking. It was out of confidence rather than despair that he published more and more in Arabic and that he labored so hard to promote the systematic study of democracy in the Middle East where he felt his efforts were most needed and would be most valued. He usually deflected my urgings to speak out more forcefully in the United States on current political controversies—not because he felt powerless, but because he preferred to exert his influence in person and with selected audiences. It took nothing less than the Hariri assassination in 2005 and the Israeli air war in 2006 to change his mind and launch a new website for discussing Middle Eastern conflicts which was active in 2006 and 2007.

To illustrate Harik's recurring concern with the connection between liberty and human interest, I will compare the reformulations of the problem as they evolved in his most influential projects: building democracy from Lebanon's community of communities, seeking social justice through mass movements in the Egyptian countryside, reconciling liberalization and equity in Middle Eastern economies, and managing differences in Western and Islamic civilizations.

The Missing Citizens of Lebanon

Harik's analysis of the social history of Ottoman Lebanon fit perfectly with the "Chicago School" of political modernization that grew out of the Committee for the Comparative Study of New Nations beginning in the 1960s. The Committee quickly became the debating society of the sociologists, anthropologists, and political scientists who pioneered the merger of fieldwork and grand theory in the interdisciplinary study of non-Western polities during the early wave of de-colonization and nation building. Each year a handful of graduate students were able to sit in on the arm-wrestling between Clifford Geertz and Edward Shils, Morris Janowitz and Lloyd Fallers, David Apter and Leonard Binder, McKim Marriott and Manning Nash, and an endless line of visitors from other campuses.

To everyone's surprise, the seminar of luminaries did produce a consensus in a few key areas, particularly the need to move beyond the dualistic notions of "modernity" and "tradition" that owed their popularity to the works of Talcott Parsons, Daniel Lerner, and Karl Deutsch. The best illustration of that consensus was the collection of essays that Geertz edited under the title, "Old Societies and New States: The Quest for Modernity in Asia and Africa." The overriding theme was the persistence and, most importantly, the potential value of "primordial loyalties"—the vast web of religious, ethnic, tribal, caste, and linguistic ties that predated the nation-state, promoting collective identities that seemed either too parochial or too universal for Western models of secular nationalism and pluralist democracy to take root.

The Chicago authors agreed that the widely heralded "passing of traditional society" was a myth. Primordial loyalties were not going to evaporate, but they might be "tamed" or "domesticated" in ways that could serve nationalist sentiments and democratic institutions instead of destroying them. The challenge was not to dissolve parochial identities but to "expand" them—to redefine them in ever more inclusive terms so that old divisions could support new solidarities and once isolated enclaves could form wider communities. Indeed, the volume's contributors showed that the construction of modern identities from pre-modern elements was already quite advanced in many countries. "Super-tribalism" was producing ethnic confederations among historic enemies; the caste system was being "reincarnated" as thousands of local fragments merged into regional and nation-wide coalitions; multilingualism reduced pressures for homogenization and cultural hegemony; and sectarian representation offered guarantees of communal autonomy and federalist power sharing. If formerly "feudal" and "primeval" domains could turn into "interest groups" and "mass constituencies," they could support or even embody the political parties and social movements that are the building blocks of tolerant nationalism and the bargaining units of stable democracy.

Harik's doctoral dissertation and first book put Lebanon at the center of these debates. He argued that as early as the eighteenth and nineteenth centuries, Lebanon's traditional system of landholding and patronage had undergone a revolutionary change that eventually triggered popular demands for social reform and national independence. Under the older "feudalism," local landlords granted their usufructs (iqta's) to neighboring villagers on the basis of personal fealty, with little regard to religious affiliations. However, the Maronite Christians of Mount Lebanon began to challenge their Druze overlords by forging stronger patronage ties within their own confessional group, even if they involved relative strangers living at greater distances from one another. The church and activist clergy were instrumental in building the organizational and communication resources that stimulated greater solidarity and assertiveness among Maronites in Mount Lebanon and beyond. In time, Druze landlords responded with similar tactics, recruiting their own followers along clearer confessional lines. The chain reaction of elite competition and mass mobilization touched off growing conflicts within the major religious communities and between them. During the nineteenth century this led to popular revolt, European intervention, and the political rise of the Maronite church at the expense of the military and official classes aligned with Istanbul.

Although Harik carefully chronicled this transformation and appreciated its contributions to a more open and inclusive polity, he never bought into the rosy portrait of "consociationalism" that captivated so many of his colleagues in Lebanon and the West before the eruption of all-out civil war in 1975. He was keenly aware that no matter how much Lebanon modernized, it remained filled with inequalities and rigidities that invited civil strife and manipulation by neighboring countries and great powers. He constantly criticized the hypocrisy of Lebanese politicians and intellectuals who thought that democracy merely gave them new tools for asserting their privileges collectively and nationally, instead of as solitary gang lords and neighborhood bullies.

In principle, liberty might benefit from proportional representation, but only if the national pacts were periodically renegotiated to broaden power sharing and to promote Lebanese sentiments as well as confessional interests and personal ambitions. Parliamentary "blocks" and multiparty "lists" could speak for their imagined communities, and they could even aspire to embody a common spirit of Lebanon; but they could not speak for real individuals, especially those who were stigmatized to permanent inferiority such as the Shiites, the Palestinian refugees, and the under-classes of all sects. And as the system sought to perpetuate itself by marginalizing more and more of the people it claimed to represent, nothing could save it from self-destruction.

Anyone who thinks that Lebanon's predicament is unique should refresh their memories of abiding Anglo-American misgivings about democracy—and there are no better guides than Mill's classic essay and the Federalist Papers. Those who taught us the most about liberty were filled with warnings about popular intolerance and the need to craft mixed forms of government that would save us from ourselves. Unfortunately, like the Lebanese, they left us convoluted representative formulas (slaves who were not citizens but whose numbers boosted white power in Congress, the disenfranchisement of women, gerrymandered state legislatures, and racially-biased immigration laws) so rigid and corruptible that they unwittingly paved the way for precisely the social upheavals that the Founding Fathers dreaded. Iliya Harik knew the worst of both Western and Middle Eastern polities, and I never tired of matching him point for point in comparing Chicago ward politics with anything he could muster from the Levant. In his mellow later years, many of Harik's colleagues and students seemed to think of him as imperturbable. In fact, no one was sharper and more unforgiving in assessing the faults of his countrymen in both Lebanon and America.

Semi-Liberating the Fellahin

In Egypt, Harik encountered a peasantry that was far more destitute than the self-sufficient yeomen he was accustomed to in the Fertile Crescent. He recognized immediately that the Egyptian fellahin could never follow the Lebanese example. They were unable to negotiate more favorable terms of patronage and land tenure because they were at the mercy of aristocratic powers and demographic forces that could only be checked by aggressive intervention from a revolutionary state. Nasser's agrarian reforms broke the back of the absentee landlords by redistributing about 20 percent of cultivated land to smallholders and landless farmers. But Harik pointed out that land grants would be meaningless unless the government also built rural organizational networks that would allow the peasantry to choose their own leaders and manage their local economies. This is why he called his landmark study of Egypt "The Political

Mobilization of Peasants" and why he focused on the new associational life that the central government promoted in the countryside, particularly the agricultural cooperatives, municipal councils, and party branches.

Saying anything positive about Nasser has never been easy in America—certainly no easier than criticizing him in Egypt while he was still alive. Nonetheless, Iliya Harik called the shots as he saw them, putting ideology aside to acknowledge sound and flawed policies as objectively as possible, regardless of prevailing prejudices. At a time when Westerners reflexively viewed Nasser as a Soviet cat's paw and as the suicidal author of the Six-Day War, Harik understood that he was also a nationalist and populist icon of the Bandung Generation that included Mao, Tito, Nehru, Sukarno, and Nkrumah.

Even at the height of the Cold War, Americans were eager for the sort of balanced assessments that were Iliya's trademark. I remember teaching a continuing education course on the International Politics of the Middle East to a group of well-heeled members of the Council on Foreign Relations who were preparing to visit the region just before, as it happened, the eruption of the 1973 War. I was still a pretty green graduate student and one of my toughest customers was an elderly gent named Max whose wife dutifully dragged him to class each week. About half-way into the sessions, we took up modern Egyptian history and for the first time Max interrupted his usual nap to thank me for giving what he considered a fresh overview of Egypt's nationalist movements including the Nasserist Revolution. "I always thought that Nasser was an Arab Hitler," he said, "but now I realize he was more like F.D.R. or at least like Perón. He really tried to do some good things for his people, especially the farmers and workers."

Fair enough. On the other hand—and with Iliya Harik there was always another hand—the agrarian reforms were at best partial and fleeting successes filled with unintended consequences. His studies of post-Nasserist society showed that Sadat and Mubarak encouraged new forms of inequality and monopoly by betting on the largest and wealthiest farmers, including descendants of the feudal families that had bolstered the monarchy for more than a century and a half. Limits on landholding were raised, the cooperatives were turned over to bureaucrats and party bosses, and the profits of agribusiness poured into partnerships with political cronies who overheated up-scale urban markets while ignoring the countryside. Excess rural workers were shipped off to the Gulf, where they retaliated by sending home their foreign exchange remittances via the black market and wildfire Islamic enterprises instead of through state-controlled banks.

Harik favored economic liberalism in Egypt and most other Middle Eastern countries, but he was quick to point out the difference between privatization and plundering, especially when liberalization went hand in hand with greater tyranny and constant warfare. Who benefited by replacing socialist corruption with capitalist corruption, military dictatorship with party dictatorship? The same sort of leftist and religious opponents rotted in jail under both regimes and the back-drafts of regional wars stoked as much violence in Egypt as anywhere.

Iliya Harik knew that the Camp David gamble of trying to slice Cairo out of the Arab world was nothing but a play for time. Sadat promised the Egyptian people that his pact with the US and Israel would bring them peace, prosperity, and democracy. In fact, neither he nor Mubarak delivered on any of those pledges. Instead, they squandered the breathing space, making things all the worse not only for Egypt but for its neighbors and much of the Islamic world as well. The fiascos of Bush 43 were rooted in the ultimately self-fulfilling nightmare that Saddam would become the Napoleon of the Mashriq and in the confidence that the US could subdue Iraq with force as long as Egypt remained neutralized by Washington's largesse. Since 9/11, new American blunders have revived long-standing skepticism about the wisdom of Camp David. Our current predicaments in Iraq, Iran, and Afghanistan cast doubt far enough into the past to make even Jimmy Carter wonder whether his momentary glory was an illusion.

States, Markets, and Social Balancing

Harik undertook several comparative studies of political economy in the Middle East, articulating in both English and Arabic a dual message: states throughout the region needed to open their economies to greater competition and foreign investment, but they also had to stand above the inevitable conflicts that liberalization engenders between rising and declining social classes. Under Sadat and Mubarak, Egypt provided an excellent example of what others should avoid. Governments had a responsibility to mitigate the disruptions of their economic reforms, particularly when nascent markets were easily manipulated and shrinking safety nets were leaving the weak unprotected. Harik urged states in the process of liberalization to avoid being captured by the newly rich and to preserve their independent power to mediate between would-be social hegemons, instead of ruling in the name of one faction against another.

In Harik's view, Middle Eastern governments could act as effective balancers domestically only if they also cooperated with other developing countries to press for greater equity in the international economic order. In this phase of his career, Iliya Harik's writings were most explicitly comparative, examining multiple countries and economic sectors. He increasingly emphasized regional over national analysis, viewing all Middle Eastern societies as struggling with similar ambitions to participate more directly in the global economy while trying to reform world capitalism at the same time.

I sensed that as Harik adopted a more global perspective of political economy, he became more pessimistic about the prospects for development in the Middle East and more concerned that national tragedies such as Sudan, Somalia, Yemen, and Iraq would spiral into full-blown regional crises. He knew that Middle Eastern economies were underperforming even by non-Western standards, falling ever further behind East Asia and Latin America and flirting with an African-style meltdown of continental proportions. Integration with global capitalism was proving to be more difficult for Middle Eastern societies because their hypothetical economic compatibilities with the West were eclipsed by political and cultural conflicts that were deepening every year.

Most political economists would have been content to spend the rest of their careers repeating such observations of Middle Eastern "exceptionalism," but Harik chose to move in a new direction altogether: contesting the primacy of economics and highlighting instead the importance of imperialism and culture, especially religion. Many of Iliya Harik's peers will regard his work on comparative and global political economy as the pinnacle of his scholarship. I would not quarrel with that assessment, yet I would invite my colleagues to consider this phase of

Harik's work as a bridge that led him to deeper inquiries into philosophy and humanism. He was always an outstanding social scientist, but in his final years he became something more: a broker of cultures as well as disciplines, whose audience was truly universal.

Liberty as Self-Knowledge and Critical Conversation

Here's my personal nomination for Iliya Harik's most lasting legacy as a political philosopher and cultural broker. It is not something he wrote. Rather, it is an interpretation of something he wrote, his essay on "Democracy and the Paradoxes of Cultural Diversity: Beyond the Veil of Difference," which appeared in an online Islamic magazine edited by one of my former law students, Asma Uddin. An American Muslim woman of South Asian heritage who is now a talented attorney and a popular writer on Islam, she wrote:

Harik's contribution to the Islam and democracy analysis, therefore, is his focus on context and its role in how democracy is defined and implemented in various countries and civilizations. By recognizing common ground among competing notions of democracy, the analysis is no longer about which civilization is better and which needs to catch up. Democracies are not judged "as better or worse, but as different." Most importantly, they are seen as "relevant to one another as part of one whole phenomenon." Contextual understandings of democracy show how various countries and civilizations are interlinked and open up possibilities for discourse and mutual exchange.[2]

[2] Uddin, Asma (2009). Parallel universe: Islam and democracy—Their relationship is all in how it's defined, *Islamica Magazine*, 19, p. 120. Available online at http://www.islamicamagazine.com/issue-19/parallel-universe-islam-and-democracy.html
Responding to Harik, Iliya (2003). Democracy and the paradoxes of cultural diversity: Beyond the veil of difference, *The Byblos Letters*, 3.

The Asma-Iliya conversation was far from unique. No doubt, everyone who knew Iliya Harik has similar memories and could cite more examples. Nonetheless, Iliya took an extra measure of gratification from this woman's reaction because he realized that he was connecting with a vast and vital new audience at the highest moral level. For writers and teachers who hope to make a difference, it doesn't get any better than that.

I'm not sure that Harik got it right in his later writings on the need to reformulate the meaning of liberty in different cultural contexts. My own stock-in-trade as an international lawyer depends on universal norms and non-derogable rights. Carving out exceptions to suit the special pleadings of cultures and religions makes me very uncomfortable, because such loopholes—whether justified by history or political necessity or level of economic development—always amount to a license to fall below international standards. Just once I'd like to hear a neo-traditionalist argument that one's heritage compelled *exceeding* the prevailing norms of human rights and democracy. But, alas, it's always the other way around.

Nonetheless, Iliya Harik was keen to reconcile two United Nations proclamations that are in clear opposition to one another: the 1948 Universal Declaration of Human Rights and the 2005 UNESCO Convention on the Protection and Promotion of the Diversity of Cultural Expression.[3] I ran across his essay on the subject only after he had passed away and the discovery made me feel doubly cheated. Not only had I lost a priceless friend in his prime, but I would also have to do without the countless arguments he owed me over his conversion to moral relativism.

[3] Harik, Iliya (2007). Reflections on cultural encounters and democracy in *Comparing Cultures and Conflicts*, eds., Peter Molt and Helga Dickow, Baden-Baden: Nomos; and Harik, Iliya (n.d.). *Violence, Cultural Identity, and Negotiated Diversity: the Arab World in the Context of the 2005 UNESCO Convention on the Protection and Promotion of Cultural Diversity*, Heinrich Böll Foundation.

Chapter 14

Leonard Binder's Islamic Liberalism: A Critique of Development Ideologies

This is a collection of engrossing and provocative essays filled with wit and irony, rich in allusion and innuendo, relentlessly hopeful in exhorting the very political forces they deconstruct but never quite demolish. The ambitious range of topics covered (development theory, orientalism, the search for cultural authenticity, the convergence of liberalism and fundamentalism, the emergence of the bourgeois state) combined with the eclectic methods used (hermeneutics, phenomenology, the sociology of knowledge, class analysis) virtually guarantee the futility of a single reading. But the second time around the "isms" become more intelligible, the "ologies" become less intimidating, and one can begin to see how the tightly reasoned analysis of texts complements the sketch of a broader argument about the complex social bases of the Islamic resurgence and their potential contribution to building pro-democratic coalitions.

Binder is challenging Middle Eastern intellectuals to refashion the Islamic heritage into a liberation theology for the Muslim World. By "liberating" one text after another, he is trying to show how far Muslim writers have gone (and how much farther they still must go) in order to emancipate their societies from multiple forms of repression—authoritarian regimes, exploitative class structures, autistic and self-defensive cultures, and overwhelming pressures from the international system. He argues that the liberals' most valuable resource is not capitalism or nationalism or the state, but the prospect of a new cultural consensus based on an Islam that is practical, rational and tolerant. "...Without a vigorous Islamic liberalism," he argues, "political liberalism will not succeed in the Middle East, despite the emergence of bourgeois states." (p. 19).

Binder sees the intelligentsia as bearing the main responsibility for mediating between a weak bourgeoisie and a burgeoning Islamic movement. Their role is to promote a cross-class parliamentary alliance that will lead civil society against the old authoritarianism of the Bonapartist state while fending off the threat of a new authoritarianism of the fundamentalists. He believes that "the resurgence of Islam is both a threat and a promise, so the task of the moment is to appropriate religion as part of a new bourgeois ideology before it is appropriated by some rival force" (p. 17).

Yet Binder cautions that Islamic liberalism may not turn out to be quite so liberating after all, particularly if it is perceived as being sacrilegious or if it joins in foolhardy coalitions with the fundamentalists. The predicament of the liberals is that they can unwittingly pave the way for new forms of repression either by stigmatizing themselves with Western culture or by "supping with the saints." While pointing to both types of risks, Binder frequently rebukes the liberals for being too timid in avoiding the former and too reckless in accepting the latter. Certainly one reason for his eagerness to revive Western scholars' shrinking dialogue with Islamic liberals is to make them think long and hard about flirting with "petit bourgeois" fundamentalists lest they fall into the same trap as their counterparts in Iran.

Although this is an apt and timely warning (especially in Egypt and Turkey), Binder underestimates the equally important danger of a liberalism that tries to base itself on a denatured Islam. In his eagerness to encourage religious currents that are pragmatic, adaptive, non-literalist, and pluralist, Binder glosses over the likelihood that Muslims will instead regard them as historicist, relativist, utilitarian, and opportunistic—in other words, from their point of view, without content or meaning. This issue is raised several times in the skillful treatment of works by Sayyid Qutb, Tariq al-Bishri, Zaki Nagib Mahmud, and Abdallah Laroui. In my opinion, these are the most masterful essays in the book. Nevertheless, Binder's preference for the rationalism and cosmopolitanism of Mahmud and Laroui should in no way dissuade us concerning the greater appeal of the eclecticism and anti-imperialism of Qutb and al-Bishri.

Binder's deconstruction of texts is more persuasive than his political sociology. There is a clear tendency to expect too much of the intelligentsia and the haute bourgeoisie while expecting too little of the masses. This bias suggests that Islamic liberalism can adopt a pretense of universalism but that it will (and should) serve only narrow interests.

How much can we expect of the intelligentsia? How are they likely to "appropriate" Islam?—to save their own necks with modest advances in the freedom of expression, or to consolidate the cultural and political hegemony of big capital, or to reconcile the internal contradictions of a democratic popular front, or to transcend their own interests and those of their most powerful allies in building a freer and more pious society? Perhaps some of them can do all of these things, but should we not expect the achievement of each stage to produce more intellectual defections to the status quo thereby making any movement to subsequent stages increasingly unlikely?

Certainly one can anticipate a bourgeois enthusiasm for limiting arbitrary government without assuming an innate hostility toward authoritarianism. Even in a bourgeois state (perhaps especially in such a state) might not the greatest appeal of religion be as an instrument of social control and a mask of class domination?

Finally, is the "glacial and pitiable presence" of "the impoverished, traditional and ignorant mass" a potential constituency for the liberals or only for their fundamentalist rivals? On this point Binder's original confidence about the liberals' ability to fashion a new cultural consensus seems to vanish inexplicably: "...it seems foolish indeed to attempt to rally the sanculottes to the barricades on behalf of a concept which is as complicated as Islamic liberalism" (p. 359). One might argue that without the masses Islamic liberalism could claim to be more Islamic (i.e., less heterodox and superstitious), but then what would remain of its claim to be liberal?

Chapter 15

Philosophers, Lawyers, and Journalists: Arab and Turkish Ventures in Modernist Islam

The challenge of modern intellectuals and professionals to the interpretive monopoly of the ‘ulama has spurred a democratization of religious knowledge throughout the Islamic world. Those who earn their living outside the madrasah and the mosque have reinvented the public sphere of Islam, provoking an unprecedented global conversation where every aspect of religion and politics is open to debate and re-imagination.[1] An increasingly common theme of modernist writers is the urgent demand for “legal pluralism”—a claim that distinct religious and ethnic communities have an inherent right to choose their own legal systems even if they are citizens of the same nation-state.[2]

Three of the most influential proponents of legal pluralism in contemporary Islam are Mohammed Arkoun, the renowned humanist philosopher from Algeria, Kamal Aboulmagd, a prominent international lawyer from Egypt, and Ali Bulaç, Turkey’s most popular Islamic newspaper columnist. Each writer struggles to reinterpret and reconcile the concepts of “ummah” and “civil society,” arguing that intentionally

---

[1] On the creation of Islamic public spaces allowing more open discourse between participants from increasingly diverse social and ideological backgrounds, see Salvatore, Armando (1997). *Islam and the Political Discourse of Modernity*, Reading: Ithaca Press.

[2] On the theory of legal pluralism and case studies at national and transnational levels, see Chiba, Masaji (1989). *Legal Pluralism: Toward a General Theory Through Japanese Legal Culture*, Tokyo: Tokai University Press; Legrand, Pierre (1997). The impossibility of ‘legal transplants,’ *Maastricht Journal of European and Comparative Law*, 4, pp. 111–24; Dupret, Boudin *et al.*, eds. (1999). *Legal Pluralism in the Arab World*, Dordrecht: Kluwer; Örücü, Esin *et al.* (1996). *Studies in Legal Systems: Mixed and Mixing*, Kluwer; Teubner, Gunther, ed. (1997). *Global Law Without a State*, Brookfield, VT.: Dartmouth; and research proposals of the Max Planck Institute project on legal pluralism in various world cultures.

incoherent systems of law can promote tolerance and blunt the totalitarian impulses of the centralizing modern state whether it dresses in nationalist or religious garb. In their hands, legal pluralism becomes the guarantor of intellectual freedom, economic innovation, and local self-rule.

Arkoun believes that Muslims must rely on Western notions of civil society to encourage the indispensable criticism and skepticism that their religious leaders have stifled for centuries. But he also contends that Western nationalism oppresses minorities while ignoring the universal ummah of humankind. Aboulmagd hedges his bets. He sees the parallel development in Egypt of Western and Islamic enterprises as healthy competition that discourages hegemonic drives from either quarter. Two sets of banks and two networks of voluntary associations show that a resurgent ummah and a nascent civil society can flourish side by side while promoting the rule of law even if different rules apply in different sectors. Bulaç advances the most radical interpretation, asserting that for the original community of Muslims in Medina, the ummah and civil society were one and the same. Muhammad was a stranger to Medinese society who accepted everyone according the principle "you are what you are." Because Islam recognizes no compulsion in religion, it also insures complete freedom of ethnic identity and grants all communities the right to rule themselves according to laws that preserve their chosen cultures.

Together Arkoun, Aboulmagd, and Bulaç build a compelling case that all unitary states and legal systems—secular or religious, Islamic or non-Islamic—threaten political, economic, and cultural freedom. They also propose a range of techniques for avoiding or undoing the oppressive fusion of modern nationalism and traditional religion that they see emerging in the East as well as the West. Arkoun urges engagement and constant debate, Aboulmagd advocates partition and market segmentation, and Bulaç champions ethnic federalism and a revival of the millets.

Mohammed Arkoun: The Ummah as Living Utopia

Mohammed Arkoun has grand ambitions even by the heady standards of philosophy. He not only challenges Western and Islamic civilizations to live up to their loftiest ideals, he also demands that they surpass those ideals by building a world community that will free them from self-imposed restraints that neither civilization can overcome without the other. He tells Muslim and Western audiences alike that they should view each other as mutual emancipators instead of as co-destroyers who threaten to burn down everyone else's house along with their own.

Arkoun insists that all cultures contain both liberating and oppressing impulses that constantly compete for preeminence. This is the ceaseless struggle between "thought" and "unthought"—the battle of creative minds against "institutionalized ignorance" that prohibits innovation by banishing it from the imagination. Arkoun believes that enlightened people in every society have a duty to push back the realm of "unthought" in the name of human freedom even while realizing that their victories will always be partial and reversible.

Arkoun unhesitatingly describes Westerners as leaders in liberation and Muslims as laggards. Contrasting the democracies of Europe and North America with authoritarian regimes in "so-called Islamic societies," he argues that contemporary Muslims are forced to fight against far greater odds because the "great Islamic tradition" has left them a legacy that is doubly distorted—first, by the traditional 'ulama and, more recently, by nation-states that turn religion into an instrument of tyranny. Historically, Islamic scholars sought a share of power by hemming in the revolutionary "thought" of prophecy with their self-interested declarations of "unthought." Worse still, today's post-colonial regimes use the myths of religious traditionalism and fundamentalism to monopolize power and to crush dissent from every quarter. The most obvious victims of nationalist intolerance are ethnic minorities such as the Berbers and Kurds—ancient cultures that arose centuries before the dawn of Islam and that increasingly face an impossible choice between assimilation and extinction. Yet for Arkoun all Muslims are crippled by the double burden of "unthought" in its modern and traditional forms—the "imagined nation" and the fictionalized "Islamic memory." This includes the numerically dominant ethnic groups who are just as powerless and just as cut off from their religious heritage. Consequently, the vast majority of today's Muslims are marginalized politically, economically, and psychologically. They have become "a people without history."

The liberating dimension of the Islamic heritage is what Arkoun calls the ummah. "Ummah as a spiritual Utopia was inaugurated with the prophetic discourse, developed and enriched through a great diversity of religious, political, ethical and social experiences, and articulated in a large number of major works. This ummah is still alive as a terrestrial and eschatological hope in the collective minds of millions of believers."[3] Muslims can rekindle these hopes by demanding the freedom of critical inquiry in all fields, especially in philosophy and ethics. They must be ready to use the complete repertoire of the social sciences and humanities in the comparative and historical study of all religions including their own. For Arkoun, this is the surest path toward reclaiming the pluralism of legal interpretation, cultural expression, and political action that was strangled by medieval orthodoxy and modern nationalism.

Arkoun believes that Muslims have no choice but to borrow from the West, yet he insists that its models of civil society are also mere ideals and unfinished experiments—more advanced than Islam's, but nonetheless flawed constructs that every culture can adapt and improve. In his view, all of humanity's major problems cut across nations and religions, and all of the most promising solutions are multicultural or, more accurately, multi-civilizational. He describes two contrasting global systems, one repressive, the other emancipating—both fashioned from a complex mixture of Western and Islamic interests and ideals.

For Arkoun, the current international system is a multi-tiered hierarchy where the capital and technology of the West join with authoritarian nationalists in the Third World to manipulate Islam and exploit indigenous populations. This is a monopolizing and totalitarian globalism that accentuates the worst in Western and Islamic traditions.

---

[3] Arkoun, Mohammed (2002). *The Unthought in Contemporary Islamic Thought*, London: Saqi Books, p. 333.

Its antidote is an egalitarian and empowering globalism that fuses the ummah and civil society—the twin quests for universalism and freedom that can unleash liberating forces at every level of the hierarchy simultaneously, from the quasi-democracies at the top to the pseudo-religious national tyrannies in the middle, and down to the excluded masses and ethnic minorities at the bottom. Together, the ummah and civil society can achieve what neither can hope to attain separately—pluralistic nations and world communities that tolerate enduring differences while promoting a common sense of humanity.

Arkoun's vision of global liberation is rooted in a series of mutually reinforcing projects of legal pluralism. The first is a reform of the democracies of Western Europe and North America where civil society is enshrined in principle but stunted in practice. He believes that even the most advanced democracies vary widely in tolerance and freedom depending on their historical obsession for centralization, assimilation, and secularism. Comparing the Catholic democracies of southern Europe, he contrasts France's militant Jacobinism with the flexible liberalism of the Italian Risorgimento and particularly with post-Franco Spain's broad concessions to local autonomy and multiculturalism. He welcomes the development of the European Union because he believes that it will dissolve the racist and colonialist legacies that make Western democracies discriminatory at home and expansionist abroad. Supranational European citizenship will allow non-Christian and non-white immigrants, including those who reject assimilation, to become full participants in a truly cosmopolitan society that will be a prototype for experiments in regional democracy all over the world.

In addition, Arkoun calls for a revival of the intellectual diversity that typified early Islamic inquiries in theology, ethics, and law. He is particularly eager for Muslims to renew their ancient interest in ethics because its focus on competing values and moral dilemmas is likely to encourage moderation in debates on doctrine and flexibility in fitting rules to changing circumstances. Arkoun aims his argument squarely at Muslims who hope to advance an independent Islamic version of civil society that can rival or complete Western models instead of merely imitating them. He insists that they will never be taken seriously unless they acknowledge the achievements of Western democracies and consciously build upon them. It is perfectly sensible for Muslims to take the lead in tailoring democratic institutions to the needs of non-Western societies, but it is futile to pretend that they are starting from scratch with purely indigenous ingredients. In fact, he sees the European Union as precisely the sort of transnational democracy that Muslims should be constructing as a modern ummah.

Moreover, Arkoun calls for an end to the internal colonialism that nationalist elites have imposed on Muslims since gaining independence from foreign rule. Federalism and multiculturalism must replace chauvinist campaigns to subjugate and assimilate ethnic minorities. A diverse and spontaneous associational life should encourage self-government in neighborhoods, workplaces, schools, religions, linguistic groups, and cultures. The monistic nationalism of the post-independence era will recede and growing freedom will inspire a resurgence of the all-inclusive popular alliances that typified early nationalist movements throughout Asia and Africa.

Currently, a "wealth-defending" hegemonic West supports nationalist tyrannies that manipulate a distorted political Islam in order to subjugate their own people. The European Union holds out the promise of a genuinely multicultural and transnational democracy that Western Muslims can help construct and that Muslims everywhere can embrace in liberating their homelands. Pluralistic legal systems will strengthen the rule of law locally, nationally, and internationally. Liberal nationalism will overtake racism and ethnocentrism, humanist Islam will prevail over traditionalism and fundamentalism, and a universal world citizenry will recognize common identities that supersede transient clashes of civilizations. In sum, the synthesis of ummah and civil society will undermine today's repressive global hierarchy and unleash an emancipating globalization of the future.

Kamal Aboulmagd: The Virtues of Dualism

Kamal Aboulmagd is a consummate bridge builder and powerbroker with an extraordinary knack for winning the confidence of people from different worlds. As Egypt's preeminent international lawyer, he fashioned a fascinating network of alliances spanning rival cultures and business circles as well as divergent political and religious groups. He advised the governments of Anwar Sadat and Husni Mubarak while retaining lifelong ties to their opponents in the Muslim Brotherhood. He drafted constitutional reforms for the royal families of the Gulf states at the same time that he co-authored manifestos of Islamic factions seeking to open up the Ba'athist regime in Syria. Although he lived in the United States and sent his children to American universities, he was also an outspoken critic of American policy in Iraq. His negotiating skills are increasingly evident in a number of international organizations where he has become a ubiquitous advocate of greater cooperation and power sharing. Most recently, he has gained notoriety for his efforts to reorganize the Arab League, to lead an administrative tribunal in the World Bank, and to broaden the "Dialogue of Civilizations" that the United Nations established to promote reconciliation between the Islamic world and the West.

One of Aboulmagd's most interesting undertakings was his highly publicized attempt to mediate the deepening division in Egypt's financial system between conventional Western-style banks and a new breed of Islamic investment firms that have attracted millions of depositors both domestically and among Egyptians working abroad. The boom in Islamic banking created a regulatory nightmare for the government. Fraud and scandal have been common, but the public's enthusiasm for Islamic enterprise is undeterred. The problem is not merely economic and legal, but political and religious as well.

Husni Mubarak's regime always tried to maintain a delicate balance toward Islam—crushing any display of armed rebellion in the name of religion while ostentatiously promoting peaceful expressions of piety, including many that openly criticized government policies. Under Mubarak, repression and tolerance worked hand in hand. Military force was regularly unleashed against religious opponents, but it could only appear to be legitimate if it seemed reserved for extreme dangers and not aimed at independent efforts to organize Islamic activity in general. In order to neutralize demands that Egypt must establish an Islamic state, Mubarak claimed that Egyptians were free to build an Islamic society and that the government itself was a key sponsor of that endeavor.

The success of Islamic banks is by no means a sign of Egypt's passage to an Islamic society, but it does reflect the emergence of an independent economic sector with multiple connections to domestic interest groups and foreign corporations. The new prominence of Islamic finance is a natural product of Mubarak's own economic reforms, particularly the privatization and liberalization spawned by three decades of "open door" capitalism. Even though the Islamic banks are straining relations in Egypt's private sector, it is now a more dominant and self-confident business community than Egypt has known since the fall of the monarchy. In fact, private sector diversification proved more destabilizing for the political system than for the economy. As greater competition in the marketplace spawned demands for democracy, Mubarak's economic success paved the way for his political demise at the hands of liberals and Islamists alike.

This is the context in which Kamal Aboulmagd sought to resolve the quarrels between the avowedly pro-Islamic regime and its restless allies in the business world. His solution was to transform an ostensibly legal battle into a religious conversation and a political bargaining process. Instead of seeking the most rational and efficient regulatory model, he proposed a deliberately inconsistent patchwork that virtually guaranteed friction and duplication. When everyone else was calling for an end to dualism, Aboulmagd seemed determined to institutionalize it.

Although Aboulmagd acknowledged the merits of both Western and Islamic financial systems, he firmly rejected the notion that either should enjoy a legal monopoly. Western banks, he noted, boasted greater experience and resources, but their power centers were far from Egypt and they would never treat Third World countries as equals. As for Islamic banks, they offered a combination of moral and practical advantages, yet most were still unknown and untested. He argued that the best path was to let both systems coexist and develop their own relationships over time—competing in some areas, cooperating in others, and growing new markets when opportunities arose.

Aboulmagd's economic logic was questionable, but his political logic made perfect sense to a nation caught between a plodding dictatorship it did not respect and a burgeoning religious movement it did not trust. Aboulmagd understood that beyond the public rhetoric no one really wanted a unified banking system. The government was accustomed to treating the private sector as its stepchild and saw little advantage in concentrating power in independent hands. Furthermore, the Mubarak regime had no appetite for needless confrontations with the popular Islamic revival. Having soundly defeated the violent fringes of the movement, the authorities had little to fear from its peaceful mainstream. Better to sponsor Islamic capitalism than to throttle it, sharing credit for its accomplishments and using its failures to justify greater regulation. For their part, the rival business factions realized that they had a common interest in conserving their political capital. Entrepreneurs in both camps argued that instead of trying to destroy one another, they should use the twilight of the Mubarak era to build alliances they would need to press their own agendas for democratization when the time was ripe.

Aboulmagd challenged proponents of Islamic and Western law to reexamine some of their most entrenched assumptions. He urged Islamists to accept once and for all the inevitability of lending money at interest and to recognize that many of their own practices accomplish the same thing under different labels. Similarly, he called on Western-trained secularists to acknowledge Islam's demand for a law that supports morality and society as well as contracts and markets. Most important, Aboulmagd flatly contradicted basic conceptions about the very nature of law that dominate both Islamic and Western traditions. He envisioned a hybrid legal system that deliberately encouraged uncertainty, incompleteness, and renegotiation—a stark contrast to the monistic and hegemonic aspirations of his colleagues in both Muslim and Western camps.

Egypt has always lived with a highly mixed legal system that blends several competing schools of Islamic and Western law. Moreover, these multiple approaches have had to adapt to important survivals of customary law and to growing intrusions from international law. Indeed, it is precisely this eclecticism that has made Egypt's legal system such a popular and durable prototype for modernizers throughout the Arab and Islamic worlds. In this sense, Aboulmagd's counsel could not have been more conservative. An elder jurist trained in both Islamic and Western traditions—with roots in the villages of Upper Egypt and clients circling the globe—he urged his country to revalue its heritage just when pressures to abandon it seemed irresistible. Although Aboulmagd's vision sounded radical, it merely asked Egyptians to consciously embrace the patchwork approach to lawmaking they had followed for generations. If the military regime and its opponents insisted on de-legitimizing one another with incompatible legal standards, Egypt would never promote the rule of law in any form.

Ali Bulaç: The Medina Constitution and the Turkish Army

Ali Bulaç is a native of Eastern Turkey who attended university in Istanbul where, like millions of other Kurdish migrants, he had to adapt to a foreign culture that refused to adapt to him. In time, his apparent handicaps proved to be precisely the assets that urban Turks most valued when they sought to reconnect with their own history and people. His multilingualism, small town origins, and religious training were indispensable to a generation that was shedding Ataturkist orthodoxy and opening their eyes to the diversity and divisions of Turkish society. Today he heads an impressive group of more than a dozen commentators at *Zaman*, Turkey's leading Islamic newspaper, where he is a gadfly and a cheerleader for all of the right-wing parties vying to create a workable fusion of religion and democracy.[4]

Bulaç's early fame was based largely on his portrayal of the Medina Constitution as the best form of government for the modern world. According to Bulaç, Muhammad and the many peoples of Medina voluntarily negotiated a social compact embodying an ideal balance of freedom and solidarity—an achievement that eluded every empire and nation-state that followed. In his view, the text and the context of that original contract provide the basic principles for a "pluralist project" of Islamic law that is more important today than ever.

[4] Morrison, Scott (2004). The life and times of the Turkish Islamist Ali Bulaç, *British Society for Middle Eastern Studies International Conference on Middle Eastern Studies*, London, 4–7 July.

Bulaç describes the Medina Constitution as a miracle that created strength out of weakness. Refugees fleeing persecution brought tolerance and objectivity to warring neighbors trying to escape a century of bloodshed. A small minority of only fifteen percent of the population provided not the "judge" but the "referee" for powerful and well-armed communities that preserved their own courts and laws. A pluralistic society allowed several legal systems to coexist, leaving the aggrieved parties free to choose among alternative rules and jurisdictions.

The essence of the formula for coexistence was freedom from coercion in all matters of "identity"—not merely in the choice of religion but also in choices of kinship, culture, and law. Bulaç sees identity as a composite of all these dimensions where a threat to any part is a threat to the whole. "If there is no coercion in the choice of religion, then there should be no pressure and compulsion on the laws embraced by different religions, philosophical beliefs, or ideologies. A person who chooses this or that religion chooses, at the same time, the legal system which is a manifestation of that particular religion. Leaving people free to choose their religion, yet creating obstacles in their choice of a legal system—and that is precisely what the modern state is doing—means interference with the essence of religion. Any interference with religion divides the personality of the believer and makes him culturally schizophrenic."[5]

According to Bulaç, that is why Muhammad carefully surveyed his new community, taking a population census to record the relative weight of Muslims, Jews, and polytheists. That is also why the social compact was a written document that listed each tribal signatory by name, including its clients and explicitly acknowledging the validity of its customary law. And that is why when the people of Medina wanted Muhammad to handle disputes they could not settle themselves, he always asked them, "How do you want me to decide, according to the Qur'an or the Torah?"

[5] Bulaç, Ali (1998). The Medina document, in Charles Kurzman, ed., *Liberal Islam: A Source Book*, New York: Oxford University Press, p. 177.

In Bulaç's view, Islamic government is most distinguished from the modern state by its insistence on participation by all social groups and its rejection of domination by any of them. "Each religious and ethnic group enjoys complete cultural and legal autonomy. In such areas as religion, law-making, judiciary, education, trade, culture, art, and the organization of daily life, *each group will remain as it is* and will express itself through the cultural and legal criteria it defines" (emphasis added).[6]

Islamic government is divided and limited whereas modern government is monolithic and totalitarian. "While the [Medina] Document transfers power to the central authority in judiciary, defense, and the proclamation of war—legislation, culture, science, arts, economy, education, health and other services are left to civil society." "In our region, where the Arab-Israeli war of many years, the recent Azeri-Armenian war, the feuding religious communities in Lebanon, the ethnic predicament in the Balkans, and the Kurdish problem exist, we need pluralist projects allowing the coexistence of all religious, ethnic and political groups based on partnership, choice, and participation."[7]

"This blueprint of an alternative social project [reduces] the state to executive activity and [limits] the executive to the provision of common and indivisible services. However, what opens the door to real pluralism is the ability of individuals and groups to define their own identities and to choose their own religions and legal systems. Experience shows that unless the realms of economy, culture, science, education, art, health, communication and so on are taken away from the control of the centralized state and transferred to groups with different religions and identities, real pluralism cannot be envisioned. The precondition for such a revolutionary design is to bring the singular quality of law to an end and leave this realm, among others, to the discretion of legal groups." "The Medina Document is the source of a blueprint that may be an alternative to a modern state that is becoming more totalitarian, overtly and covertly. Whoever deals with the "state" or "modernity" realizes immediately that one has to deal with both."[8]

---

[6] *Ibid.*, p. 174.

[7] *Ibid.*, p. 176.

[8] *Ibid.*, p. 178.

Bulaç's preference for weak central government does not discourage him from advancing bold proposals for deploying Turkey's army—the institution that Turkish Islamists usually identify as the very embodiment of state repression and secularist intolerance. After the pro-Islamic Justice and Development Party swept the national elections and formed one of the few single-party governments in decades, Bulaç was the only prominent Muslim writer who called on Turkey to supervise the military occupation of post-war Iraq. In October 2003, Turkey's foreign minister asked the Organization of the Islamic Conference (OIC) to authorize an "Islamic Peace Force" for Iraq that would be led by Turkey and composed of troops "that the region will accept," including Egyptians, Saudis, Iranians, Pakistanis, and Malaysians.

Acknowledging that Turkish public opinion flatly rejected the plan, Bulaç nonetheless supported it, claiming that former President Clinton was on board and wrongly assuming that OIC troops would be more welcome in Iraq than American and British forces. "Turkey's Iraq policy should not consist only of Northern Iraq and finding jobs for Turkish businessmen." "By acting according to the Bush administration's demands, Turkey weakens the hand of international legitimacy, deeply strains its relations with the Islamic and Arab world, and causes long-term hostility against us by the Iraqi people." "The only possible option before Turkey is to spearhead the [OIC] initiative itself even if Islamic countries are not ready for this move."[9]

In fact, other than Bulaç and his friends in the new government, no one was ready for such a move. The prospect of exporting the Turkish army might have reassured Islamists in Istanbul and Kurds in Diyarbakir, but it alarmed Turkey's neighbors and nearly everyone else in the Muslim world. At home, Bulaç may have hoped that emptying the barracks could pave the way for a Medinese federation of ethnic and religious equals, but beyond Turkey the idea evoked unwelcome

---

[9] Bulaç, Ali (2003). Türkiye farklı bir şey yapmalı (Turkey must do something different), *Zaman*, 23 September; Bulaç, Ali (2003). İslam barış gücü (The Islamic peace force) *Zaman*, 18 October.

memories of Ottoman imperialism. If Bulaç is correct in asserting that modern Turks suffer from a dangerous surplus of militarism and repressive capacity, then there should be no surprise when Iraq and similarly fragile societies are reluctant to expose themselves to that Turkish malady.

The Many Uses of Legal Pluralism in Turath Discourse

Each of these writers uses legal pluralism to supplant the more fixed rules of Islamic law (shari'a) with broader and more malleable principles culled from the Islamic heritage or legacy (turath). Their common goal is to dissolve the interpretive monopoly of the conservative 'ulama while preserving the broad outlines of the traditional Islamic legal schools (madhab, pl. madahib). Instead of trying to discard classical legal scholarship, they surround it with multiple sources of competing knowledge that can claim similarly illustrious histories in Islamic civilization—philosophy, mysticism, dialectical reasoning, and natural science. They seek to adapt Islamic law to modern needs by harmonizing it with other legal traditions that it cannot ignore or replace, particularly with customary law, administrative regulation, Western codes, and international law.

By pluralizing legal genres, they hope to prevent any tendency from gaining the power to repress the others. They intentionally avoid theoretical coherence in favor of eclecticism and indeterminacy that they regard as more suitable to the social and political realities of their time. In their hands, legal pluralism is a safeguard against the repressive impulses they see lurking in religious, nationalist, and foreign agendas. Suspicion of these potentially dominant tendencies is paired with a clear desire to rehabilitate and reform customary law—the most endangered and marginalized current of all.

IV: Diplomacy and Great Power Politics

Chapter 16

Morsy in Beijing: Implications for America's Relations with China and the Islamic World

President Mohamed Morsy's historic visit to Beijing has once again thrust Egypt to center stage in world affairs after three decades of isolation and passivity.[1] Egypt is joining a long line of regional powers in the Middle East and the Islamic world that are holding the United States at arm's length while moving closer and closer to China. Turkey, Saudi Arabia, Iran, Pakistan, and Indonesia all started down this road much earlier than Egypt, and they have gone further in asserting independent foreign policies that fill Washington with resentment and confusion. Afghanistan and the Central Asian successor states of the Soviet Union are tilting in a similar direction.[2] Even Russia, whose elite long viewed modernization as synonymous with Europeanization, is redefining itself as a Eurasian bridge linking the aging societies of the European Union with the booming markets of the Asia-Pacific basin.[3]

---

[1] For a sample of international commentary on Morsy's visit to China, see Bhadrakumar, M.K. (2012). Egypt thumbs the nose at U.S., *Asia Times Online*, 21 August; Aneja, Atul (2012). Morsy on path-breaking visit to China, Iran, *The Hindu*, 21 August; Schenker, David and Christina Lin (2012). Egypt's outreach to China and Iran is troubling for U.S. policy, *Los Angeles Times*, 24 August; Gong Shaopeng (2012). Aid no longer buys affection for U.S. on Egypt's streets, *Global Times*, 27 August; Halime, Farah (2012). Chinese firms brave uncertainty in Egypt to gain a foothold in Middle East, *New York Times*, 29 August; and O'Reilly, Brendan (2012). Egypt joins China club, *Asia Times Online*, 31 August.

[2] Bianchi, Robert R. (2013). China-Middle East relations in view of Obama's pivot to the Pacific, *China Report*, forthcoming.

[3] Putin, Vladimir (2012). An Asia-Pacific growth agenda, *Wall Street Journal*, 5 September; Herszenhorn, David M. (2012). Putin's ambitions turn to the Far East, *New York Times*, 6 September; and Trenin, Dmitri (2012). Russia's stake in Asia-Pacific, *China Daily*, 6 September.

The multipolar world is in full bloom. No longer a hypothetical scenario for future generations to grapple with, America's economic decline has sparked the rebirth of diplomacy and maneuver in aspiring powers everywhere, particularly in the Middle East and Asia. In this increasingly pluralistic world, spheres of influence aren't what they used to be, and formal alliances have few takers in an era filled with hedgers and freelancers who want to see which way the wind is blowing before they make commitments they might regret later.

The rest of the world is adapting to the new reality much faster than the United States. A recent report of the National Intelligence Council (NIC)—the super-agency that coordinates long-term strategic analysis for America's defense and intelligence community—sounds the alarm with unusual clarity.

In its latest forecast entitled "Global Trends 2030: Alternative Worlds," the NIC stresses Washington's persistent underestimation of China's rise and its stubborn reluctance to acknowledge the end of American hegemony in world affairs. The authors challenge the foreign policy bureaucracy on the very first page with a barb from John Maynard Keynes: "… the idea of the future being different from the present is so repugnant to our conventional modes of thought and behavior that we, most of us, offer a great resistance to acting on it in practice.[4]"

The gist of the report echoes what most independent observers of international politics have known for years—if American leaders expect to retain even a modest claim to global influence, they must rediscover diplomacy and learn to play weaker hands more skillfully. They have to realize that their military advantage is often a trap that lures them into one quagmire after another. Superior firepower is no match for guerrilla stamina and counter-insurgency becomes a euphemism for a wounded empire that bleeds itself to exhaustion.

---

[4] National Intelligence Council (2012). *Global Trends 2030: Alternative Worlds*, Washington, D.C.: Office of the Director of National Intelligence, p. i.

Morsy's overtures to Beijing underscore the gravity of the NIC's warnings. The Obama Administration is trying to stretch diminishing resources over an even wider geographic area by plunging into Pacific conflicts while it is losing its grip in the Middle East and Afghanistan. The Obama-Clinton pivot to the Pacific is a belated answer to China's westward expansion into what Americans had come to see as their zones of privilege in the Middle East, the Caspian Basin, Central Asia, and the Indian Ocean. But bringing the battle to China's shores merely makes Washington weaker without slowing Beijing's momentum in economic and political expansion.[5]

The more the United States tries to tie down the Chinese in their own neighborhood, the more the Chinese are encouraged to push back in every other region where America is vulnerable and overextended. Washington cannot seal off flashpoints from one another, hoping to prevent chain-reaction conflicts and transcontinental escalations. Such efforts are bound to backfire because there are too many moving parts and too many opportunities for miscalculation.

America doesn't make itself safer by adding the deep-seated hatreds of the Pacific-Indian Ocean region to the full-blown calamities of the Middle East. No matter how many aircraft carrier groups are relocated to Australia, they will never be enough to put out all the fires between Suez and the Yellow Sea.

Above all, America's foreign policy needs to respect its domestic demands and limits. The United States cannot squander its resources trying to parry Chinese influence in every corner of the globe and then expect to have enough left over to fix its own crippling economic and social problems. President Obama should take to heart his own admonition in his acceptance speech at the Charlotte convention that

---

[5] Tisdall, Simon (2012). Hillary Clinton won't unite South-East Asia against China, *The Guardian*, 3 September; Cunningham, Philip J. (2012), Deceit pivots U.S. foreign policy, *China Daily*, 3 September.

America needs to focus on nation-building at home before it tries to heal the rest of the world.[6]

In her effort to sell the Pacific pivot, Secretary of State Hillary Clinton's greatest assistance has come from the hawks in Beijing who are pushing a more assertive stance in pressing maritime claims. China is its own worst enemy in frightening neighbors whose goodwill and trust it needs for peaceful development and economic cooperation. Sooner or later, China has to stop flouting the law of the sea and listen to its own maritime lawyers who include some of the world's leading experts in the field.[7]

The weakness of the current Chinese claims will become increasingly evident and embarrassing as Beijing petitions for inclusion in the Arctic Council's deliberations over transit rights through the northern shipping routes to Europe that are being created by global warming. China can hardly expect to muscle its way in the Western Pacific while pleading for fair play in distant waters where it has no territorial or historical claims at all.[8] The moment China's leaders embrace a sensible split-the-difference approach to maritime disputes they will undercut the regional support for a stronger American military and diplomatic presence, and most Pacific nations will be happy to keep the US Navy out of sight and well beyond the horizon in Guam and Hawaii.

---

[6] Text of Obama's Acceptance Speech at the Democratic National Convention, *Washington Post*, 6 September 2012.

[7] For an excellent summary of the World Court's approach to recent maritime disputes, see the definitive article by the retired judge who represented China on the Court: Shi Jiuyong (2010). Maritime delimitation in the jurisprudence of the International Court of Justice, *Chinese Journal of International Law*, 9:2, pp. 271–291.

[8] Erickson, Andrew and Gabe Collins, (2012). China's new strategic target: Arctic minerals, *Wall Street Journal*, 18 January; Jian Junbo (2012). China, seeking a voice in Arctic affairs, says it has Swedish support for Arctic Council role, *Associated Press*, 16 April; China won't be frozen out of the Arctic, *Asia Times*, 3 May. See also Jakobson, Linda (2010). China prepares for an ice-free Arctic, *SIPRI (Stockholm International Peace Research Institute) Insights on Peace and Security*, March.

In a deeply flawed attempt to do more with less, Secretary Clinton has put a brave face on a grim predicament. But too often she is seen as scolding and hectoring, quickly wearing out her welcome and leaving US interests more exposed than before. Her apparently imminent retirement will give President Obama a freer hand in shaping more pragmatic approaches to foreign policy that lower the decibel level of political conversations.

Egypt's budding friendship with China suggests a new direction for American diplomacy that moves beyond both Secretary Clinton's muscle-flexing and the NIC's hand-wringing. For at least the next generation or two, the United States will have to cope with a more powerful China and with a more self-confident set of resource-rich Muslim nations espousing independent ideas about reshaping global governance. Instead of trying to weaken these forces or hoping to turn them against one another, Washington would be well advised to offer them all a greater share in the collective management of world economic and political crises before they reach the point where no set of alliances or institutions can save the day.

The whole world knows where that effort must lead—to insuring equitable access to vital sources of energy, water, and food, to developing a multi-currency standard for global commerce, to broadening representation in the United Nations Security Council, and to forging a global ethic based on the shared wisdom and experience of Western and non-Western civilizations. China and the Islamic world are indispensible partners in all of these ventures and many more. As America becomes more aware of its inability to lead alone, it should make every effort to turn the most likely rivals into friends instead of enemies.

What qualities does America's next chief diplomat need to bring to the job in order to make these goals achievable? Probably not the epic vision of a Marshall or Acheson, who presided over the birth of an elaborate institutional architecture, nor the cunning of a Kissinger or Brzezinski, who outmaneuvered the would-be challengers to that edifice. Instead of a midwife or chess master, we might be better served by a more modest politician who can cope with deadlock and uncertainty without becoming dispirited or disagreeable—someone very similar to

President Obama himself when doggedly wearing down his Republican opponents and, with a knowing smile, exposing their disregard for the public good. A Secretary of State who sees counterparts from countries such as Egypt, Turkey, Indonesia, and China as equals and even as prospective teammates—that's something to cheer the soul as we head into the windy season of presidential campaign madness.

Chapter 17

China–Middle East Relations in Light of Obama's Pivot to the Pacific

China's leaders usually view the Middle East in the larger context of global strategies that can advance national wealth and power. They see the Middle East as part of a wider region including Central Asia that borders China and shares cultural and religious ties with China's vast Muslim population.[1] From this perspective, Central Asia is China's backyard and the Middle East is a neighbor's neighbor. Equally important, Middle Eastern ports connect with China across long sea routes spanning the Indian and Pacific Oceans where navigation is controlled by American warships that can disrupt Chinese commerce at several choke points in case of hostilities. Thus, by land and by sea, China's lifelines pass through the length and breadth of the Islamic world with the Greater Middle East—including Caspian and Central Asian pipelines—and the Indian Ocean Basin at the center.[2]

Chinese policy-makers also see the Middle East–Central Asia region as a gateway connecting the Western Pacific with Europe, South Asia and Africa, and eventually with Latin America as well. Since the collapse of the Soviet Union, China has become the leading proponent of

[1] Liu Xin Hua (刘新华) (2004). 试论中亚对中国地缘战略的重要性 (The significance of Central Asia viewed from China's geo-strategy), *Journal of Wuhan Economic Administration Cadre's College*, 18:2, 20–24; and Zhang Xin Ping and Li Wei Liang (张新平, 李维亮) (2004). 中亚与伊斯兰世界关系的地缘政治思考 (Geopolitical thinking on relations between Central Asia and the Islamic World), *Journal of the Northwest University for Nationalities*, 6, 66–71.

[2] Qian Xue Wen (钱学文) (2007). 中东、里海油气与中国能源安全战略 (*The Middle East, Caspian Oil and Gas, and China's Energy Security Strategy*), Beijing: Current Events Press.

Eurasian integration. This means not merely a revival of the continental and maritime Silk Roads, but an assertive post-colonial vision of "Eurasia for the Eurasians" where non-Western civilizations regain equal respect and influence and where "New World" guests are welcome as partners but not as masters. As wealth and power shift to the east, China's influence is spreading rapidly to the west. Bankers and engineers from China are teaming up with counterparts from Turkey, Germany, Korea, Pakistan, and the Persian Gulf to build transcontinental networks of trains, roads, pipelines, dams, and power stations running from London and Vienna to Shanghai and Guangzhou.

American military and diplomatic strategists are acutely aware of the dangers of a more integrated Eurasian landmass, particularly if it is fashioned to suit China's economic and political preferences. Many in Washington fear that China's Eurasian vocation goes far beyond rivaling Russian influence in Central Asia. They suspect that Beijing also seeks to pull the European Community further away from a divided Atlantic alliance, to exploit America's self-inflicted wounds in the Middle East, and to corner the market on Africa's minerals and development projects. Most of all, they dread the prospect of a Eurasian superpower that could hamper American action in the Eastern Hemisphere and undermine Washington's claims to exclusive control over Latin America.

From the Monroe Doctrine to the Marshall Plan the cardinal rule of United States diplomacy has been to preserve the Western Hemisphere as America's sphere of influence while preventing any other nation or coalition from gaining similar dominance in the Eastern Hemisphere.[3] This is the "core interest" that guides Washington's consideration of all other interests. Unlike China's definition of core interests as concrete territories—Taiwan, Tibet, Xinjiang and more recently the South China Sea—America's red line is drawn around more subjective and shifting assessments of relative power and global intentions.

As the United States perceives the westward expansion of China's influence as threatening both regional and worldwide balances of power, it has responded with an understandable but ill-conceived

---

[3] Walt, Stephen M. (2011). Explaining Obama's Asia policy, *Foreign Policy*, 18 November.

counter-action—the "Obama pivot" from the Middle East to the Western Pacific. The new American thinking aims to divide the intercontinental and transoceanic regions that China and other nations want to integrate while encouraging an "encircle China" coalition among smaller maritime powers from India and Singapore to Australia and Vietnam and on to the Philippines, Japan and South Korea.

The blind spot in the American plan is that all of these countries need China more than they need the United States. None of them wants a military alliance with Washington that will antagonize Beijing because their economic futures pull them inexorably to greater integration with the mainland's vast and growing markets. China's neighbors might feel vulnerable enough to welcome outside guarantees against any temptation for Beijing to play the bully instead of the benefactor, but their nationalist traditions deeply resist moving in a pro-American orbit. Even as they warm to the prospect of continued American visits to their ports, many of them suspect that eventually the United States will hang them out to dry by cutting a deal with China to divide the Pacific into spheres of influence.

Obama's eastward focus attempts to stem the powerful current of Islamic countries that have strengthened ties with China while quarrelling more and more with the United States. A growing number of former American allies, including some that were virtual US dependencies, are now hedging their bets with more independent foreign policies that actively court Chinese investment, trade, military cooperation and diplomatic support. The most notable examples are Indonesia, Turkey, Pakistan, the states of the Gulf Cooperation Council and, more recently, Egypt, Afghanistan and Iraq.

Indonesia flatly rejected American efforts to mediate conflicting territorial claims in the South China Sea and to lead patrolling the Makassar and Malacca Straits. Turkey frequently angers Washington by siding with Iran, Palestine and Iraqi Sunnis, and when NATO backed out of joint military exercises in Turkey because Ankara excluded Israel, the Chinese air force was quick to fill the gap making its first overseas flights in history over Konya. Pakistan was so infuriated by American military incursions and sponsorship of India's nuclear program that it pledged to expand its Chinese-backed arms industry and to accelerate pipeline construction linking Iran to Xinjiang. The Gulf Cooperation Council states offered China a handsome package of long-term energy deals, construction projects and joint investments in return for Beijing's abstention from United Nations Security Council votes to impose sanctions against Iran's nuclear enrichment activities. And now that American-sponsored rule is crumbling in Afghanistan, Iraq and Egypt, those countries are adding to the ranks of independent-minded actors seeking a counter-balance to excessive dependence on Washington's largesse.

Obama's foreign policy team would like to disengage from the string of Middle Eastern failures that has sapped American prestige and influence for more than a decade and shift to the more urgent task of parrying China's expansion in the Pacific and Indian Oceans. In fact, the United States will probably have to deal with a series of crises in both the Middle East and Asia at the same time and flashpoints in one region will more quickly aggravate tensions in the other. Washington's desire to separate the Middle Eastern and Far Eastern theaters seems particularly futile as the forces of integration and interdependence gather steam throughout Asia and Europe inspiring visions of a seamless market and community from the Atlantic to the Pacific.

At most, the Obama administration might hope to slow the momentum of China's westward push, but they cannot reverse it. Washington wants to put China on the defensive, but that is precisely where Chinese diplomats and soldiers are most comfortable and most skilled. They are accustomed to deflecting the advances of stronger powers—particularly distant nations that are overextended geographically and economically—and to focusing stress on their weakest points until they flounder and retreat. A frustrated superpower licking its wounds from defeat after defeat in the Middle East could find no more certain graveyard than the endless seas and struggles of a rising Asia riven by nationalist hatreds and caught in a spiraling arms race.

China's Dual Destiny—The Mongol Vocation and the Celebration of Zheng He

The transcontinental ambitions of Chinese nationalism are vividly portrayed in the official reworkings of history that popularize and romanticize pre-modern imperial connections across the Eastern Hemisphere and throughout the Indian Ocean Basin, including the Persian Gulf, the Red Sea and the farthest shores of Africa. Chinese historical imagination increasingly highlights the legacy of the Chinese Mongol dynasty, the Yuan, and its affinities with other Mongol successor states that briefly ruled the vast realms of Confucianism, Buddhism, Islam and Christianity. In their Sinicized incarnation, the Yuan have been rehabilitated as a Chinese dynasty instead of a barbarian occupation and their hybrid culture and ethnicity are viewed as natural bridges between China and other world civilizations both Western and non-Western.

Admiral Zheng He, the Chinese Muslim explorer of the Ming dynasty who led seven maritime expeditions of "treasure ships," has been transformed into a marvelously multivalent icon of peaceful expansion, Sino-Islamic brotherhood and Third World solidarity. From the perspective of Chinese domestic politics and foreign relations, Zheng He's personal journey of assimilation and empowerment is as important as his voyages. His legendary rise from prisoner of war to imperial confident and then to China's most famous ambassador holds a special attraction for the Muslims of China—particularly the pivotal Han-speaking Hui who reside in every corner of the country—as well as for Muslims around the world who want to know where China stands in the so-called clashes and dialogues of civilizations.

The Mongol and Zheng He narratives frequently intersect and reinforce one another. Nanjing University is the home of a new Yuan Studies Center that explores the history of Islam in China, portraying Muslim cultures as national resources instead of subversive dangers and as indigenous creations instead of foreign implants. It gathers top Muslim students from across the nation, particularly multilingual Hui from the strategic borderlands of Yunnan, Xinjiang, and Ningxia, who shift freely between Chinese, Arabic and English as they compare notes on how their communities manage to blend local traditions with universal Islamic principles. Over the last decade, the Center has also taken the lead in organizing a series of international dialogues between Confucian, Islamic and Western scholars in China, North America, Europe, and Southeast Asia. It has become a hub of China's triple outreach to its own Muslims, to Islamic markets abroad and to reform-minded scholars of Confucianism and Christianity.[4]

Nanjing was also the capital of the early Ming dynasty where Zheng He supervised the shipyards that built his armadas. When China celebrated the six hundredth anniversary of his earliest voyage in 2005, Nanjing was the center for a yearlong flood of exhibitions and festivities not only on the mainland, but in the Chinese diaspora communities throughout Southeast Asia and beyond.[5] Islamic historians and scholars were invited to international conferences that produced at least a dozen anthologies showcasing China's ancient and continuous exchanges with Muslim lands in every part of Asia and Africa. The political messages were timely and well-articulated: China expanded its influence through peaceful trade instead of military conquest; China respected and partnered with other cultures, valuing mutual learning and eschewing interference with local traditions; China is a sister civilization of Islam that has survived similar humiliations at the hands of Western imperialism and is now recovering its historic dignity and grandeur.

During the last decade, Zheng He has grown into the essential synthesis of China's ideal self-image at home and abroad—the organic link between assimilated Mongol rule and Han restoration after the Ming insurgency; the trusted imperial commander who planned decisive campaigns on land and at sea; the loyal Muslim who combined the best of traditional religion, modern science and patriotic dedication; and the

---

[4] Hua Tao (华涛) (2006). 穆斯林社会与全球文明对话 (Muslim society and the global dialogue of civilizations), *Journal of Hui Muslim Minority Studies*, 61:1, 24–26, available online at http://ishare.iask.sina.com.cn/f/19875247.html (accessed 14 January 2013); and Hua Tao (华涛) (2003). 文化对话与中国传统文化范式中的障碍 (Cultural dialogue and obstacles in the paradigms of traditional Chinese culture), *Journal of Nanjing University,* 40:1, 45–51.

[5] Wang Gungwu (2005). China's cautious pride in an ancient mariner, *Yale Global*, 4 August.

peaceful messenger who spread China's influence and glory to the farthest frontiers.[6]

Equally important is the persistent and pointed contrast between Zheng He and his European successors, particularly Christopher Columbus. Chinese depictions commonly stress the puniness of Columbus' ships compared to Zheng He's floating cities. They highlight Columbus' confusion over what he had discovered, his extermination of native populations, his perfidious dealings with European monarchs and clerics, and his tragic humiliation after a lifetime of self-aggrandizement.

Mainstreaming Chinese Islam

Islam is flourishing in China today primarily because the party and government have struck a bargain with much of the Hui community's religious and professional leadership on how they can enhance the goals of economic development, political quiescence and international acceptance. The core of the bargain is an official pledge to condemn the atheistic excesses of the Cultural Revolution in return for Muslim denunciations of the "three evils" of terrorism, extremism and separatism. Under this formula, Hui Muslims enjoy unprecedented freedom of religion while the security forces turn their sights on more troublesome targets, including the Turkic-speaking Uyghurs, Tibetan Buddhists, Catholics who remain loyal to Rome, the Protestant home church movements and wildfire "cults" such as the Falun Gong.[7]

The benefits for Chinese-speaking Muslims have been enormous. The state encourages and actively sponsors a host of Islamic activities including religious education, mosque building, charitable work, Hajj organization, halal food production, religious tourism, publishing, internet communities, overseas study, exports to Muslim markets, joint ventures with foreign businesses and foundations and,

---

[6] Branigan, Tania (2010). Zheng He: Messenger of peace, or of power? *The Guardian*, 25 July.

[7] Hayoun, Massoud (2012). Islam with Chinese characteristics, *The Atlantic*, 18 January.

occasionally, even religious instructors from Pakistan where Beijing is particularly eager to build independent relations with private Islamic associations. In villages and towns where the wounds of the Cultural Revolution are still healing, local party and government leaders openly recruit Islamic teachers and imams to mediate their relations with business and citizens' groups who remain suspicious of central authority.[8] In return, Muslim religious and business elites often urge their most promising students to join the Communist Party, hoping they will rise to positions of authority that will eventually benefit their kinsmen even at the price of abandoning public worship.

State patronage extends far beyond the religious officialdom to promote a rising middle class of Muslim businesses, professionals and intellectuals. Muslim university graduates can now look beyond their families' traditional niches in the private sector to find positions in the many state-run companies with overseas operations, especially the energy, construction and financial firms springing up across the Middle East and Africa. Students trained in Arabic, Persian or Islamic studies take up faculty positions in the string of "nationalities universities" that connect the interior provinces with the big cities and the east coast.

More and more young Muslims are moving into top-flight universities and government think tanks where they quickly transition from religious and humanistic studies to the social sciences and international relations. Their scholarly works and policy analyses have become regular features in the established area studies journals, the press and television news programs. Several of these Muslim scholars have become prominent advisors on foreign policy, widely respected for their expertise on the Middle East and the Islamic world.[9]

---

[8] Gui Rong (桂榕) (2009). 村的权力文化网络：云南沙甸和谐社会的政治人类学研究 (Cultural networks of power in a Hui village: A political anthropology study of the harmonious society of Shadian Yunnan), *Journal of the Yunnan University of Nationalities*, 26:4, 49–52.

[9] Ma Li Rong (马丽蓉) (2009). 全球化进程中清真寺功能影响研究 (The functions and influence of mosques in the globalization process), *Journal of Hui Muslim Minority Studies*, 2, March, 54–64; and Ma Li Rong (马丽蓉) (2007). 西方霸权语境中的阿拉伯-伊斯兰问题研究 (*The Arab-Islamic Question in the Context of Western Hegemony*), Beijing: Current Events Press.

The Hajj and the Great West

One of the most extraordinary signs of Islamic vitality in China is the rapid growth of the state-sponsored pilgrimage to Mecca. Until the 1980s, the Communist Party obstructed and suppressed the Hajj, fearing that exposure to international Islamic currents would radicalize Chinese Muslims, especially in the tense borderlands where the Soviets were always ready to exploit ethnic and religious conflict. The post-Mao reform and opening gradually relaxed these restrictions, allowing a trickle and then a steady flow of pilgrims that now exceeds 14,000 per year.

The bulk of China's Hajjis come from the predominately Hui communities of the northwest provinces—the multi-ethnic and multi-religious crossroads where Han, Hui, Mongol, Tibetan and Turkic cultures intersect.[10] This is precisely the region that Beijing's planners and strategists have identified as China's future heartland in terms of economic development, security threats and political rivalries.

Developing the Great West is the linchpin of Chinese economic growth for the next generation because it will spread prosperity from the privileged coast to the secondary cities of the neglected interior. It is central to security not only because of the volatile brew of ethnic animosities in the borderlands, but because China's air force has repositioned its land-based nuclear deterrent to the west to protect it from the naval and air attacks that are certain to capture or destroy the coastal cities in case of all-out war. Moreover, the west is vital politically because it will likely hold the balance of power in future showdowns between the evenly matched northern and the southern regions if China moves toward electoral democracy or regional tests of strength.

[10] *Al-Jazeera* (2009). From Xian to Mecca: A road to Hajj, 24 November; and Han Shu Yun (韩淑云), 女哈吉与通过仪式—基于青海循化穆斯林女性朝觐者的调查研究 (Female Hajjis and the rites of passage—A survey of female Muslim pilgrims in Xunhua, Qinghai province), *Journal of Beifang Ethnic University*, 2, 70–73.

In this context, the loyalty and patriotism of Hui Muslims tops the list of military, economic and political concerns of any government in Beijing. The Hui are too powerful to suppress and too unreliable to ignore. They must be carefully managed, regulated, subsidized, indoctrinated, assimilated, coopted and prominently displayed as model citizens and modern achievers.

Having consolidated the government-led Hajj as a perquisite of northwestern Hui Muslims, Beijing is now eager to expand the project to include the rebellious Uyghurs of Xinjiang. After decades of avoidance and denial, the government has at last admitted that most Chinese Hajjis are illegal pilgrims from Xinjiang who travel without visas and often without passports, transiting through Pakistan and Turkey with the aid of overseas kinsmen who frequently are political exiles and campaigners for independent statehood.[11] The escalation of communal violence in Xinjiang has finally convinced Beijing that only a combination of jobs and religious freedoms can save their vital link to Eurasia's indispensible energy resources and markets. Hence, the simultaneous decisions to transform Xinjiang into western China's largest international free trade zone and its preeminent staging center for the Hajj.

Currency Wars

In addition to the Hajj, Saudi Arabia plays a central role in China's aspiration to promote its currency in international trade while dethroning the dollar as the global standard of value. Chinese analysts correctly conclude that Saudi Arabia's policy of conducting oil transactions exclusively in dollars is vital to America's financial and political dominance. As American politicians increase their demands on China to revalue the Yuan, the Chinese fight back with mega-

---

[11] Yao Chun Jun (姚春军) (2009). 对新疆维吾尔宗教信仰者朝觐问题的心里探析 (A psychological analysis of Uyghur Muslims' beliefs about the Hajj), *Xinjiang Social Science*, 2, 52–57.

transactions that internationalize their currency as an alternative medium of exchange.[12]

While economists disagree on whether the Yuan is undervalued, international lawyers generally concur that there is no remedy available to plaintiff nations in these types of disputes. Indeed, some economists argue that an overvalued Yuan is a proper tradeoff for China's agreement to abide by World Trade Organization prohibitions on direct government subsidies to exporters.[13] This leaves Chinese bankers enormous latitude to woo trading partners into currency swaps and special investment packages that no other nation can provide. As the members of the Gulf Cooperation Council become increasingly critical of America's positions toward Palestine and Iran, they are more receptive to China's attack on the dollar. Washington is on notice—it can adjust its Middle Eastern policies or jeopardize its financial integrity in the region and around the world.

The Libya Expedition

China's evacuation of nearly 36,000 nationals during the Libyan revolution was a heroic rescue operation by sea and air that would have been the envy of Zheng He himself. Chinese warships moved from the Gulf of Aden where they were hunting Somali pirates through the Suez Canal and into the Mediterranean for the first time in history. They were soon followed by a group of transport planes that flew directly from Xinjiang to the Libyan desert to collect the remaining workers who were unable to reach the coast.

In less than a month, Beijing had impressed several audiences with its global military reach. It showed nationalist critics at home that it would spare no effort to protect its teeming communities of overseas

[12] Fisk, Robert (2009). The demise of the dollar: Arabs, Asia, Russia said planning to drop dollar in oil trade, *The Independent*, 6 October.

[13] Rodrik, Dani (2009). Making room for China in the world economy, *American Economic Review*, 100:2, 89–93.

workers. It alerted Middle Eastern and African nations that its rising commercial profile would be backed up with force when necessary. And, most importantly, it reminded NATO powers that they no longer enjoyed exclusive access to North African territory and resources.

Pondering the New Egypt

Just when Chinese investments in Libya seemed to slip away because of Beijing's belated embrace of the revolution, Egypt offered even greater opportunities for political as well as economic gains. A more independent Egypt seeking new friends and ready to trade its diplomatic influence for economic relief holds tantalizing possibilities for every wing of China's interlocking military-commercial-political elite. As tensions multiply between Washington and Cairo, China weighs the countless routes that an Egyptian partnership could open to the Middle East, Africa and Europe.

Many Chinese writers expect that Egypt will move closer to Turkey, creating its own version of democracy and capitalism inspired by Islamic principles. They opine that a budding Turkish-Egyptian connection might help China by counter-balancing Iran and better managing its hostilities with the Persian Gulf Arabs and Israel.[14] The more fluid balance of power that China contemplates in the Middle East is a perfect counterpart to the multi-polar international system it envisions in the post-American world order. On both levels, numerous nations would be free to form and break quasi-alliances instead of herding into rigid blocks dominated by opposing superpowers. Of course, no one really knows if multi-polar politics will encourage more conflict or less, either regionally or globally. However, from the perspective of a rising but still secondary world power, the obvious advantage lies in the ability to erode the influence of a stronger rival without having to fight wars that you will probably lose.

[14] Wu Bing Bing (吴冰冰) (2011). 中东多极化是中国新机遇 (Middle East multipolarization is a new opportunity for China), *Global Times*, 30 August.

The Problem of Timing

There is still no consensus in Beijing on overall Middle East policy, particularly in the wake of the Arab uprisings. Where some see opportunities others see traps. For every voice urging the leadership to exploit America's misfortunes, there is a counter-argument that the United States should be left to stew in its own mess. And there is always a faction of inveterate skeptics, including those who claim to see "two Asias"—the Far East basking in progress and harmony versus the Middle East consumed by hatred and producing nothing but oil and war.[15]

China's foreign policy journals and think tanks are filled with cost-benefit analyses of countless policy options for dealing with Middle Eastern problems.[16] Even when writers recognize a substantial upside, their lists of caveats and warnings of unanticipated consequences must chill the bones of all but the most intrepid decision-makers. In the wider context of the ongoing debate over whether China's overseas presence is too timid or too bold, the violence and unpredictability of the Middle East tip the scales in favor of prudence.[17] America's desire to look toward the Pacific is read as an admission of failure—a thin cover for hasty retreat from a land of sorrows and humiliations. Why take over America's headaches when it feels so good to see their pain? Better to wait and see what they're willing to offer us in return.

China is preparing to help clean up the mess in Afghanistan and Iraq, but only with plenty of company from neighbors and international organizations. Iran is worth propping up as long as sanctions-busting is profitable and war is continually postponed, but China is in no hurry to

[15] Yin Gang (2008). Two Asias: The Middle East in an Asian century, *Bitter Lemons*, 8 May.

[16] Li Yi (李意) (2010). 海湾安全局势与中国的战略选择 (*The Security Situation in the Arab Gulf and China's Strategic Choices*), Beijing: World Knowledge Press.

[17] Dong Wang and Li Kan (2010). Eying the crippled hegemon: China's grand strategy thinking in the wake of the global financial crisis, *Social Science Research Network*, September 8; and Godement, François *et al.* (2011). China debates its global strategy, *European Council on Foreign Relations*, April.

throw more men and money into oil fields that are certain to be prime targets. The same logic applies to Syria where China is free of the frozen commitments that tie Russia to Assad and the Americans to Israel. Beijing has no need to save the Ba'athists, but it is determined to restore the leash that NATO snapped during the Libyan operation. When a Western sphere of influence is in turmoil, what is the point of helping to shore up the status quo? After the smoke begins to clear, there will be plenty of time to mend fences and make friends with the survivors.

The Virus in the Homeland

The detachment and objectivity that Chinese leaders show concerning upheavals in the Middle East quickly evaporate when they contemplate the reverberations among their own people. When the Arab peoples speak so eloquently of re-launching their unfinished revolutions, how can patriotic Chinese with any sense of history fail to recall the origins of their own modern Renaissance in the May Fourth Movement and the New Culture Movement? And how can one invoke the glories of 1919 without confronting the tragedies of 1989?

Whether or not they admit it in public, China's leaders know that their society is already in a constant state of revolt. The new Arab Awakening has hit the Communist Party's rawest nerve—the open secret that one-party rule is exhausted and that nothing exists to replace it. The democratic surge in the Middle East has not created any of China's domestic discontents, but it has emboldened people from all walks of life to say candidly what they only dared to whisper before—that China's rulers can punish and steal, but they cannot govern.

The great irony of the Arab revolts is that just when China's leaders see America losing ground in its prized overseas dominions, they are feeling the ground crumble beneath their own feet at home. "Reform" is on the lips of every Chinese politician and commentator, including multiple proposals for freedom of expression and competitive elections.[18]

---

[18] *Strategypage.com* (2010). Chinese general declares democracy the ultimate weapon, 19 August; and Bandurski, David (2011). Turning back to 'new democracy'? *China Media Project*, 19 May.

Infighting among party factions is increasingly public and pervasive in Beijing and particularly in the provinces. These are exactly the cracks in elite consensus that aggrieved groups commonly interpret as openings for greater protest and opposition. Hence, the more the party debates its future, the more it fills the jails to convince its critics and itself that it remains alive. The ruling establishment has good reason to cringe and scowl when they look to the Middle East because they suspect they are watching a preview of their own rapidly approaching fate.[19]

Three Pillars of China's Greater Middle East Strategy

Given China's profound ambivalence toward most Arab countries, it seems only natural that Beijing should look elsewhere to safeguard its growing dependence on the long-distance transportation of Middle Eastern energy. China's leaders have paid special attention to a handful of large and strategically positioned Muslim nations that bridge the increasingly integrated markets and societies of the Middle East and Asia. Above all, Beijing has focused its alliance-building on Turkey, Pakistan and Indonesia—military and economic centers that can provide or restrict access to several of the most important land and sea routes in the Eastern Hemisphere. Indeed, Obama's eagerness to reengage the Pacific is a belated and stumbling response to China's rapid success in pushing its power and prestige westward not only in the Greater Middle East, but to the heart of Europe and Africa as well.

Leaders in Turkey and China share a common awareness that they are heirs of rich diplomatic traditions from Ottoman and Qing eras that distilled centuries of Islamic and Confucian statecraft blended with more recent Westphalian principles of power politics. Representatives from both countries thrive in the fluid and uncertain world of multilateral bargaining and they are utterly convinced that the historic resurgence of balance of power diplomacy is tailor-made to showcase their skills.

---

[19] LeVine, Mark (2012). The Arab spring's Chinese roots...and future? *al-Jazeera*, 2 February.

Moreover, they share a tendency to view their nations' interests in terms of increments of geography and power where every diplomatic link connects multiple neighbors in far-reaching networks that quickly dissolve the boundaries between local, regional and intercontinental politics. Turkish diplomats and scholars never tire of explaining that they belong to a Mediterranean society that is simultaneously Balkan, Black Sea, Caucasian, Caspian, Middle Eastern, Central Asian—and, when it suits them, Mongolian and Chinese.[20] Their counterparts in China describe a similar progression of westward circles of influence, stressing culture and commerce instead of race and religion.

The match between China and Turkey is a recent and stormy affair made not in heaven but in hard-nosed bargains of realist politicians with overlapping visions of Eurasian leadership.[21] Ankara and Beijing have had to devise concrete solutions to a constant flow of disputes from turf battles in Central Asia to the plight of Uyghurs in Xinjiang and, most importantly, enormous trade imbalances that infuriate powerful business lobbies in Istanbul and Anatolia. Both sides have given ground on every issue. Turkey scaled back its ambitions in Central Asia to trade and education instead of political reform; China accepted regular closed-door meetings with Turkish nationalist parties that champion Uyghur causes; and Beijing has pledged huge investments in Turkish industry and infrastructure. In a particularly symbolic gesture, China even agreed to halt exports of popular Hajj apparel and equipment so that Turkish producers could begin to recover their own domestic markets.

---

[20] Davutoğlu, Ahmet (2001). *Stratejik Derinlik: Türkiye'nin Uluslararası Konumu* (*Strategic Depth*), Istanbul: Küre Yayınları.

[21] Adibelli, Barış (2007). *Çin'in Avrasya Stratejisi* (*China's Eurasia Strategy*) Istanbul: IQ Kültür Sanat Yayıncılık; and Adibelli, Barış (2006). *Büyük Avrasya Projesi: ABD, Rusya ve Çin'in Varolma Mücadelesi* (*The Greater Eurasia Project: The Struggle for Survival between the United States, Russia and China*), Istanbul: IQ Kültür Sanat Yayıncılık.

Compromise has paid handsome dividends to both parties. Turkey links up to the only economy in the world that is growing faster than its own and reminds its overbearing Atlantic friends that Ankara has heavyweight partners in all directions. China gains a privileged export platform to its biggest customer in Europe and an on-site broker enmeshed in the daily affairs of every Middle Eastern country where superpowers are as welcome as the plague.

Chinese ties with Pakistan have soared to new heights thanks to the spillover of the Afghanistan war and Washington's aggressive courtship of India. The "enemy of my enemy" logic is irrefutable when the common adversary is so transparent in its long-term intentions. New Delhi's military establishment has responded to increasing Chinese presence in the Indian Ocean by dispatching its own warships to the South China Sea and by aiding Vietnamese oil exploration in disputed waters.

In telegraphing its willingness to join an encircle China strategy, India has virtually guaranteed a Chinese push at counter-encirclement that corrals the smaller states of South Asia against Delhi's over-confidence. The cornerstone of China's South Asian strategy has always been Pakistan, but Obama's Af-Pak War has sealed that alliance more tightly than ever.[22]

For over a decade, the turmoil in Afghanistan and Pakistan has frozen competing pipeline projects supported by China and the United States. But with Pakistan tilting decisively toward Beijing, there is every prospect that Iranian oil and gas will eventually flow through Baluchistan and the Northern Territories to Kashgar and then to all corners of mainland China. Islamabad has already given China top billing in the deep-water port of Gwadar on the Arabian Sea, threatening to transfer management from Singaporean operators to Chinese rivals and urging Beijing to build additional facilities for hosting submarines. For Beijing, the combined economic and military benefits could be incalculable.

[22] Lieven, Anatol (2011). *Pakistan: A Hard Country*, New York: Public Affairs Books.

Pakistan would be providing a triple windfall—overland routes bypassing the dreaded Straits of Hormuz, eliminating at least part of China's "Malacca dilemma," and offering Zheng He's modern counterparts a permanent home away from home right on India's doorstep.

Indonesia is the guardian of China's maritime lifelines to the Middle East and Africa. Less than fifty years ago, its army slaughtered hundreds of thousands of its own citizens because their Chinese race implied Communism and disloyalty. Today, that same nation views China as the driving force of its development and as a historic contributor to its own conversion to Islam. That dramatic turnabout places Indonesia squarely in opposition to any Pacific power—real or imagined—that would target or antagonize Beijing.

Indonesia has long been the center of Southeast Asia's international relations and in the past decade it has become a global actor as well thanks to its democratic vitality, natural resources and religious pluralism.[23] It has evolved into China's easternmost anchor in Islamic Asia, complementing Turkey in the west and Pakistan in the center. The inauguration of the China-ASEAN Free Trade Area in 2010 paves the way for massive Chinese investments in infrastructure and industry—investments that Indonesia needs desperately as its oil reserves decline and that it cannot hope to obtain from Japan or more distant capital markets.

The pro-American posture that India is currently trying to assume in the Pacific is precisely the role that Indonesia abandoned after the fall of Suharto. Like Turkey, Indonesia sees its best interests in playing the indispensible balancer between its neighbors and the great powers instead of becoming locked into permanent commitments with a single block. Jakarta has stymied Secretary Clinton at every step in her efforts to internationalize territorial disputes in the South China Sea and to insert the US Navy into policing the Pacific-Indian Ocean junctions.

---

[23] Sukma, Rizal (2009). A post-ASEAN foreign policy for a post-G8 world, *Jakarta Post*, 5 October.

Muslim politicians in Indonesia are highly critical of Washington's assertions that Indonesia is a center of international terrorism. They regularly accuse America of Islamophobia and charge that Washington is attempting to undermine their political influence by frightening Indonesian voters. Meanwhile, the same Muslim leaders are warming to China after decades of alienation. Although they denounce Chinese actions in Xinjiang, they take advantage of every opportunity to expand contacts between Muslims in China and Indonesia. Jakarta has hosted rich exhibits of Islamic arts and culture from China and Beijing has eagerly publicized the small but thoroughly Indonesianized communities of Chinese Muslims in northern Java. Barack Obama enjoys enormous affection in his childhood home, but America is increasingly viewed as a clumsy outsider that requires careful handling by a region determined to chart its own course.

President Obama is quick to assure us that his reengagement of Asia is not aimed at containing China's dramatic but unsettling rise. Indeed, he often notes that the United States has no choice but to engage Beijing in compromise and collaboration because China's achievements have placed it far beyond containment. Having grasped this much, he must also realize that China is equally beyond encirclement.[24] As the heads of America's security establishment try to disengage from the Middle East and to execute his Pacific project, they might well ask, "Mr. President, how do we surround an adversary that has already surrounded us?"

[24] Johnson, Ian and Jackie Calmes (2011). As US looks to Asia, it sees China everywhere, *New York Times*, 15 November.

Chapter 18

China and the United States in the Middle East and the Islamic World

Leaders in China and the United States are struggling to restrain their great power rivalries before they destroy the global order that sustains them both. Viewing US–China affairs as the world's most important and most dangerous bilateral relationship, a growing number of scholars and policy-makers are urging Washington and Beijing to share power instead of plunging into a futile and ruinous quest for superiority. For supporters of international cooperation, these are hopeful signs that history can move beyond the mutual fears and security dilemmas that haunt our basic assumptions about human nature and world politics.

Nonetheless, calls for a US–China diarchy do not go far enough toward sharing power in an increasingly multipolar world. They do not include what Sino-American-centric thinkers condescendingly term "second and third-tier" nations—the older powers of Europe, Russia, and Japan or the many rapidly emerging countries in non-Western regions. Most of all, they underestimate the current importance and future potentials of the Middle East and the Islamic world. The resources and transport links of these countries are paramount to American and Chinese strategists, but the people and their aspirations receive scant regard unless crisis and upheaval threaten great power interests.

In the four decades since Henry Kissinger's diplomatic breakthroughs, China and the United States have gradually learned to cooperate in ways that previously seemed inconceivable. However, today both superpowers are stumbling in efforts to deal with the rising powers of the Islamic world, particularly Turkey, Iran, Egypt, Saudi Arabia, Pakistan, Indonesia, and Nigeria. Neither China nor the West can expect a peaceful international environment or economic prosperity unless they accord Islamic nations the same levels of respect and accommodation that they extend to one other. In terms of their relations with Middle

Eastern and Islamic powers, China is more advanced in the diplomatic realm, the United States is ahead in academic expertise, and both nations are woefully backward in building fruitful person-to-person relationships between ordinary people, which is the most important dimension of all.

During Barak Obama's presidency, China has continued the steady westward expansion of its economic and political influence into Central Asia and the Middle East as well as in Europe, Africa, and Latin America. Recent efforts to redeploy American power from the Middle East and Afghanistan to the Western Pacific are a belated and ill-advised counter-offensive to China's ascendance in areas that the United States has long regarded as buffer zones or as its exclusive spheres of influence. China's multiple alliances throughout the Islamic world are particularly alarming to Western powers because they crisscross the land and sea routes that dominate the lifelines of global commerce and raw materials supplies. The US pivot to Asia will heighten tensions with China not only in Asia, but in the Middle East and many other regions as well.[1]

Power Sharing and Power Struggles

Much of the current desire to promote Sino-American power sharing is driven by the conviction that war is a choice rather than an inevitability and by the realization that military conflict has become an overt preference for hawks in Washington and Beijing alike. Arguments for the rationality and desirability of war are chillingly clear in both capitals. Military projections and countermeasures are revealed in a cascade of reports that ignore scruples of secrecy and prudence in an apparent attempt by both sides to scare the wits out of one another. Indeed, many who worry that this sabre rattling can produce self-fulfilling fears of war

[1] Bianchi, Robert R. (2012). Morsy in Beijing: Implications for America's relations with China and the Islamic world, *Middle East Institute Insights*, 12 September, available online at http://www.mei.nus.edu.sg/publications/mei-insights/morsy-in-beijing-implications-for-america%E2%80%99s-relations-with-china-and-the-islamic-world; and Bianchi, Robert R. (2013). China-Middle East relations in light of Obama's pivot to the Pacific, *China Report*, forthcoming.

have taken the lead in portraying a Chinese-American partnership as the best safeguard of peace in our time.[2]

The problem with diarchy is that it is just as likely to lead to war by another road. If the United States concludes that it can no longer afford to deny China a larger share of power in world affairs, then why should anyone believe that the two together can shut out countless other countries with growing strength and ambition? And if Sino-American cooperation stems from their reluctance to clash over access to vital resources and trade routes, then how long will their accord last in an era when the nations that own those strategic assets are finding their voices and demanding a new deal?

Diarchy alone cannot dispense with the quest for spheres of influence. In fact, it encourages—and virtually guarantees—the great games and proxy wars that typically escalate and suck in generals and statesmen against their will. There is no clearer example of regional flashpoints waiting to ignite a chain-reaction of global confrontation than today's Middle Eastern and Pacific-Indian Ocean mine fields. These are the very regions that Obama's pivot and rebalancing seek to sever and compartmentalize. But that effort is doomed in advance precisely because the Middle East and the Far East are already more intimately linked than at any time in modern history.

The best hope for avoiding Chinese-American confrontation—intentional or not—is to look beyond both diarchy and spheres of influence to fashion more inclusive and effective institutions of global governance (see Figure 18.1). This requires that both American and Chinese leaders promote wider power sharing coalitions to give new prominence to the Middle Eastern and Asian nations whose vital assets they covet but cannot possess and whose disruptive dangers they dread but cannot prevent. This is a grand but eminently achievable task. It does not mean reinventing human nature or starting from scratch. In fact, we are better prepared than ever for exactly such a venture because of our rich experience in fashioning international regimes and our growing

---

[2] Kissinger, Henry A. (2012). The future of US-Chinese relations: Conflict is a choice, not a necessity, *Foreign Affairs*, March/April; White, Hugh (2012). *The China Choice: Why America Needs to Share Power*, Collingwood, Australia: Black Inc.

insight into the practical possibilities of rational choice and collective action.[3]

Figure 18.1. Strategic alternatives and their consequences.

Conquest and Exclusion	➔	War
Partition	➔	Spheres of Influence 🡅
Co-hegemony	➔	Diarchy 🡅
Broad-based Cooperation	➔	Global Governance

Source: Author

Building Regimes Instead of Empires

If China and the United States want to avoid war, they will have to devise equitable formulas for sharing access to vital resources and areas that have become an increasingly contested set of global commons. Above all, they must agree to abandon any effort to exclude one another from trade and transport across the full length of the Eurasian continent and through the vast seas between the eastern Mediterranean and the northern Pacific. Soon they will have to add a third zone as well—the northern maritime passages near the Arctic Circle that are becoming navigable because of global warming.

Focusing on access instead of control serves many purposes at once. It leaves ownership and sovereignty undisturbed—respecting the historical and legal rights of governments and peoples whose consent is indispensable. It allows decisions about production and pricing to remain in the hands of impersonal markets instead of potential enemies. And it highlights mutual benefits and responsibilities rather than mutual fears about survival. As a result, two supposedly ineluctable nightmares—"the tragedy of the commons" and "the tragedy of great power politics"—are

[3] Ostrom, Elinor *et al.* (1999). Revisiting the commons: Local lessons, global challenges, *Science*, 284:5412, 278–282; Hasenclever, Andreas *et al.* (1997). *Theories of International Regimes*, New York: Cambridge University Press.

reduced to manageable proportions that invite creative thinking and experimentation instead of fatalism and despair.[4]

There is a great distance between conceiving contested commons as power sharing opportunities and building international regimes that can further global governance, but the road map is clear and the route is well traveled. In fact, there are three interconnected paths to traverse simultaneously and progress in one can promote progress in the others as well. Identifying common problems, fostering mutual trust, and fashioning effective institutions are the essential processes of regime building. Each process is a series of wagers that repeated interactions will encourage learning, socialization, and reliance so that eventually cooperation will develop a life of its own that can withstand inevitable setbacks and disappointments (see Figure 18.2).

Why should sober minded statesmen risk their nations' futures on such capers? The simple answer is that, for one thing, they often work in coping with complex problems and inspire similar efforts to tackle related issues. Moreover, in matters of global peace and planetary sustainability, the alternative to collective action could well be collective suicide. Besides, Winston Churchill's reasoning is as sound today as when he first declared, "To jaw-jaw is always better than to war-war."

The greatest hurdle for Chinese and American power brokers might not be accommodating one another, but expanding their vision of collective leadership to include the rising nations of the Islamic world who inhabit most of the lands, straits, and archipelagos that superpowers usually treat as bargaining chips or battle grounds. Beijing's central party-state is eager to convince Muslims at home and abroad that China is an Islam-friendly country, but its pool of social science and humanities expertise is weak after decades of isolation and recurrent political upheavals. The United States can draw on a rich community of scholars, business people, and volunteer workers with direct experience in all

---

[4] Hardin, Garrett (1968). The tragedy of the commons, *Science*, 162, 1243–1248; Mearsheimer, John J. (2003). *The Tragedy of Great Power Politics*, New York: W.W. Norton.

Figure 18.2. Power sharing, regime building, and global governance.

Power Sharing Coalitions

US-China

US-China-Islamic World

G20-Regional Groupings

United Nations System

↓

Regime Building Processes

↓

Identifying Shared Interests and Dangers	Fashioning Multilateral Institutions	Fostering Trust and Learning
Managing Contested Commons	Pooling Information	Dialogues and Group Conversations
Correcting and Redesigning	Monitoring and Renegotiation	Concerts of Leaders and Innovators

↓

Global Governance

Source: Author.

Muslim societies, but their insights carry little weight in foreign policy circles. In both countries, diplomacy and public opinion are heavily influenced by security and military preoccupations with battling terrorism and religious extremism.

Under these circumstances, it is very difficult to establish trust between Muslims and Sino-American leaders. Engrained assumptions about the clash of civilizations and neo-imperialism cast a long shadow over all efforts to demonstrate basic good will, let alone business-like working relations. No wonder we see all sides pouring great energy into countless international conclaves on civilizational dialogue, universal ethics, and cross-cultural borrowing.[5] Sometimes, the talk about brotherhood is loudest when the underlying feelings are weakest.

A Sino-American Agenda for the Middle East and the Islamic World

Henry Kissinger's admirers are fond of saying that in the realm of forging US–China relations he owns the franchise.[6] Grand as that achievement may be, it falls short of both countries' needs for a more flexible international order that must be able to bend periodically without shattering into pieces. Kissinger recently joined a panel discussion that gave a cogent summary of the core principles that he and Zhou Enlai followed in gradually transforming the two superpowers from enemies to partners. Both countries must have a broad strategic vision that inspires determination to cooperate in order to avoid disaster for the whole world. Cooperation requires respect for other cultures even when they hold different values. It is more important to reconcile conflicting interests than to insist on conformity with unitary values. Diplomacy and personal communication are crucial no matter how rigid the geopolitical logic appears. Leaders have many choices and can make countless miscalculations, but skillful diplomacy can prevent inevitable conflicts from turning into war. Above all, we must focus on common projects that enlist the best minds of both sides so that the pursuit of shared objectives counterbalances the incessant exchange of grievances.[7]

---

[5] For example, see the international congress sponsored by the Organization of Islamic Cooperation and the Chinese Academy of Social Sciences (2012). *China and the Muslim World: Cultural Encounters*, Beijing, 28–29 June. Available online at http://www.ircica.org/international-congress-on-china-and-the-muslim-world-cultural-encounters/irc902.aspx.

[6] Frankel, Max (2011). Henry Kissinger on China, *New York Times*, 13 May.

[7] Woodrow Wilson Center (2012). *China's New Leadership: Opportunity for the United States?*, 3 October. Available online at http://www.wilsoncenter.org/event/china%E2%80%99s-new-leadership%E2%80%94opportunity-for-the-united-states.

All of these principles are equally valid for guiding Chinese and American policies toward the Middle East and the Islamic world. Kissinger's list of common projects for Sino-American talents can include no higher priority than creating working alliances and genuine friendships with Muslims at home and abroad. In fact, there is much to learn from America's experiences with China when thinking about improving relations with the Islamic world. There is good reason to believe that insights developed in the troubled Sino-American context can be transferred to pivotal Middle Eastern and Islamic countries that can either nourish or cripple much of the global economy and polity.

Let me illustrate some of the key parallels by suggesting a few fundamentals that Chinese and Americans ought to keep in mind when dealing with non-Western societies generally and with Islamic cultures in particular. Try to appreciate different perspectives; understand that, like China, Muslim nations also see themselves not as "rising" and "emerging," but as "returning" to positions of strength they held for centuries before Western empires pushed them aside. Learn from world history; recognize mutual debts and borrowings instead of claiming human civilization as your exclusive property. Encourage reformers and modernists; connect with progressives from all traditions instead of assuming that one side is enlightened and peaceful while others are backward and aggressive. Realize that cosmopolitanism and humanism have deep roots in Western, Chinese, and Islamic civilizations—roots we all need to nourish and cannot afford to see wither.[8]

On the emotional and interpersonal levels, the core issue is respect. Chinese and Americans consistently underestimate the arrogant and bullying images they project in other cultures. That blindness not only plagues Sino-American encounters, it taints both would-be hegemons in the eyes of everyone else. In terms of psychology, the proper approaches seem so obvious that one wonders why they are so scarcely practiced. Don't lecture; use reason, persuasion, and appeals to

[8] For similar views in recent mainstream American media, see Hiatt, Fred (2012). No escape from the Middle East, *Washington Post*, 8 October; Zakariya, Farid (2012). For conservatives, a Middle East divide, *Washington Post*, 10 October.

self-interest. Avoid the use of force; it will incite sustained resistance and the memories will embitter future generations. Don't provoke needlessly; respect the sacred whether it be one's flag, one's prophets or one's borders.

Beyond Trust

Building trust with Middle Eastern and Islamic countries is the highest hurdle for China and the United States, but defining common problems and projects requires the most imagination and willingness to experiment. Part of the difficulty is the sheer irrelevance of the conventional geographic terminology that has been ossified by bureaucratic routine and area studies.[9] Americans usually assume that the Middle East is a flexibly defined region centered—spiritually if not physically—in Jerusalem, the disputed capital of Israel, their most reliable friend in the area. On the other hand, Chinese officials and scholars see the same lands as inseparably linked to Central Asia which includes Xinjiang and touches Tibet—China's westernmost provinces where separatism and defense are paramount concerns just as in Taiwan at the other end of the country.[10] As for the people we call "Middle Easterners," the vast majority are Muslims who identify with the global community of Islam even when they feel varying attachments to the Arab world or Turkic speakers or Persian civilization.

In today's highly networked global economy, connections between big metropolitan centers are at least as important as borders

---

[9] On the cultural and political misconceptions embedded in conventional geography, see Lewis, Martin, W. and Karen E. Wigan (1997). *The Myth of Continents: A Critique of Metageography*, Berkeley: University of California Press; and Andaya, Barbara Watson (2006). Oceans unbounded: Transversing Asia across 'Area Studies,' *Journal of Asian Studies*, 65:4, 669–690.

[10] Wong, Roy Bin (2001). Entre monde et nation: les régions Braudéliennes en Asie, *Annales*, 56:1, pp. 5–41; and Wong, Roy Bin (2004). East Asia as a world region in the 21st century, *Nihon Kezai Shimbun*, 13 August. Available online at http://www.international.ucla.edu/asia/article.asp?parentid=14604.

between national and regional jurisdictions. The fabric of modern life is built around the uninterrupted flow of goods, information, capital, and people between conurbations—groups of cities with fairly integrated transportation systems and labor markets which support (and often exploit) wider and more populous hinterlands.[11] There is no Christian, Confucian or Islamic formula for sustaining these networks, but people of all creeds and colors need them just as surely as they need food and air.

These are the overriding interests and vulnerabilities that connect the United States, China, and the Middle Eastern–Islamic nations. The more interdependent they become, the more they realize the devastation they will inflict on themselves and everyone else if they disrupt the networks or let them break down. And the growing vulnerabilities are there for all to see: meltdowns in the financial markets, terrorism and piracy, revolutions and civil wars, the scramble for all types of raw materials, competing projects for new energy pipelines and deep sea ports, collisions and standoffs on the high seas, diversions of cross-border river waters—and these are merely the top of the list.

From this perspective, the Obama administration is caught in an anachronism when it claims that America should scale down its efforts in the Middle East and Afghanistan in order to refocus on the Pacific. When so much of Asia is coming together, why should America's leaders be trying to push it back into separate pieces—either conceptually or politically? The generous answer is that they're behind the times and imprisoned by Eurocentric geography. In other words, they're slow learners, but they can catch up eventually.

The ungenerous answer—and, in China, the prevailing interpretation—is that a more integrated Asia is precisely what America wants to prevent. Asian coalescence would probably revolve around China's economic dynamism and political heft. It would gradually draw Russia and perhaps the European Union into its orbit, creating an even

[11] Beavestock, Jonathan V. *et al.* (2000). World-city network: A new metageography? *Annals of the Association of American Geographers*, 90:1, 123–134.

greater nightmare for Washington strategists—a Eurasian community linking all the lands between the Atlantic and Pacific Oceans.

In this view, separating the Middle East and the Far East is just what the Pentagon and White House doctors ordered. It lets India become a swing state, guarding China's sea lanes to the Persian Gulf and helping to split the ASEAN countries into America-leaning and China-leaning factions. Moreover, a US–India alignment can stiffen Japanese and South Korean spines in standing up to any bullying from Beijing.

In fact, the Chinese worrywarts had little to fear from these supposed schemes of containment and encirclement. To shepherd America's policy of rebalancing away from Middle East distractions and toward Asia-Pacific opportunities, President Obama traveled to Myanmar, Cambodia, and Thailand—where he was tied up in urgent telephone conversations with the leaders of Israel, Palestine, Egypt, and Turkey. So much for trying to keep one's crises in separate pockets. This time it was not China but the American president himself who was encircled—by the fallout of all the unfinished business that Washington has in the part of the world it now loves to hate.

Pretending that the Middle East and Asia are severable contradicts the long-standing American practice of seeking China's cooperation by linking negotiations over Sino-American disagreements in both regions. The essence of being a modern superpower is having multiple interests everywhere in the world that demand constant co-management and periodic tradeoffs. The British Empire routinely marshaled Indian manpower to suppress rebellions in Iraq, to build railroads in Africa, and to police the neighborhoods of Singapore and Shanghai. Reliance on Indian talent was so extensive that some historians describe the Raj's cohorts as junior partners in the Indo-British Empire—partners who became increasingly resentful of being treated as mere subalterns rather than proper British subjects.[12]

America's frantic efforts to keep the lid on multiple crises in the Middle East has long depended on Chinese sufferance—and that always comes with a price tag for concessions on what Beijing regards as its

---

[12] Metcalf, Thomas R. (2007). *Imperial Connections—India in the Indian Ocean Arena, 1860-1920*, Berkeley: University of California Press.

core interests close to home. Every veteran of a global consultancy, investment bank or foreign affairs think tank knows that the sun never sets on Sino-American horse-trading, including explicit package deals covering the Middle East.

If Americans object to China selling missiles to Saudi Arabia and buying advanced radar from Israel, then they must be willing to limit US arms sales to Taiwan. When they want Beijing to join the fight against global terrorism, they have to blacklist Uyghur nationalists from Xinjiang and help in persuading Turkey to stop giving them refuge. Imposing United Nations sanctions on Iran requires reining in human rights criticisms and trade restrictions on China. And renewing those sanctions sets the stage for an elaborate swap of benefits in the Middle East itself—long-term oil contracts with Saudi Arabia, visas for Chinese contractors in the states of the Gulf Cooperation Council, and cross-investments between Chinese and Middle Eastern megabanks and sovereign wealth funds. When Washington wants to lead from behind in Libya, Beijing knows how to say "Yes" while displaying its air and sea power to evacuate thousands of its citizens on the other side of the world. And when the United States seeks a repeat performance in Syria, China reminds everyone that it can always say "No."

Coming Out of the Closet

Interregional bargaining between the two superpowers is already routine and it is likely to increase in the future. Instead of trying to keep the global game behind closed doors, Chinese and American leaders should consider opening it up to more issues and participants so that it can benefit wider communities in the Middle East and elsewhere. Moving the conversations from private whispers to public debates could produce a wider range of viable solutions and a greater likelihood of successful implementation. Besides, some of the most important issues have been on the global agenda for decades and there is nothing to gain from further delay.

Every international affairs scholar has her own short list of pressing business that Sino-American brainpower should try to expedite if the superpowers want to behave like grownups. I've already suggested some principles for regime-building in the Middle East and the Islamic world, opining that trust is the most difficult factor and institutions are the most familiar terrain. Now I would like to focus on the third process of international cooperation—defining shared interests and vulnerabilities by employing the notion of mutual access to interregional and intercontinental commons.

Let's start by thinking big. The entire land mass between Europe and China is a vital source of energy and transport for the whole world. China and the United States can diversify their purchases and conserve their usage as much as they choose, but they cannot wean themselves from the oil and gas of the Persian Gulf and the Caspian Sea. And energy doesn't move itself—it passes through pipelines and tankers over thousands of miles of land and water, through countless jurisdictions, including virtual no man's zones and multiple chokepoints. Much of this transit area encompasses a sparsely settled continent of oceanic proportions and vast seas infested with marauding nomads.[13] What more do we need to recognize this sprawling and fragile system as a transnational commons?

The next logical step is to remove the threat of anyone being denied access to the resources by agreeing upon fair arrangements for acquisition, safe passage, and sustainable exploitation. This is exactly what people the world over have been doing for centuries with local resources. It is what governments and international organizations routinely do on much larger scales to resolve competing demands for resources that cross national borders. It is what the entire world has agreed to do concerning the use and exploration of outer space, the moon, and other planets.

We already have many of the necessary building blocks for managing a Middle Eastern–Asian commons. There is a steadily growing awareness of shared needs and dangers across a continuous geographic

---

[13] Linn, Johannes F. and David Tiomkin (2005). *Economic Integration of Eurasia: Opportunities and Challenges of Global Significance*, Warsaw: Center for Social and Economic Research; Pearson, Michael Naylor (2003). *The Indian Ocean*, London: Routledge; and Escobar, Pepe (2009). Welcome to Pipelineistan, *Mother Jones*, 24 March.

area. There is a vast repertoire of institutional methods for coping with complex systems of adaptation.[14] And fostering intercultural trust and respect has become the mantra—if not the living reality—of every leadership with pretentions to global influence.

Why not push these capabilities to their limits by bundling cross-regional issues instead of splitting them into separate bins? Here's a package deal that could yield a dozen Nobel Peace Prizes and a thousand new fortunes. Offer China free access and safe passage for Persian Gulf energy via the Indian Ocean and the Straits of Malacca.[15] Let them build all the land-based redundancy they want with pipelines through Central Asia, including their dream route from Iran and Pakistan to Xinjiang. Not sweet enough? Throw in a seat at the table in the Arctic Council negotiations where they have no historical or legal claims whatever. That will give them three parallel routes linking European and Pacific markets. How could any self-respecting Chinese mercantilist resist?

And in return…? The obvious starting point is for Beijing to get real in the South China Sea where it has become a pest by pretending that international law has no bearing on its blanket assertions of sovereignty—if, indeed, sovereignty is what they want the world to think they're angling for.[16]

---

[14] Concerning current trends in interdisciplinary research on complex systems, see Sedlacko, Michal and André Marinuzzi (2012). *Governance by Evaluation for Sustainable Development: Institutional Capacities and Learning*, Cheltenham, U.K.: Edward Elgar; The Santa Fe Institute, available online at http://www.santafe.edu; and The Stevens Institute of Technology Center for Complex Systems and Enterprises. Available online at http://www.stevens.edu/ccse.

[15] For a similar suggestion that India, China, and the United States co-manage "the Indo-Pacific" as a maritime commons, see Mohan, C. Raja (2012). *Samudra Manthan: Sino-Indian Rivalry in the Indo-Pacific*, Washington, D.C.: Carnegie Endowment for International Peace.

[16] Some of China's most respected international lawyers have criticized the legitimacy of Beijing's South China Sea claims. See, for example, Li Ling Hua (李令华) (2012). 关于南海九段线的法律地位问题 (On the Legal Status of the Nine-Dash Line in the South China Sea). Available online at http://blog.ifeng.com/4523016.html.

Current speculation attributes Beijing's assertiveness to historical grudges, chauvinist populism, turnover in the top leadership, and growing confidence in its military capacities. Perhaps. But the fact remains that China is extremely vulnerable because its global economic interests have vastly overtaken its ability to protect them militarily or politically. That is the open secret that Beijing cannot hide from itself, its neighbors or the world beyond. And that is precisely the reason that China might be delighted to abandon its games of chicken in the Western Pacific in return for benefits in far-flung regions where its ambitions are unbounded but its power is still quite paltry.[17] In other words, don't try to contain or encircle China; invite it to the dinner table and offer it a supersized portion as long as it minds its manners.

The Road More Traveled By…to the Dark Side

This might seem like lot to digest even for those wistful souls who believe that something called long-range planning is possible in international politics. But realistically speaking—and these days we're all Realists—business as usual is taking us nowhere. Shoring up the status quo and kicking the can down the road to the next administration or the younger generation is not an option—it's a cop out.

The Middle East is not going to settle down because Obama brings the troops home from Iraq and Afghanistan. Muslims will not become less outraged by intentional insults from foreign bigots and by civilian casualties from Predator drones. And China is not about to pop back into its long discarded shell because Washington courts its hedging neighbors. The imaginary regional boxes linger only in our minds. The hatches that are supposed to seal off the separate compartments will not hold.

Quite the reverse, all of these pressure points are waiting to burst in a dozen directions. If Iran is attacked, it will retaliate where it can

---

[17] Dai Bing Guo (戴秉国) (2010). For a candid assessment of China's global limits by a top foreign policy adviser, see 中国取代美国称霸？那是神话 (China replacing America as a hegemon? That's a fairy tale), *Zhong Xinwen*, 7 December. Available online at http://www.chinareform.org.cn/open/view/201012/t20101208_54169.htm.

inflict the quickest damage—against the weakest and wealthiest countries on its doorstep. If the city-states along the Persian Gulf implode, the dominoes can fall all the way to Madrid and Tokyo and make the suffering of the Arab Spring look like a day at the beach. If China's lifelines are in jeopardy, it has all the time in the world to lure its overconfident foes into futile campaigns that can bleed them dry. What other society has more practical experience in relying on its own resources and riding out times of turmoil? And Heaven help the rest of us if they should fail because China's collapse could unleash human catastrophes beyond imagination and perhaps beyond repair.

Tailoring the Bargain for the People Who Matter Most

The natural riches and lands of the Middle East and the Islamic world belong to their citizens and their future descendants—not to their rulers and certainly not to foreigners. For generations, many of these people have seen their patrimony monopolized and squandered by corrupt regimes and multinational corporations. Much of that system of internalized colonialism still survives, but it's legitimacy and opaqueness vanished long ago. The chain of siphons that channels their wealth abroad is under constant assault, including the overseas bank accounts of princes, presidents, and their extended families. Under such circumstances, why would these citizens have any interest in the notion that their collective properties are part of a common pool of resources that sustains all of mankind?

In fact, many of these people already know all about the need for collective action in preserving the great chain of being. Most of we city folk learned the basics of ecological systems and sustainability from the farmers, pastoralists, and fishing communities who invented what we still regard as best practices. And their economics are pretty sharp as well. They're perfectly happy to sell their natural wealth to foreigners who can use it more efficiently—as long as they see a fair profit that stays at home and benefits their children.

What if the Sino-American grand bargain included incentives for the rulers of resource exporting countries to be more responsive to their own citizens? Political inclusion and popular consent could help legitimize new transnational trade arrangements with clear benefits for previously marginalized communities. If the entire citizenry is involved in the negotiation, they are more likely to endorse bargains with foreigners that might otherwise be seen as self-dealing or as surrenders of sovereignty. Fairness and equity could replace theft and collusion as the hallmarks of the bargaining process.

This gives existing regimes a clear path to survival if they are wise enough to choose it. Their task is to negotiate dual pacts with foreign purchasers and with their own people. This is a tall order that might take a generation or more to accomplish. But it could improve the chances for gradual reform instead of violent revolution, particularly in the most authoritarian countries of the Persian Gulf, the Caspian Basin, and Central Asia. The only pacts likely to survive are those forged by freely chosen representatives, not by self-imposed tyrants or foreign-backed puppets. Surely, it's time to reverse one of the most flawed and outdated assumptions about the political requisites of energy security. For resource importers, the more reliable negotiator is not a Shah but a Mosaddeq, not a Suharto but a Sukarno.

The Arab Spring is but a moment in the historic sweep of social and political change in the Islamic world. From Turkey and Egypt to Pakistan and Indonesia, the unstoppable trend has been the swelling of popular demands for the devolution of power and for a wider sharing of national wealth. And in many countries—despite recurrent coups and dictators—those demands have prevailed whether through elections or revolutions or both.

The spread of majority rule has resulted in profound transformations in power relations, socioeconomic conditions, and cultural-religious attitudes. Well-educated and Westernized elites in the biggest cities have seen their customary privileges shrivel as provincial towns and villages gained greater strength and confidence. In terms of income and status, military and bureaucratic cadres have been overtaken by business owners, professionals, and rich farmers. Urban migration, rural prosperity, and mass media have thrust every region's religious and cultural preferences on top of one another, inviting mixtures and adaptations that seemed inconceivable a generation ago.

The proliferation of national and local syntheses of Islam, capitalism, and democracy have provided countless models and variations that are avidly debated and dissected by Muslims everywhere. At this point, it is very hard to imagine that any Middle Eastern or Islamic country can stand outside of such colossal change. The monarchies and Soviet-vintage police states that have managed to hang on thus far are living on borrowed time. Even an energy hungry Sino-American diarchy would find it difficult to prop them up indefinitely and it would be foolish to try.

Disposition and Potential: The Other China Model

The thought of China encouraging democracy in the Islamic world challenges the popular assumption that Beijing is committed to exporting its own version of authoritarianism in opposition to Western-inspired liberalism. I would argue instead that China's leaders are truly committed only to their own best interests and not to any model or set of abstract principles. There is no consensus about the so-called Beijing consensus in Beijing itself. On the contrary, party officials and intellectuals increasingly agree on the urgency of political reform and they quarrel incessantly over the alternative formulas and timetables for guiding it. Particularly after the latest transfer of power, espousing democracy is all the rage—provided that it's Chinese democracy, properly adapted to the special conditions and sensibilities of the People's Republic.[18]

Of course, that probably leaves Liu Xiao Bo and countless others behind bars for years to come. Nonetheless, it shows that nervous party

---

[18] A recent petition for democratic reform signed by more than seventy leading party leaders and intellectuals is available at 改革共识倡议书 (Proposing a consensus for reform) *Radio France Internationale*, 26 December 2012, available online at http://www.chinese.rfi.fr). For a scathing critique of the Hu Jin Tao-Wen Jia Bao era, see Deng Yu Wen (邓聿文) (2012) 胡温的政治遗产, 财经网 (The political legacy of Hu and Wen), *caijing.com*, 2 September. Available online at http://www.politicalchina.org/newsinfo.asp?Newsid=226783. For an example of the Communist Party School's discussions of democracy, see Keping Yu (2009). *Democracy Is A Good Thing: Essays on Politics, Society, and Culture in Contemporary China*, Washington, D.C.: Brookings Institution Press.

leaders know which way the global political winds are blowing and that they would rather sail with them as far as possible instead paying a much higher price by defying democracy in principle as well as in deed. If China's rulers are willing to be this flexible and adaptive at home, then why should we doubt their capacity for bending at least as much in dealing with distant countries whose internal politics matter far less to them? After all, the touchstone of Chinese foreign policy is not anti-liberalism but indifference to (or as they put it, tolerance of) other nations' choices of political and economic models. They have no reason whatever to bet on likely losers. If they conclude that a foreign tyranny is bad for business, why should they waste their efforts and damage their credibility by going against the flow?

If we want to find guideposts of China's strategic thinking, we're better off consulting enduring classical writings than dwelling on stale socialist dogma. One of the most powerful teachings of the ancients is that all situations possess inherent dispositions that create natural potentialities or tendencies independent of any human plan or intervention. Recognizing these potentialities and seizing their opportunities rank among the highest skills of statecraft, warfare, and diplomacy. Wisdom lies in manipulating and exploiting what is already given in a particular set of circumstances—letting it carry you along toward a distant shore instead of rowing furiously to reach a preconceived endpoint.[19]

Applying Practical Knowledge to Profit from Ripening Potentials

In just this manner, I argue that a confluence of current circumstances contain multiple potentials that we have yet to fully appreciate and exploit. China and the United States are worried about the growing risks of going to war, prompting urgent calls for a more explicit

---

[19] Jullian, François (1995). *The Propensity of Things: Toward A History of Efficacy in China*, New York: Zone Books; Jullien, François (2004). *A Treatise on Efficacy: Between Western and Chinese Thinking*, Honolulu: University of Hawaii Press; and Zhang Dainian (2002). *Key Concepts in Chinese Philosophy*, New Haven: Yale University Press.

Sino-American partnership to stabilize the international system. But multi-polarization has passed the point where even the strongest diarchy between Washington and Beijing could satisfy the deepening need for inclusive global governance. The rising power and turbulence of nations in the Middle East and the Islamic world poses a particularly acute problem because they both possess and jeopardize resources and transit zones that are vital to an increasingly fragile global economy.

Fortunately, during the past four decades, American and Chinese leaders have learned valuable lessons about reversing longstanding enmities between rival civilizations—lessons that can and should be applied in nurturing Sino-American relations with Muslims everywhere. Moreover, diplomats and scholars are drawing on a growing reservoir of experience and insight in building international regimes that foster collective management of contested commons, including common pool resources. These advances are helpful in considering how to manage the increasingly interdependent regional and transcontinental commons of Eurasia and the Indian-Pacific Ocean Basins.

Meanwhile, political and economic progress in the Islamic world—not only during the Arab Spring, but throughout Asia and the wider Middle East over several decades—has generated multiple experiments with capitalism and democracy that appeal to Muslims everywhere. This progress places enormous pressures on would-be authoritarian holdouts, particularly the isolated resource-rich states of the Persian Gulf and Central Asia who cannot survive without great power protection. Rulers in these nations face mounting demands to negotiate new pacts with foreign importers and with their own citizens—simultaneous bargains that will insure equitable access and predictability to resource consumers while benefiting and enfranchising the marginalized majorities of their people.

Chapter 19

The Lands of Islam in a China-Led Afro-Eurasia

The Obama administration's efforts to "pivot" or "rebalance" American foreign policy away from the Middle East and Afghanistan toward the Asia-Pacific region have triggered spirited debates in China over how Beijing should adjust its deepening relations with the Islamic world. These debates can teach us a number of lessons at the same time: About inherent tensions in China's geostrategic thinking, about the skillfulness of Beijing's overtures to rising Muslim societies that Chinese leaders increasingly view as vital to China's future—particularly when compared with the stumbling of the United States—and about the advantages of viewing global politics from the perspective of non-Westerners who appreciate the contributions of Asian and African peoples to world history and civilization.

The Debates and Their Implications

In October 2012, one of China's leading scholars of international politics, Wang Ji Si, argued that China should respond to Obama's Pacific pivot by "marching west"—by shifting its strategic focus from the looming maritime confrontations with American-backed adversaries in the Far East to exploiting the new opportunities that beckoned China in Central Asia, South Asia, and the Middle East.[1] Wang saw multiple advantages in turning away from provocations at sea and taking advantage of power vacuums on land. China could correct its lopsided economic development model by channeling resources from the wealthy coastal cities toward the depressed frontier provinces where ethnic

[1] Wang Ji Si (王缉思) (2012). "西进",中国地缘战略的再平衡, 环球时报 ("March West," Rebalancing China's Geostrategy), *Global Times*, October 17. Available online at http://opinion.huanqiu.com/opinion_world/2012-10/3193760.html.

violence and separatist sentiments fed on a toxic combination of economic and cultural discrimination. As the United States retreated from its misadventures in Afghanistan, Pakistan, and Iraq, China could lead coalitions of regional states in rebuilding these shattered economies and societies. The resulting influence and goodwill would consolidate China's sway in Central Asia and bolster its growing role in the Persian Gulf and the Eastern Mediterranean.

Best of all, in Wang's view the Americans would be grateful for China's assistance in stabilizing volatile countries, protecting the flow of energy and raw materials, and keeping the lid on terrorism and Islamic extremism. Sino-American relations would flourish in a new era of cooperative solutions for common global problems that no great power could tackle alone. Instead of being dragged into a Pacific war by opportunists and ultranationalists, China and America would seal their partnership as the guarantors of world peace and prosperity for generations to come.

Refutations of the "march west" proposal were both swift and scathing. A retired admiral and popular writer, Yang Yi, insisted that China's security interests were multidirectional, requiring a comprehensive and balanced strategy that prepared for all contingencies.[2] To be sure, he said, China needed a "stable" west, but it also required a "solid" north and a "secure" east. Above all, Yang asserted that China had to create an "expanding" south because its far-flung commerce was the key to global strength and domestic stability.

Because China's intercontinental commerce was vulnerable at so many points to disruption from potential adversaries, China's future depended on building and deploying a modern navy not only in the Pacific and the Malacca Straits, but throughout the vast Indian Ocean Basin, including the Middle East and Africa. Yang Yi characterized China's maritime weaknesses as an Achilles' heel that hostile nations—particularly Japan and the United States—could exploit to impose a de facto "containment" or "encirclement" that would stifle China's

---

[2] Yang Yi (杨毅) (2012). 周边安全需要全方位战略, 环球时报 (Peripheral Security Requires a Comprehensive Strategy), *Global Times*, October 26. Available online at http://news.xinhuanet.com/world/2012-10/26/c_123875252.htm.

expansion and even threaten its existence. Yang insisted that China had no choice but to "break out" of this southern maritime encirclement and that there was no point in delaying the challenge even if it increased the dangers of military conflict.

A widely read journalist, Feng Hai Wen, supported Yang's views but went much further in criticizing Wang Ji Si.[3] Feng claimed that an explicit strategy to "march west" would put China on a collision course with Russia because Moscow continued to view Central Asia as its "near abroad" and would never tolerate a Chinese military presence there. Indeed, Feng accused Wang Ji Si of floating a trial balloon that served Washington's interests instead of China's.

According to Feng Hai Wen, the Americans were hoping to kill two birds with one stone—they would force China to "retreat" from Pacific trouble spots and to destroy its budding alliance with Russia by stirring up resentments on its southern borders. This was a brazen American attempt to revive the divide and rule tactics that pitted China and Russia against one another during the Cold War. Worse yet, Washington was trying to lure China into the very quagmires that had sapped America's strength and prestige for decades—the endless ethnic and religious quarrels that stoked civil war and imperial overreach all across Central Asia and the Middle East. Feng even suggested that Wang's long associations with American universities and think tanks had undermined his objectivity in weighing China's national interests, particularly when Chinese military experts offered more informed opinions on security issues.

Even when Wang Ji Si's colleagues at the Brookings Institution advised President Obama to tone down the aggressive rhetoric of the "Pacific rebalancing" during his second term, Feng Hai Wen chose to interpret the gesture as nothing more than a shift "from hard containment

---

[3] Feng Hai Wen (冯海闻) (2012). 中国大国战略选择南进还是西进？环球网 (China's Great Power Strategic Choice, Sail South Or March West?), *Global Times Online*, November 1. Available online at http://opinion.huanqiu.com/opinion_world/2012-11/3235465.html.

to soft encircling."[4] This appeared to be a clear endorsement of the views of a hawkish military writer—Dai Xu, a retired air force colonel—who was calling on China and Russia to "establish a Eurasian Alliance to prevent the United States from eating weak countries."[5] Dai Xu claimed that a Sino-Russian partnership would attract Iran, Pakistan, Afghanistan, Central Asian countries, and perhaps even Turkey against America's efforts to split up the Eurasian continent and to keep the fracturing Europe Union bound to the North Atlantic alliance.

Ironically, whether or not Feng Hai Wen realized it, he was in fact enlisting one "march west" advocate against another. For, like Wang Ji Si, Dai Xu also described his Sino-Russian alliance as a "Long March westward into the Eurasian interior." According to Dai Xu, "marching west" meant moving in tandem with Russian not against it. Moreover, he saw "marching west" as a complement to Yang Yi's strategy of "sailing south" not as a substitute for it. Dai explained, "The goal is to exchange space for time by associating with others in responding to America's blatant strategy of encirclement and to win greater opportunities for modernization and development."[6]

In other words, for geostrategic thinkers of every stripe, all of China's roads lead through the Islamic world to Europe and Africa—westward through Central Asia, the Caspian Basin, and the Middle East or southward through the Pacific-Indian Ocean-Mediterranean sea routes. Some argue for the primacy of the land routes, others for the maritime routes, and still others for coordinating both together. The more heated the argument becomes, the more it reveals an underlying Chinese

---

[4] Feng Hai Wen (冯海闻) (2013). 美国对华政策或从硬围堵变软包围, 环球网 (America's China Policy Or From Hard Containment to Soft Encirclement), *Global Times Online*, January 22. Available online at http://opinion.huanqiu.com/opinion_world/2013-01/3568348.html.

[5] Dai Xu (戴旭) (2012). 中俄应构建欧亚大联盟阻止美国屠戮弱国 (China and Russia Should Establish a Eurasian Alliance to Prevent the United States from Eating Weak Countries), Global Times, January 29. Available online at http://opinion.huanqiu.com/1152/2012-01/2385635.html.

[6] Dai Xu, *ibid.* See also, Dai Xu (戴旭) (2009). C-形包围：内忧外患下的中国突围, 上海文汇出版社 (*C-Shaped Encirclement: China's Breakout From Internal Troubles and External Aggression*), Shanghai: Wenhui Publishing.

consensus about the long-term indispensability of cultivating Islamic connections regardless of whether pro-American or pro-Russian relations are seen as more useful stepping stones. China's future depends on the lands and seas of Islam—not only because of their locations and riches, but also because of their links to markets and resources in Europe and Africa. This century is often described as an Asian Century or as a Chinese Century, and it appears to be starting out that way. But we might see it play out as a Eurasian Century or even an Afro-Eurasian Century with growing Sino-Islamic overtones.

Chinese and American Approaches to the Islamic World

The most striking feature of Chinese writings on Islamic societies is the frequent emphasis on their embeddedness in broader contexts and relationships, particularly in multiple and overlapping networks that transcend national boundaries and ethnic differences. In this sense, Chinese see Muslims very much the way that Muslims (and Chinese) would like to see themselves—as a single transcontinental community with an ancient civilization and a shared destiny, as a leader of the pre-modern world that is regaining its confidence and trying to rediscover its universal ideals after two centuries of subjugation and revolution.

These views could not be more at odds with the American-inspired traditions of area studies and international relations which stress the divisions between nations, ideologies, languages, and races while treating religion—and especially Islam—as a vestige bound to wither in the light of science and freedom. Ever since the end of World War II and the beginning of decolonization, much of the non-Western world has regarded these disciplines as appendages of neo-imperialism. The end of the Cold War has merely heightened suspicions that they are being retooled for a new fight and that Islam and China happen to be in the right place at the right time.

Today's emerging American-led coalition to "balance" China also carries an underlying hostility to the Islamic world, particularly when it accents the roles of India, Israel, Singapore, and Australia, which are also strengthening ties with one another. This could encourage Sino-Islamic cooperation to become openly hostile against a Western-backed alliance that both Chinese and Muslims see as targeting their rising power.

To the extent that Chinese writers view Islam as a dynamic and multicultural civilization, they are less prone to fall into the classic Orientalist trap of focusing on a historic "center" and privileging it over a supposedly marginal "periphery." This might account for the tendency of Chinese scholars and policy-makers to be skeptical of Westerners who identify Islam with the Middle East and who conflate the Middle East with the Arab world, and particularly with the Arabian Peninsula. Even when Chinese writers identify themselves as "Middle East" experts, they frequently insist that Beijing pursues a "balanced" and "comprehensive" set of relationships with all of the major ethnic and religious communities in the region, meaning Arabs, Turks, Persians, and Jews.

Paradoxically, China's growing dependence on Persian Gulf energy imports has probably reinforced its determination to diversify its Islamic connections to include non-Arab countries, including many that are far from the constant turmoil and unpredictability of the Arab Spring and Israel's battles with Palestine and Iran. The most prominent examples are Turkey, Pakistan, and Indonesia—rising powers that Chinese writers see as vital crossroads and invaluable allies who are eager to expand their markets and to reduce their over-dependence on the United States and Europe.[7] Recently, this list has expanded to include overland ties to Central Asia, Afghanistan, the Caspian Basin, and the Caucasus as well as maritime links with Bangladesh, the Maldives, Kenya, Sudan, and Nigeria.

China's strategists realize that they cannot follow the American example of diversifying their energy sources away from dependence on the Persian Gulf and the Caspian Sea. Nor can they effectively challenge American command of the sea routes that transport most of that energy to China's shores. Instead, they believe that China must skillfully diversify its political and diplomatic efforts to win friends far beyond the limited reach of Beijing's modest military assets.

---

[7] Bianchi, Robert R. (2013). China-Middle East relations in light of Obama's pivot to the Pacific, *China Report*, 49:1, 103–118.

Above all, China wants to avoid the familiar American pattern of entanglement in foreign wars, guerrilla insurgencies, and endless quarrels between irreconcilable neighbors. The more Beijing sees Washington's blundering and bleeding in the Middle East, the more determined it is to hedge its bets and bide its time—watching Obama struggle with a long backlog of unfinished business in the very region he claims to be downgrading while making renewed pledges of protection to distrustful leaders in the Asia-Pacific theater.

In dealing with Islamic countries, hedging seems to come effortlessly to Chinese diplomacy.[8] Unlike the United States, China sees no single focal point of good or evil—no Jerusalem to defend at all costs and no Tehran to bring down by any means. Instead, Chinese strategists view the Muslim world as filled with fresh opportunities, much as their counterparts in Ankara and Jakarta see it—not simply as a new railroad here or a bigger bridge there, but as a complex series of transcontinental networks in which neighboring societies are linked in all directions, as long chains of multinational regions that overlap with one another across the length and breadth of the Eastern Hemisphere and beyond.

This is a vision of a fluid and polycentric order where the balance of power can shift in several directions depending upon changing perceptions of threat and interest, of identity and values, and—most of all—on diplomatic skill and political prudence. In this world, every dream of building a New Silk Road must be measured against the dangers of stumbling into a New Great Game. Any breakthrough of economic integration on a regional or continental scale also implies inevitable social upheavals and redistributions of power within nations and between them.

When Chinese writers debate the consequences of "marching west" and "sailing south," they often arrive at a similar conclusion—all paths lead through the Islamic world and all sub-regions of that universe can quickly turn into Silk Roads and Great Games at the same time.

[8] One of the best Chinese studies of quasi-alliances was authored by a specialist in Middle East politics. Sun De Gang (孙德刚) (2007). 多元平衡与"准联盟"理论研究, 时事出版社 (Multi-polarity and the Theory of "Quasi-Alliances"), Beijing: Current Events Press.

Whether the flag follows trade or vice-versa, great power rivalries will pull rising societies—Muslim and non-Muslim alike—in multiple directions at once. The appeal of permanent alliances has given way to pervasive hedging and constant recalculations of ad hoc coalitions, issue by issue and year by year. Networking is welcome, hierarchy is disfavored, and divorce is accepted as a fact of life. Indeed, it is precisely China's reputation for detachment and pragmatism—its image as the modern embodiment of amoral mercantilism—that makes it appealing to many countries that want to keep their options open while feeling their way through the post-American world order.

American and European writers frequently opine that many of China's gains in the Islamic world—and elsewhere—have been possible because the United States is doing the "heavy lifting" of providing global public goods while opportunists in Beijing are behaving like "free riders."[9] In this view, American investments in protecting the world's sea lanes and fighting international terrorism benefit China at home and abroad with virtually no cost to Beijing. Of course, the audience for this discussion extends far beyond American ears to include dozens of societies that live and breathe the experiences of colonialism and neo-colonialism. In that arena, the distinction between "free riders" and "heavy lifters" is overshadowed by the accompanying gap in power between "rule makers" and "rule takers"—and non-Western publics tend to sympathize with China's frustrations in trying to gain a more equitable role in international institutions. From this perspective, the currently dominant states of Europe and North America cannot reasonably expect China and other rising nations to pay the full price of admission to global governance until they are prepared to share more control over the levers of decision-making.

Even if China's leaders enjoy—at least for now—an inherent advantage of position in competing for influence in Muslim countries, they still must confront China's deep-seated fears of Islam and of

---

[9] Eyal, Jonathan (2013). Entangling the Dragon in Arab Quicksands, *The Straits Times*, May 20.

religion in general.[10] Compared to their American counterparts, however, Chinese elites are learning to restrain their Islamophobia instead of letting it drive their social policies and poison their foreign relations. Both at home and abroad, Beijing increasingly distinguishes between mainstream Islam, which it openly supports, and extremist groups, which it tries to crush. Naturally, these are always subjective judgments that invite refutation. Nevertheless, by explicitly discriminating in favor of non-threatening Islamic majorities and singling out violent fringes, China's rulers join a centuries-old tradition of pragmatically and cynically manipulating religion in ways that Muslims have routinely encountered—and often turned to their own advantage—under both foreign and nominally Islamic governments.

Religious practice is enjoying a state-sponsored revival throughout China, including "imported" faiths such as Buddhism, Islam, and Christianity as well as "indigenous" religions such as Daoism, Confucianism, and many popular traditions.[11] Chinese Muslims have seized the opportunity of this relative religious tolerance to enhance their material well-being and political clout. Mandarin-speaking Muslims, the Hui, have been particularly adept at leveraging their cultural and personal ties with global Islam in advancing China's trade and diplomacy at the same time that they earn greater rewards for their extended families and communities. Even the long-suffering Turkic-speaking Muslims of Xinjiang, particularly the Uyghurs, are being courted with highly touted campaigns to develop the Great Western Region, including industrialization, international trade, bilingual education, and a dedicated fleet of jumbo jets to carry pious Muslims on the hajj at discounted fares.

---

[10] Horner, Charles and Eric Brown (2010). Beijing's Islamic Complex, *The American Interest Magazine*, May-June; Bovingdon, Gardner (2010). *The Uyghurs: Strangers in Their Own Land*, New York: Columbia University Press.

[11] Lagerwey, John (2010). *China: A Religious State*, Hong Kong: Hong Kong University Press; Oakes, Timothy and Donald S. Sutton, eds. (2010). *Faiths on Display: Religion and Tourism in China*, Lanham, Maryland: Rowman & Littlefield; Ashiwa, Yoshiko and David L. Wank, eds. (2009). *Making Religion, Making the State: The Politics of Religion in Modern China*, Stanford: Stanford University Press; Goossaert, Vincent and David A. Palmer (2007). *The Religious Question in Modern China*, Chicago: University of Chicago Press.

Meanwhile, in the United States, President Obama is still struggling with his stigmatic "Muslim" persona, Qur'an-burning pastors, and far right-wing assertions that national educational standards are part of a Chinese-Islamic conspiracy to corrupt American culture.[12] The steady flight of Muslim—especially Arab—students, professionals, and tourists to Europe and Asia is convincing many Americans that Islamophobia is bad for business, but the hemorrhaging continues unabated.[13]

Why Asians and Africans Might Be Learning More Than Westerners from New Scholarship on Global Connectivity

China's strategists constantly stress their country's role in building a more integrated Eurasian community—economically, physically, and diplomatically—that will also strengthen ties with Africa and Latin America. Their transcontinental and global aspirations quickly lead them to view Islamic societies as indispensable partners in those efforts. Much of the current debate in China revolves around the specific kinds of Eurasian coalitions that are most promising and realistic. Hence, the frequent arguments about tradeoffs and inherent tensions in competing proposals to "march west" and "sail south" or about reconciling the unavoidable contradictions between Silk Roads and Great Games.

In following the twists and turns of these debates, I have noticed that Chinese writers increasingly frame their analyses in terms of well-known international relations concepts that have been popularized by American and European theorists. However, I also detect a clear tendency in recent years to favor the thinking of Zbigniew Brzezinski over the views of Henry Kissinger. For many Chinese policy-makers and scholars, the key difference is that Kissinger wants to draw China eastward—toward a trans-Pacific partnership with the United States—

---

[12] Webster, Stephen C. and Glen Beck (2013). Education standards are a Chinese-Muslim conspiracy, Democraticunderground.com, March 29. Available online at http://www.democraticunderground.com/10022585696.

[13] Hayoun, Massoud (2013). Islamophobia is bad for business, Boston Review, January 16. Available online at http://www.bostonreview.net/BR38.1/massoud_hayoun_islamophobia_business_china_middle_east.php

whereas Brzezinski sees China's destiny in the west—as the leading continental power in a unifying Eurasia. Seen from Beijing, Kissinger describes a China that can merely follow while Brzezinski envisions a China that dares to lead.[14]

Kissinger believes that the United States can continue to split China and Russia as he and Richard Nixon did forty years ago.[15] On the other hand, Brzezinski sees China as a logical partner for a weaker but resurgent Russia that wishes to leverage its north-central position between Europe and the Far East—just as many Islamic countries make a similar effort from the south-central direction. In this view, Kissinger's China would be little more than an apprentice of the United States whereas Brzezinski's China would become Russia's bigger brother in fashioning a grand coalition with Eurasian powers such as Turkey, Iran, Pakistan, Germany, and many more. Kissinger voices America's fondest dream—a China that can slip into the mainstream of global order without sinking the commander's boat. Brzezinski recalls America's worst nightmare—a Eurasian confederation controlled by Eurasians, led by a core of Sino-Russian and Islamic powers, and ready to cast its net not only over Africa's riches but on America's doorstep.

Chinese writings on geopolitics and Islam are highly compatible with the dominant themes of recent scholarship on global history, post-colonialism, and world systems theory.[16] The common threads are the

---

[14] Kissinger, Henry A. (2012). *On China*, New York: Penguin Books; Brzezinsky, Zbigneiw (2012). *Strategic Vision, America and the Crisis of Global Power*, New York: Basic Books; Brzezinski, Zbigniew (1997). *The Grand Chessboard: American Primacy and Its Geostrategic Imperatives*, New York: Basic Books.

[15] "Kissinger Returns," *Harvard Magazine*, May–June 2013; Kissinger, Henry A. (2012). The future of U.S.-Chinese relations: Conflict is a choice, not a necessity, *Foreign Affairs*, March–April.

[16] Hua Tao (华涛) (2006). 穆斯林社会与全球文明对话，回族研究 (Muslim Society and the Global Dialogue of Civilizations), *Journal of Hui Muslim Minority Studies*, 1; Ma Li Rong (马丽蓉) (2007). 西方霸权语境中的阿拉伯-伊斯兰问题研究, 时事出版社 (*The Arab-Islamic Question in the Context of Western Hegemony*) Beijing: Current Events Press; Zhu Wei Lie (朱威烈) (2007).伊斯兰文明与世界, 世界政治 (Islamic Civilization and the World), *World Economics and Politics*, 7; Wu Bing Bing (吴冰冰) (2006). 从伊斯兰文明看文化自觉, 回族研究 (Cultural Consciousness from the Perspective of Islamic Civilization), *Journal of Hui Minority Studies*, 1.

focus on global connectivity and the enhanced appreciation of the contributions of non-Western civilizations. From this perspective, the Western policy-makers who urge containing China, dividing Eurasia, and reconstructing Islamic societies are sadly out of touch with their own intellectual communities. Washington, in particular, clings to Cold War habits and unipolar moments that are at odds with swelling demands around the world for parity among cultures and multilateralism in global governance. The new learning of Western universities—invigorated by infusions from the South Asian and Far Eastern Diasporas—is embraced more readily in Beijing and Ankara than in Washington and Brussels.

While Chinese writers increasingly portray the Islamic world as a sister civilization and a valued partner, American and European politicians persist in characterizing Islam as an alien and frequently hostile ideology that requires periodic intervention by non-Muslims to subdue and reshape entire nations and regions, particularly in the Middle East. The growing scholarship on global connectivity gives the ideas and ideals of Islamic globalization a solid foundation by placing them in historical and comparative perspective. Nevertheless, the political implications of that learning are grasped and applied in Asian and African statecraft more than in Western halls of power.

Efforts to deal with the simultaneous rise of China and the Islamic world must adopt the widest possible vision—encompassing the oceanic continent of Eurasia and the sprawling highways of the Indian-Pacific Ocean Basin. The lands that American leaders and scholars conventionally term the Middle East—or more recently the Greater Middle East—are merely a small segment of these transcontinental mega-regions. Both American and Chinese leaders have begun to stress the wider contexts of their relations instead of viewing Middle Eastern issues in isolation or as deserving higher priority than others. President Obama has described his eastward pivot to the Asia-Pacific as a correction of over-investments in Iraq and Afghanistan. In response, several Chinese writers have suggested that Beijing redirect more of its energies westward to fill the anticipated power vacuums and to parry American encroachments into China's spheres of influence with counterthrusts into supposed preserves of the United States.

In fact, China's westward march is nothing new. The current episode began at least a quarter century ago—right after the fall of the Soviet Union—and many similar examples fill the histories of the great dynasties, particularly the Qing, Ming, Tang, and Han. [17] Obama's decision to refocus on the Pacific was a belated effort to stem China's growing gains throughout the Muslim world—including the American-dominated Middle East, but by no means limited to that area. Wang Ji Si and his critics are overly modest when they suggest that China is now reacting to America's strategic initiatives instead of vice-versa.[18]

The overarching conflict between American and Chinese approaches is that Washington still wishes to divide Afro-Eurasia whereas Beijing seeks to unify it. The United States would prefer a collection of segmented and compartmentalized mini-regions and quasi-nations that must deal separately with powerful outsiders. China's leaders, in contrast, are transcending many of their geostrategic debates to invest mightily in a transcontinental and hemispheric future where they can project their power while supporting other non-Western nations in their demands for more equal shares of global wealth and power. China is certainly not an altruistic actor in these matters, but its efforts are also likely to benefit several other countries that it supports and that return the favor. As long as Muslim societies perceive their options in this context, we should expect them to continue tilting evermore eastward.

---

[17] Perdue, Peter C. (2010). *China Marches West: The Qing Conquest of Central Eurasia*, Cambridge: Harvard University Press; Fletcher, Jr., Joseph F. (1995). Studies *on Chinese and Islamic Inner Asia*, Surrey, UK: Ashgate; Adshead, Samuel Adrian M. (2000). *China in World History*, New York: Palgrave Macmillan.

[18] Wang Ji Si also understates China's extensive history of "sailing south," including many well-known navigational innovations, Zheng He's multiple voyages to the Indian Ocean and East Africa decades before Columbus and da Gama, and the far-flung Diasporas that Chinese seafarers and merchants founded throughout Southeast Asia.

Chapter 20

Conclusion: Toward a New Concert of Civilizations

A new era of cooperation between Western, Chinese, and Islamic governments will require more than elite bargaining and institutional innovation. All three civilizations are riven by a deep contradiction between their aspirations to universalism and their ethnocentric self-perceptions of superiority and entitlement. Each has an impressive core of cosmopolitan reformers that champions civilizational interchange instead of domination and hegemony. But none of them are strong enough to prevail by relying exclusively on their own resources.

If Western and Chinese internationalists promote closer ties with Islamic liberals, they will be advancing several goals simultaneously—they boost the prospects for peace and progress in some of the world's most volatile regions, they strengthen themselves against hardline nationalists at home, and they take concrete steps toward developing a global ethic of humanitarianism that draws on the shared experience and wisdom of all civilizations.

Empowering Muslims Instead of Trying to Subdue Them

The most important goal for the two superpowers is to avoid a war with one another, but that will be impossible unless they resist the growing temptation to undermine one another's vital interests in the Middle East and the Islamic world. Just as neither superpower is capable of unilaterally leading the wider international system, neither can control the people and resources of Muslim nations. For Washington and Beijing, the wiser course is to renounce efforts to undermine one another or to divide Muslims into feuding blocks of superpower dependents.

A Sino-American cold war in the Islamic world would devastate all three regions and many others who depend on their well-being. China and the United States cannot rule the Islamic world—either separately or together—and they dare not destabilize it further lest they weaken themselves. To protect their own core interests, the great powers have little choice but to strengthen the Muslim world and the best way to do that is by encouraging the progressive trends of Islamic globalization.

Reclaiming the Homelands from the Xenophobes

By improving relations with the Islamic world, China and the West can advance domestic goals that are at least as important as their foreign policy aims. China and most of the North Atlantic community are struggling with powerful nativist and chauvinist groups that contradict their humane and universalist ideals, threaten their social fabrics, and erode their civil liberties. Heirs of the Western Enlightenment and its Chinese counterparts are as deeply embattled with fundamentalism and anti-foreign prejudice as any Islamic modernist. The virus of Islamophobia has produced as many strains in China and the West as the multiple jihads ravaging Muslim societies.

If globalization has common characteristics that are truly universal—and not merely Western, Chinese, Islamic or other variants—then it also faces powerful anti-globalization oppositions in every society and culture, including those that regard themselves as the earliest and most advanced civilizations of all. Just as we see world civilization as a common achievement of humanity as a whole, we should also realize that its contradictions can be equally ubiquitous and persistent. The same societies that appear to be the strongest pillars of progress can also be its weakest links. The internal crises of China, the West, and the Islamic world are local and global at the same time—it's hard to imagine remedying any of them if the others remain untreated.

Building a Global Ethic for World Governance

A common theme running through the internal struggles of Chinese, Western, and Islamic societies is the battle between universalists and exceptionalists—the cosmopolitan groups stressing common links with other cultures against the ethnocentric groups trying to preserve differences that underpin their supposed uniqueness and superiority. In China, the unfinished revolution of the May Fourth Movement's call for science and democracy clashes with the revival of Chinese traditional culture, including multiple schools of modern Confucianism. Muslims quarrel over literalist versus literary interpretations of the Qur'an and over the public versus private relevance of religious principles. And Western nations are riven by culture wars concerning the very definition of basic identities such as family, gender, and citizen.

There have never been so many different ways of being Chinese or Muslim or American or European. In each case, those who wish to preserve and expand that freedom of choice look to other societies and to global trends for common standards and solutions. On the other hand, those who wish to limit or retract those freedoms look for standards in the past—real and imagined—of their own people, often defined in terms of race or sect. Looking outside helps to increase freedom at home while promoting mutual understanding around the world.

International law and universal norms have always flourished when societies have been willing to compare their current predicaments with those of others in different places and times. Despite its many shortcomings, today's globalized environment is a high point in looking outside and surveying everyone's history instead of merely looking at ourselves and our own mythologies. In part, this greater open mindedness reflects a growing tolerance of differences and an appreciation that world history is a creation of all civilizations. On the other hand, looking outside is also motivated by a profound sense of inadequacy in all of the would-be leaders of the international system, both Western and non-Western.

Ironically, the most globalized nations also have become the most isolated in the sense that few people regard them as successful models worth emulating. China is filled with candid writers who see their country as out of touch with ever-increasing demand for democracy and as destined to follow the universal trend toward greater freedom. American commentators widely acknowledge their nation's sinking esteem around the world and its near pariah status in many Muslim lands. Europeans still cling to the notion that theirs is the pioneering experiment in regional integration, but even they are skeptical of its durability and its relevance elsewhere. As for Islamic writers, they know perfectly well that their societies are locked in a chain reaction of revolutions and civil wars that use religion as a rallying cry and a battle ram more than as a source of creative inspiration for fashioning modern institutions.

Why should so many struggling countries look to one another for help in devising solutions that none has found separately? Perhaps they realize that their common weaknesses and failures threaten them all. On their own, neither Western nor Chinese nor Islamic nations can set the world right—but each of them is more than capable of turning it upside down. When hegemony remains beyond everyone's reach, what alternative is there to cooperation—even if it is a coalition of the wounded? Better to collaborate while most of the injuries are still self-inflicted instead of waiting for multi-sided resource battles and proxy wars that have no victors.

If Western, Chinese, and Islamic leaders choose to look to one another for support and inspiration, they will soon discover very similar efforts to promote an international system that is based on legitimacy more than power and on collective action more than hegemony. Americans and Europeans are in the forefront of activists without borders committed to strengthening transnational civil society and international law. Chinese students of philosophy and world politics are determined to show that their history and culture can foster humane values and prudent statecraft with universal appeal to a world with little tolerance for superpower arrogance. And Islamic reformers are struggling to define human rights, social justice, and scientific inquiry as the essence of their religion and its constantly evolving civilization.

There is no assurance that future generations will be more successful than our own in translating these common ideals into something approaching a global ethic or effective world governance. Nevertheless, the building blocks of that vision are already well formed in all of the major civilizations and there is no time to spare in putting them in place.

Bibliography

Abdalghani, Karima (2011). Bil-asma' wa al-arqam: Nata'ij al-maqa'id al-fardiya wa qua'im al-ahzab fil-marhala al-'uwla lil-intikhabat (With Names and Numbers: Results for Individual and Party-list Seats in the First Round of the Elections), *Al-Ahram*, 7 December.

Abdel Malik, W.E.Y., A.S. Ibrahim, S.K. Youssef, M. Aziz and Rifaat M.K. El-Shinawy (2010). Radiological review studies on Ismailiya canal ecology, *Tenth Radiation Physics and Protection Conference*, Nasr City Cairo, Egypt, 27–30 November.

Abdel Salam, Mohamed (2010). Egypt's Qena unrest continues, sectarianism feared, *Bikyamasr.com*, 23 April.

Abdellah, Adel (2011). George Ishaq: Revolution figure seeking a majority, *Egyptvotes.org*, 29 November.

Abdoun, Safaa (2011). FJP contest all single winner seats in Sharqiya run-offs, *Daily News* (Egypt), 21 December.

Abouzeid, Rania (2011). Why the Muslim Brotherhood isn't all that fraternal, *Time*, 29 September.

Abu Dahab, Mohammad (2012). Gharbia Copts reluctant to run in elections, *Egyptvotes.org*, 11 January.

Accounting and Auditing Organization for Islamic Financial Institutions. *The Shari'a board.* Available online at http://www.aaoifi.com/aaoifi/TheOrganization/AAOIFIStructure/AAOIFIShariaBoard/tabid/71/language/en-US/Default.aspx (accessed 13 January 2013).

Adam, Nathif J. and Abdulkader Thomas (2004). *Islamic Bonds: Your Guide to Issuing, Structuring and Investing in Sukuk*, London: Euromoney Books.

Adibelli, Barış (2006). *Büyük Avrasya Projesi: ABD, Rusya ve Çin'in Varolma Mücadelesi* (The Greater Eurasia Project: The Struggle for Survival between the United States, Russia and China) (IQ Kültür Sanat Yayıncılık: Istanbul).

Adibelli, Barış (2007). *Çin'in Avrasya Stratejisi* (*China's Eurasia Strategy*) (IQ Kültür Sanat Yayıncılık, Istanbul).

Adshead, Samuel Adrian M. (2000). *China in World History*, New York: Palgrave Macmillan.

Afify, Heba (2011). In Sharqiya, Islamists are poised to sweep seats, *Al-Masry Al-Youm*, 14 December.

Ahmad, Khurshid and Zafar Ishaq Ansari, eds. (1979). *Islamic Perspectives: Studies in Honour of Mawlana Sayyid Abul A'la Mawdudi* (Islamic Foundation, Markfield, Leicestershire).

Ahmed, Abdulhadi (2005). Malaysia seeks dramatic O.I.C. reform, *IslamOnline.net*, 28 June. Available online at http://groups.yahoo.com/group/MahdiUnite/message/7476 (accessed 13 January 2013).

Ahmed, Amel (2011). Revolutionary blind-spots: The politics of electoral system choice and the Egyptian transition, *Middle East Law and Governance*, 3, 3–12.

Ahmed, Yasmine Moataz (2012). Who do Egypt's villagers vote for? And why? *Egypt Independent*, 10 April.

Ajijola, Alhaji Adeleke Dirisu (1998). The problem of *'ulama*, in Charles Kurzman, ed, *Liberal Islam: A Sourcebook*, New York: Oxford University Press.

Al-Ahram (2012). Al-nata'ij al-niha'iya li-intikhabat majlis al-sha'ab (Final results of the parliamentary elections), 21 January.

Al-Ahsan, 'Abdullāh (1988) *The Organization of the Islamic Conference: An Introduction to an Islamic Political Institution*, Herndon, Vancouver: International Institute of Islamic Thought.

Al-Amin, Esam, (2011). Understanding Tunisia's elections results, *Counterpunch*, 28 October.

Al-Bishry, Tariq (2011). Al-Tawari' intahit (The emergency has ended), *Al-Dostor*, 24 September.

Al-Dasuqi, Mahmud (2012). 'Iada bayn al-Ghul wa Qandil bi Qena wa al-Jama'a al-Islamiya wa al-Hurriya wa al-'Adala yu'aradan (Run-off between al-Ghul and Qandil in Qena; the Islamic Society and Freedom and Justice Object), *Al-Ahram*, January 11.

Al-Dasuqi, Mahmud (2012). Amin al-hurriya wa al-'adala bi Naga Hamadi: al-Salafiyun ankaru tahalafhum ma'a 'Abdalrahim al-Ghul (The Leader of Freedom and Justice in Naga Hamadi: The Salafis deny allying with Abdalrahim al-Ghul), *Al-Ahram*, 15 January.

Al-Dasuqi, Mahmud (2012). Baltajiya yamn'aun ahali qariya Abu Shusha bi Qena min al-khuruj lil-taswit (Thugs prevent the villagers of Abu Susha in Qena from going out to Vote), *Al-Ahram*, 15 January.

Al-Diasty, Karem (2011). Salafi Nour Party: The largest political force in the governorate, *Egyptvotes.org*, 20 December.

Al-Ghwell, Hafed (2010). Les inégalités spatiales sont une question de choix politique, et non une fatalité géographique, *worldbank.org*, 15 June.

Al-Hey'a al-'Aliya al-Mustaqila lil-Intikhabat (2011). *Al-Farz al-ma'lumati al-daqiq li intikhabat al-majlis al-watani al-ta'sisi 23 Uktober 2011, al-nata'ij al-niha'iya* (Supreme Independent Commission on Elections, Final Results of the Detailed Reporting of Information on Elections for the National Constituent Assembly of 23 October). Available online at http://www.isie.tn/ (accessed 13 January 2013).

Al-Husaini, Hujaj (2012). Al-Hurriya wa al-'Adala wa al-Nur yiqtisaman 8 muqa'd lil-fardi bil-Minya (Freedom and Justice and Nur divide eight individual seats in Minya), *Al-Ahram*, 14 January.

Al-Jazeera (2009). From Xian to Mecca: A road to hajj, 24 November.

Al-Jumhuriya al-Tunsiya Wizara al-Tanmiya wa al-Ta'awun al-Duwali (2008). *Al-Masah al-watani hawl al-sukan wa al-tashghil lisSana 2008*, al-Ma'ahad al-Watani lil-Ihsa', Tunis (Republic of Tunisia Ministry of Development and International Cooperation, National survey of population and employment for 2008, National Statistics Institute, Tunis).

Al-Jumhuriya al-Tunsiya wizara al-tanmiya wa al-ta'awun al-duwali (2005). *Al-Masah al- watani hawl al-infaq wa al-istihlak wa mustawa 'aish al-usra li sana 2005*, al-Ma'ahad al-Watani lil-Ihsa' (Republic of Tunisia Ministry of Development and International Cooperation, National survey of household expenditures, consumption and living standards for 2005, National Statistics Institute, Tunis).

Al-Masry Al-Youm (2011). Experts say Turkish model cannot be imported as is, 7 July.

Al-Masry Al-Youm (2011). Al-Wafd yurad 'ala al-Kutla: hasalna 'ala 15 muqa'da wa haqaqtum 8 faqat (The Wafd responds to the Egyptian Block: we won fifteen seats and you got only eight), 19 December.

Al-Masry Al-Youm (2011). Ba'd sa'at min 'ilan da'ma lil-Musilhi: al-Wafd yutifiq ma' 3 min murashshai al-'iada (Hours after announcing support for al-Musilhi, the Wafd allies with three run-off candidates), 19 December.

Al-Saati, Abdul Rahim (2002). Shar'ia compatible futures, *Journal of King Abdulaziz University: Islamic Economics*, 15:3.

Al-Shami, Khalad (2011). Nata'ij al-Minufiya al-niha'iya: fawz al-Sadat wa 'iada bayn al-Hurriya wa al-'Adala wa al-Falul wa al-Nur (Final results of Minufiya: victory of al-Sadat and run-offs between Freedom and Justice, the National Party, and Nur), *Al-Masry Al-Youm*, 17 December.

Al-Tabrani, Hana' (2012). Fawz al-Shurbaghi murashshaha al-Ikhwan wa akhar mustaqil fil-'iada bi Shimal Sina' (Victory of al-Shurbaghi candidate of the Ikhwan and of an independent in the run-off in North Sinai), *Al-Ahram*, 14 January.

Ali, Mostafa (2011). Alexandria votes for Its Islamist sons, with dangerously high expectations, *Ahramonline*, 5 December.

Alker, Hayward (1979). *Mathematics and Politics*, New York: Macmillan.

Almasry, Farah (2011). Civil forces ally in run-offs to confront Islamist landslide, *Egyptvotes.org*, 5 December.

Amara, Tarek (2011). Tunisia security forces fire in air during protest, *Reuters*, 23 November.

Amara, Tarek (2010). Tunisia's Ennadha to oppose Sharia in constitution, *Reuters*, 24 March.

Amin, Shahira (2010). Egypt's farmers desperate for clean water, *CNN,* 10 November.

Andaya, Barbara Watson (2006). Oceans unbounded: Transversing Asia across 'area studies,' *Journal of Asian Studies*, 65:4, 669–690.

Archer, Simon, Rifaat Ahmed Cox and Bryan Kraty, eds. (2005). *Structuring Islamic Finance Transactions*, London: Euromoney.

Arkoun, Mohammed (2002). *The Unthought in Contemporary Islamic Thought*, London: Saqi Books.

Ashiwa, Yoshiko and David L. Wank, eds. (2009). *Making Religion, Making the State: The Politics of Religion in Modern China*, Stanford: Stanford University Press.

Ashour, Omar (2011). Egypt secularists and liberals afraid of democracy? *BBC News*, 13 July.

Attia, Habib (1986). Problématique du developpement du Nord-Ouest tunisien, *Revue de l'Occident musulman et de la Méditerranée*, 41–42, 264–280.

Attia, Habib (1982). Propositions pour l'élaboration d'un plan de développement régional de la région du nord-ouest de la Tunisie centrale, Tunis: Commissariate général au développement régional.

Ayhan, Veysel (2011). Results of the Tunisian constituent assembly elections: Winners and losers after a revolution, *ORSAM Center for Middle Eastern Strategic Studies*, October 31. Available online at http://www.orsam.org.tr/en/showArticle.aspx?ID=887 (accessed 13 January 2013).

Baker, Raymond William (2003). *Islam Without Fear: Egypt and the New Islamists*. Cambridge: Harvard University Press.

Bandurski, David (2011). Turning back to 'new democracy'? *China Media Project*, 19 May.

Bank for International Settlements, Basel Committee on Banking Supervision (2006). *Basel II: International Convergence of Capital Measurement and Capital Standards: A Revised Framework*, Basel, Switzerland.

Bank Negara Malaysia (2012). *The National Syariah Advisory Council on Islamic Banking and Takaful*. Available online at http://www.bnm.gov.my/index.php?ch=174&pg=467&ac=371 (accessed 13 January 2013).

Basha, Mona (2012). Hisara Murtada Mansur wa 6 maq'aid lil-Hurriya wa al-'Adala wa 2 lil-mustaqalin fil-Daqhaliya (Loss of Murtada Mansur, six seats to Freedom and Justice and two to independents in Daqhaliya), *Al-Ahram*, 14 January.

Beaverstodk, Jonathan V. *et al.* (2000). World-city network: A new metageography? *Annals of the Association of American Geographers*, 90:1, 123–134.

Belhedi, Amor (1999). Les disparités spatiales en Tunisie, état des lieux et enjeux, *Méditerranée*, 91, 63–72.

Belhedi, Amor (2006). Territoires, appartenance et identification: Quelques réflexions à partir du cas Tunisien, *L'Espace géographique*, 4:35, 310–316.

Belhedi, Amor (2007). Le rayonnement spatial des villes tunisiennes à travers la diffusion des entreprises multi-établissements pour l'innovation, *Cybergeo: European Journal of Geography*, 16 April.

Bellahgua, Abderrahmane (2012). Élections du 23 octobre: Le profil des électeurs, *mosaiquefm.com*, 22 February.

Ben Mahmoud, Mounir (2012). Sondage sur l'action du gouvernement Jebali, *BusinessNews.com.tn*, 11 April.

Bhardwaj, Surinder M. (1998). Non-Hajj pilgrimage in Islam: a neglected dimension of religious circulation, *Journal of Cultural Geography*, March.

Bianchi, Robert R. (1984). *Interest Groups and Political Development in Turkey*, Princeton: Princeton University Press.

Bianchi, Robert R. (1989). *Unruly Corporatism: Associational Life in Twentieth-Century Egypt*, New York: Oxford University Press.

Bianchi, Robert R. (2004). *Guests of God: Pilgrimage and Politics in the Islamic World*, New York: Oxford University Press.

Bianchi, Robert R. (2013). China-Middle East relations in light of Obama's pivot to the Pacific, *China Report*, 49:1, 103–118.

Binder, Leonard (1978). *In a Moment of Enthusiasm: Political Power and the Second Stratum in Egypt*, Chicago: University of Chicago Press.

Binder, Leonard (1988). *Islamic Liberalism: A Critique of Development Ideologies*, Chicago: University of Chicago Press.

Birks, J. S. (1978). *Across the Savannas to Mecca: The Overland Pilgrimage Route from West Africa*, London: C. Hurst & Co.

Bistolfi, Robert and Françios Zabal, eds. (1995). *Islams d'Europe: Intégration ou insertion communitaire*, Paris: Editions de l'Aube.

Blalock, Hubert M. (1965). *Social Statistics*, New York: McGraw-Hill.

Bogle, John C. (2005) *The Battle for the Soul of Capitalism*, New Haven: Yale University Press.

Bovingdon, Gardner (2010). *The Uyghurs: Strangers in Their Own Land*, New York: Columbia University Press.

Branigan, Tania (2010). Zheng He: Messenger of peace, or of power? *The Guardian*, 25 July.

Brittain-Catlin, William (2005). *Offshore: The Dark Side of the Global Economy*, New York: Straus and Giroux.

Brown, Nathan J. (2011). Egypt's syndicalist future? *Foreign Policy*, 8 March.

Brzezinski, Zbigniew (1997). *The Grand Chessboard: American Primacy and Its Geostrategic Imperatives*, New York: Basic Books.

Brzezinsky, Zbigneiw (2012). *Strategic Vision, America and the Crisis of Global Power*, New York: Basic Books.

Bulaç, Ali (1998). The Medina Document, in Charles Kurzman, ed., *Liberal Islam: A Source-Book*, New York: Oxford University Press.

Campo, Juan Eduardo (1991). *The Other Sides of Paradise: Explorations into the Religious Meanings of Domestic Space in Islam*, Columbia: University of South Carolina Press.

Chabbi, Morched and Hassen Abid (2008). La mobilité urbaine dans le Grand Tunis: evolutions et perspectives, *Plan Bleu-Centre d'Activités Régionales*, May.

Chabbi, Morched (2007). L'urbanisation en Tunisie, transformations et tendance d'évolution, *Archi-Mag*.

Chapra, M. Umer (2004). Mawlana Mawdudi's Contribution to Islamic Economics, *Muslim World*, 93, 163–180.

Chayes, Abram and Antonia Handler Chayes (1995). *The New Sovereignty: Compliance with International Regulatory Agreements*, Cambridge: Harvard University Press.

Chélini, Jean and Henry Branthomme (1987). *Histoire des pèlerinages non-chrétiens*, Paris: Hachette.

Chiba, Masaji (1989). *Legal Pluralism: Toward a General Theory Through Japanese Legal Culture*, Tokyo: Tokai University Press.

China's New Leadership: Opportunity for the United States? (2012). *Woodrow Wilson Center*, 3 October.

Chiu, Shirley, Robin Newberger and Anna Paulson (2005). Islamic finance in the United States: a small but growing industry, *Chicago Fed Letter*, May.

Chrisafis, Angelique and Ian Black (2011). Tunisia elections winner: 'We're hardly the Freemasons, we're a modern party,' *The Guardian*, 25 October.

Cole, Juan (2012). South Carolina and Gingrich; Egypt and the Muslim Brotherhood, *CNN*, 23 January.

Coser, Lewis A. (1956). *The Functions of Social Conflict*, Glencoe: Free Press.

Coulson, Noel J. (1969). *Conflicts and Tensions in Islamic Jurisprudence*, Chicago: University of Chicago Press.

Couvas, Jacques N. (2011). Turkey admires Tunisia's secular facelift, *Asia Times*, 9 November.

Dai Bing Guo (戴秉国) (2010). 中国取代美国称霸？那是神话 (China replacing America as a hegemon? That's a fairy tale), *Zhong Xinwen*, 7 December.

Danarto (1989). *A Javanese Pilgrim in Mecca*, translated by H. Aveling, Clayton, Australia: Monash University.

Daoudov, Murat (2011). Can Turkey inspire Tunisia? *ArabNews.com*, 24 November.

Davutoğlu, Ahmet (2001). Stratejik Derinlik: Türkiye'nin Uluslararası Konumu (Strategic Depth: Turkey's International Relations), Istanbul: Küre Yayınları.

de Tocqueville, Alexis (orig. pub. date 1866) (1998). *The Old Regime and the Revolution, Volume I*, translated by Alan S. Kahan, Chicago: University of Chicago Press.

de Tocqueville, Alexis (orig. pub. date 1835) (2011). *Democracy in America*, translated by Harvey C. Mansfield and Delba Winthrop, Chicago: University of Chicago Press.

Dai Xu (戴旭) (2009). C-形包围：内忧外患下的中国突围，上海文汇出版社 (C-Shaped Encirclement: China's Breakout From Internal Troubles and External Aggression), Shanghai: Wenhui Publishing.

Dai Xu (戴旭) (2012). 中俄应构建欧亚大联盟阻止美国屠戮弱国 (China and Russia Should Establish a Eurasian Alliance to Prevent the United States from Eating Weak Countries), *Global Times*, January 29. Available online at http://opinion.huanqiu.com/1152/2012-01/2385635.html.

Demir, Ömer, Mustafa Acar and Metin Toprak (2004). Anatolian tigers or Islamic capital: prospects and challenges, *Middle Eastern Studies*, 40:6 166–188.

Deng Yu Wen (邓聿文) (2012). 胡温的政治遗产, 财经网 (The political legacy of Hu and Wen), *caijing.com*, 2 September.

Dhehibi, Boubaker (2006). Productivity and economic growth in Tunisian agriculture, *International Association of Agricultural Economists Conference*, Gold Coast, Australia, 12–18 August.

Dong Wang and Li Kan (2010). Eying the crippled hegemon: China's grand strategy thinking in the wake of the global financial crisis, *Social Science Research Network*, 8 September.

Dudley, Nigel (2004). Pioneers of a Burgeoning Market, *Euromoney*, December, pp. 66–82.

Dupret, Baudouin, Maurits Berger and Laila al-Zwaini, eds. (1999). *Legal Pluralism in the Arab World*, Dordrecht: Kluwer.

Edge, Ian, ed. (2001). *Comparative Law in Global Perspective,* Ardsley, N.Y. Transnational Publishers.

Eickelman, Dale F. and James Piscatori, eds. (1990). *Muslim Travellers: Pilgrimage, Migration, and the Religious Imagination*, Berkeley: University of California Press, Berkeley.

El Diwany, Tarek (2003). *The Problem With Interest*, London: Kreatoc Ltd.

El-Ashker, Ahmed (1987). *The Islamic Business Enterprise*, London:Taylor & Francis.

El-Bey, Doaa (2011). Compare and contrast: Can the Turkish constitution serve as a model for Egypt? *Al-Ahram Weekly*, 7–13 July.

El-Deeb, Sarah (2011). Stunned by bloodshed, Egyptians torn over army, *Associated Press*, 16 October.

El-Gamal, Mahmoud A. (2004). 'Interest' and the Paradox of Contemporary Islamic Law and Finance, *Fordham International Law Journal,* 27, 108–09.

El-Gamal, Mahmoud A. (2005). Mutuality as an antidote to rent-seeking shari'ah-arbitrage in Islamic finance, *Rice University*, April. Available online at http://www.ruf.rice.edu/~elgamal/files/islamic.html (accessed 13 January 2013).

El-Gergawi, Sherry (2012). Egyptian Copts call for 'Brotherhood' of their own, *Ahram Weekly*, 31 March.

El-Mahdy, Osama and Mohamed Abu Elenen (2011). Sufi sheikh warns of sectarian war with Salafis, *Al-Masry Al-Youm*, 5 April.

El-Sharnoubi, Osman (2011). Despite recent violence, Kafr El-Sheikh ready for smooth Egypt elections, *Ahramonline*, 28 November.

El-Sherif, Ashraf (2011). Islamism after the Arab Spring, *Current History*, December.

Eliade, Mircea (1954). *The Myth of the Eternal Return; or, Cosmos and History*, translated by Willard R. Trask, Princeton: Princeton University Press.

Ellali, Ahmed (2012). New survey points to fluctuations in popularity of Tunisian political parties and leaders, *Tunisialive.com*, 23 March.

Elyan, Tamim and Tom Heneghan (2011). Egyptian voters reject Salafi hardliner in run-off, *Reuters*, 7 December.

Escobar, Pepe (2009). Welcome to Pipelineistan, *Mother Jones*, 24 March.

Esty, Benjamin C. (2000). The Equate project: An introduction to Islamic project finance, *Journal of Structured Finance*, 5:4, 7–20.

European Stability Initiative (2005). Islamic Calvinists: change and conservatism in central Anatolia, *esiweb.org*, 19 September.

Eyal, Jonathan (2013). Entangling the Dragon in Arab Quicksands, *The Straits Times*, May 20.

Fam, Mariam and Alaa Shahine (2011). Tunisa Islamists back tax cuts, stock sales to create jobs, *Bloomberg*, 28 October.

Farwell, James P. and Marvin Weinbaum (2011). Egypt's Brothers Rise, *The National Interest*, 29 June.

Feng Hai Wen (冯海闻) (2012). 中国大国战略选择南进还是西进？环球网 (China's Great Power Strategic Choice, Sail South Or March West?), *Global Times Online*, November 1. Available online at http://opinion.huanqiu.com/opinion_world/2012-11/3235465.html.

Feng Hai Wen (冯海闻) (2013). 美国对华政策或从硬围堵变软包围, 环球网 (America's China Policy Or From Hard Containment to Soft Encirclement), *Global Times Online*, January 22. Available online at http://opinion.huanqiu.com/opinion_world/2013-01/3568348.html.

Firestone, Reuven (1990). *Journeys in Holy Lands: The Evolution of the Abraham-Ishmael Legends in Islamic Exegesis*, Albany: State University of New York Press.

Fischer, Michael M.J. and Mehdi Abedi (1990). *Debating Muslims: Cultural Dialogues in Postmodernity and Tradition*, Madison: University of Wisconsin Press.

Fletcher, Jr., Joseph F. (1995). *Studies on Chinese and Islamic Inner Asia*, Surrey, UK: Ashgate.

Florini, Ann M., ed. (2000). *Third Force: The Rise of Transnational Civil Society*, Carnegie Endowment for International Peace, Washington, D.C.

Food and Agriculture Organization (2012). Wheat production potential in Tunisia, *Tunisia-FAO Wheat Database*, Italy: Food and Agriculture Organization.

Francis, David R. (2005). Uncle Sam's rich uncles overseas, *The Christian Science Monitor*, 19 September.

Frankel, Max (2011). Henry Kissinger on China, *New York Times*, 13 May.

Gana, Alia, Gilles Van Hamme and Maher Ben Rebah (2012). Géographie électorale et disparités socio-territoriales: les enseignements des élections pour l'assemblée constituante en Tunisie, *L'Espace Politique*, 18.

Geriesh, Mohamed H. *et al.* (2008). Problems of drinking water treatment along Ismailia canal province, Egypt, *Journal of Zhejiang University Science*, 9:3, 232–242.

Ghannoushi, Soumaya (2011). Revolution hijacked, *Guardian*, 27 September.

Gladston, David L. (2005). *From Pilgrimage to Package Tour: Travel and Tourism in the Third World*, London: Routledge.

Glenn, H. Patrick (2004). *Legal Traditions of the World: Sustainable Diversity in Law*, New York: Oxford University Press.

Godement, François *et al.* (2011). China debates its global strategy, *European Council on Foreign Relations*, April.

Goodman, David J. (2011). Tempers flare at birthplace of Arab Spring after some Tunisian votes are nullified, *New York Times*, 28 October.

Goossaert, Vincent and David A. Palmer (2007). *The Religious Question in Modern China,* Chicago: University of Chicago Press.

Gran, Peter (1979). *Islamic Roots of Capitalism: Egypt, 1760-1840*, Austin: University of Texas Press.

Gui Rong (桂榕) (2009). 回族农村的权力文化网络：云南沙甸和谐社会的政治人类学研究 (Cultural networks of power in a Hui village: A political anthropology study of the harmonious society of Shadian Yunnan), *Journal of the Yunnan University of Nationalities*, 26:4, 49–52.

Habermas, Jurgen (1972). *Knowledge and Human Interests*, Boston: Beacon Press.

Halawa, Omar (2011). In Suez, tribal loyalties raise fears of Islamist and liberal parties alike, *Al-Masry Al-Youm*, 14 December.

Hammoudi, Abdellah (2006). *A Season in Mecca: Narrative of a Pilgrimage*, translated by Pascale Ghazaleh, New York: Hill and Wang.

Han Shu Yun (韩淑云) (2010). 女哈吉与通过仪式—基于青海循化穆斯林女性朝觐者的调查研究 (Female hajjis and the rites of passage—A survey of female Muslim pilgrims in Xunhua, Qinghai Province), *Journal of Beifang Ethnic University*, 2, 70–73.

Hardin, Garrett (1968). The tragedy of the commons, *Science*, 162, 1243–1248.

Hardt, Michael and Antonio Negri (2011). Arabs are democracy's new pioneers, *Guardian*, 24 February.

Harik, Iliya (1968). *Politics and Change in a Traditional Society: Lebanon, 1711–1845*, Princeton: Princeton University Press.

Harik, Iliya (1974). *The Political Mobilization of Peasants: A Study of an Egyptian Community*, Bloomington: Indiana University Press.

Harik, Iliya (1992). Privatization and Development in Tunisia, in *Privatization and Liberalization in the Middle East*, Iliya Harik and Denis J. Sullivan, eds., Bloomington: Indiana University Press.

Harris, Caroline and Ray Harris (2008). Tunisia: Geography on the edge, *Geography Review*, September.

Harvard Magazine, "Kissinger Returns," May–June 2013.

Hasenclever, Andreas, Peter Mayer and Volker Rittberger (1997). *Theories of International Regimes*, Cambridge: Cambridge University Press.

Hassan, Amro (2011). Muslim Brotherhood announces new political party, *Los Angeles Times*, 30 April.

Hassan, Bahey el-Din (2011). Why Tunisia succeeds while Egypt fails, *al-Masry al-Youm*, 2 November.

Hayoun, Massoud (2012). Islam with Chinese characteristics, *The Atlantic*, 18 January.

Hayoun, Massoud (2013). Islamophobia is bad for business, *Boston Review*, January 16. Available online at http://www.bostonreview.net/BR38.1/massoud_hayoun_islamophobia_business_china_middle_east.php

Hegazy, Yamen M. *et al.* (2011). Ruminant brucellosis in the Kafr El Sheikh Governorate of the Nile Delta, Egypt: Prevalence of a neglected zoonosis, *Public Library of Science: Neglected Tropical Diseases*, January.

Henry, Clement M., ed. (1999). Special Issue on Islamic Finance, *Thunderbird International Business Review*, 40, July.

Henry, Clement M. and Rodney Wilson eds. (2004). *The Politics of Islamic Finance*, Edinburgh: Edinburgh University Press.

Hiatt, Fred, No escape from the Middle East (2012) *Washington Post*, 8 October.

Hopkins, Nicholas S. and Reem Saad, eds. (2004). *Upper Egypt: Identity and Change,* Cairo: American University in Cairo Press.

Hopkins, Nicholas S. and Kirsten Westergaard, eds. (1998). *Directions of Change in Rural Egypt,* Cairo: American University in Cairo Press.

Horner, Charles and Eric Brown (2010). Beijing's Islamic Complex, *The American Interest Magazine*, May-June.

Hua Tao (华涛) (2003). 文化对话与中国传统文化范式中的障碍 (Cultural dialogue and obstacles in the paradigms of traditional Chinese culture, *Journal of Nanjing University*, 40:1, 45–51.

Hua Tao (华涛) (2006). 穆斯林社会与全球文明对话 (Muslim society and the global dialogue of civilizations), *Journal of Hui Muslim Minority Studies*, 61:1, 24–26.

Hudson, Michael C. (2011). Rescue the revolution, *Foreign Policy*, 6 April.

Hussein, Abdel-Rahman (2011). After crushing defeat, Wafd wonders what's next, *Al-Masry Al-Youm*, 8 December.

Ibn Khaldun (1989). *The Muqaddimah: An Introduction to History*, translated by Franz Rosenthal, Princeton: Princeton University Press.

Ibrahim, Saad Eddin (2011). Ikhwan wa Qatariyun...wa Salafiyun wa Sa'udiyun (The Ikhwan and the Qataris; the Salafis and the Saudis), *Al-Masry Al-Youm*, 17 December.

Ihsanoglu, E. (2010). *The Islamic World in the New Century: The Organization of the Islamic Conference, 1969–2009*, New York: Columbia University Press.

Institut National de la Statistique (2010). *Annuaire Statistique de la Tunisie 2005-2009*, Tunis: République Tunisienne Ministère du Développement et de la Coopération Internationale.

Institut National de la Statistique (2010). *La Tunisie en Chiffres 2007-2009*, Tunis: République Tunisienne Ministère du Développement et de la Coopération Internationale.

Institute of Islamic Banking and Insurance (1995). *Encyclopedia of Islamic Banking and Insurance*, London.

Iqbal, Munawar and Philip Molyneux (2005). *Thirty Years of Islamic Banking: History, Performance, and Prospect*, New York: Palgrave MacMillan.

Iqbal, Munawar (1986). *Distributive Justice and Need Fulfillment in an Islamic Economy*, Islamabad, Pakistan: International Islamic University.

Iriye, Akira (1997). *Cultural Internationalism and World Order*, Baltimore: Johns Hopkins University Press.

Islamic Development Bank, *IDB's Cooperation with Islamic Banks and National Development Financing Institutions, 2004–2005.* Available online at http://www.isdb.org/irj/go/km/docs/documents/IDBDevelopments/Internet/English/IDB/CM/About%20IDB/Annual%20Reports/AnnualReport_30th.html (accessed 13 January 2013).

Islamic Financial Services Board (2005). 10-Year Master Plan Set to Chart Future Directions of the Islamic Financial Services Industry, 23 June. Available online at http://www.ifsb.org/preess_full.php?id=62&submit=more (accessed 13 January 2013).

Jadaliyya.com (2012). Egyptian elections: Preliminary results, 9 January. Available online at http://www.jadaliyya.com/pages/index/3331/egyptian-elections_preliminary-results_updated- (accessed 13 January 2013).

Jaffer, Sohail, ed. (2004). *Islamic Asset Management: Forming the Future for Shari'a-Compliant Investment Strategies*, London: Euromoney Books.

Jaffer, Sohail, ed. (2005). *Islamic Retail Banking and Finance: Global Challenges and Opportunities*, London: Euromoney Books.

Johnson, Ian and Jackie Calmes (2001). As U.S. looks to Asia, it sees China everywhere, *New York Times*, 15 November.

Jouili, Mustapha (2009). Tunisian agriculture: Are small farms doomed to disappear? *Seminar on Small Farms: Decline or Persistence?*, Canterbury, U.K.: University of Kent.

Jullien, François (1995). *The Propensity of Things: Toward A History of Efficacy in China*, New York: Zone Books.

Jullien, François (2004). *A Treatise on Efficacy: Between Western and Chinese Thinking*, Honolulu: University of Hawai'i Press.

Kamal, Ahmad (1964). *The Sacred Journey: The Pilgrimage to Mecca*, New York: George Allen & Unwin.

Kamal, Ashraf (2012). I'lan nata'ij al-maq'aid al-fardiya bil-Minya (Announcement of the results for individual seats in Minya), *Al-Wafd*, 11 January.

Kaminski, Matthew (2012). Islamists inside the gates, *Wall Street Journal*, 10 April.

Karim, Abdel and Rifaat Ahmed (2006). Aligning the Architecture of Islamic Finance to the Evolving Industry Needs, *The Islamic Financial Services Board 3d Summit*, Beirut 17–18 May.

Karim, Abdel, Rifaat Ahmed and Simon Archer (2002). *Islamic Finance: Innovation and Growth*, London: Euromoney Books.

Kassem, Mahmoud and Anita Greil (2001). Islamic banking reputation suffers in wake of Sept. 11, *Dow Jones International News*, 5 November.

Kazarian, Elias (1993). *Islamic versus Traditional Banking: Financial Innovations in Egypt*, Boulder: Westview.

Keefe, David (2004). Bringing Shariah and Basel into accord, *Global Risk Regulator Newsletter*, January.

Kenzari, Bechir (2004). Lake Tunis, or the concept of the third centre, in Yasser Elsheshtawy, ed., *Planning Middle Eastern Cities: An Urban Kaleidoscope in a Globalizing World*, London: Routledge.

Key, V.O. Jr. (1984). *Southern Politics in State and Nation*, Knoxville: University of Tennessee Press.

Khan, Shahrukh Rafi (1987). *Profit and Loss Sharing: An Islamic Experiment in Finance and Banking*, New York: Oxford University Press.

Kimbell, Deborah (2004). Etisalat deal breaks record for Islamic financing, *Euromoney*, November.

Kirkpatrick, David D. (2001). Egypt elections expose divisions in Muslim Brotherhood, *New York Times*, 19 June.

Kirkpatrick, David D. (2001). Egypt Islamists demand the end of military rule, *New York Times,* 18 November.

Kirkpatrick, David D. (2001). Egypt's vote puts emphasis on split over religious rule, *New York Times*, 3 December.

Kirkpatrick, David D. (2001). Egypt's military retracts plan to extend influence over constitution, *New York Times*, 9 December.

Kirkpatrick, David D. (2001). In Egypt, a conservative appeal transcends religion, *New York Times*, 10 December.

Kissinger, Henry A. (2012). *On China*, New York: Penguin Books.

Kissinger, Henry A. (2012). The future of U.S.-Chinese relations: Conflict is a choice, not a necessity, *Foreign Affairs*, March/April.

Kotb, Tarek H.S., Tsugihiro Watanabe, Yoshihiko Ogino and Kenneth K. Tanji (2000). Soil salinization in the Nile delta and related policy issues in Egypt, *Agricultural Water Management*, 43, 239–261.

Kramer, Martin (1990). Khomeini's messengers: The disputed pilgrimage of Islam, in Emmanuel Sivan and Menachem Friedman, eds., *Religious Radicalism and Politics in the Middle East*, Albany: State University of New York Press.

Kremer, Alex *et al.* (2010). *Poor Places, Thriving People: How the Middle East and North Africa Can Rise Above Spatial Disparity*, Washington: World Bank.

Kristof, Nicholas D. (2011a). Joining a dinner in a Muslim Brotherhood home, *New York Times*, *9* December.

Kristof, Nicholas D. (2011b). Democracy in the Brotherhood's birthplace, *New York Times*, 10 December.

Kuran, Timur (2004). *Islam and Mammon: The Economic Predicaments of Islamism*, Princeton: Princeton University Press.

Kurzman, Charles and Ijlal Naqvi (2010). Do Muslims vote Islamic? *Journal of Democracy*, 21, 50–63.

Labidi, Mehrezia (2012). Tunisia's women are at the heart of its revolution, *The Guardian*, 23 March.

Lagerwey, John (2010). *China: A Religious State*, Hong Kong: Hong Kong University Press.

Lapidus, Ira (1975). Hierarchies and networks: A comparison of Chinese and Islamic societies, in Frederic E. Wakeman and Carolyn Grant, eds. *Conflict and Control in Late Imperial China*, Berkeley: University of California Press.

Legrand, Pierre (1996). How to compare now, *Legal Studies*, 16, 232–243.

Legrand, Pierre (1997). The impossibility of 'legal transplants,' *Maastricht Journal of European and Comparative Law*, 4, 111–124.

LeVine, Mark (2012). The Arab Spring's Chinese roots...and future? *Al-Jazeera*, 2 February.

Levmore, Saul (2002). Ruling majorities and reasoning pluralities, *Theoretical Inquiries in Law (Online Edition)* 3. Available online at http://www.degruyter.com/view/j/til.2002.3.issue-1/til.2002.3.1.1043/til.2002.3.1.1043.xml (accessed 13 January 2013).

Lewis, Martin W. and Karen E. Wigan (1997). *The Myth of Continents: A Critique of Metageography*, Berkeley: University of California Press.

Lewis, Mervyn K. and Latifa M. Algaoud (2001). *Islamic Banking*, Cheltenham, U.K.: Edward Elgar.

Li Ling Hua (李令华) (2012). 关于南海九段线的法律地位问题 (On the legal status of the nine-dash line in the South China Sea). Available online at http://blog.ifeng.com/article/11000072.html (accessed 13 January 2013).

Li Yi (李意) (2010). 海湾安全局势与中国的战略选择 (*The Security Situation in the Arab Gulf and China's Strategic Choices*), Beijing: World Knowledge Press.

Lieven, Anatol (2011). *Pakistan: A Hard Country*, New York: Public Affairs Books.

Linn, Johannes F. and David Tiomkin (2005). *Economic Integration of Eurasia: Opportunities and Challenges of Global Significance*, Warsaw: Center for Social and Economic Research.

Linz, Juan J. and Armando de Miguel (1966). Within-nation differences and comparisons: The eight Spains, in Richard L. Merritt and Stein Rokkan, eds., *Comparing Nations: The Use of Quantitative Data in Cross-National Research*, New Haven: Yale University Press.

Liu Xin Hua (刘新华) (2004). 试论中亚对中国地缘战略的重要性 (The significance of Central Asia viewed from China's geo-strategy), *Journal of Wuhan Economic Administration Cadre's College*, 18:2, 20–24.

Long, David Edwin (1979). *The Hajj Today: A Survey of the Contemporary Makkah Pilgrimage*, Albany: State University of New York Press.

Lowe, Christian (2011). Tunisian Islamist wants convertible currency, *Reuters*, 28 October.

Luyken, Jorg (2011). Who wants to foil Egyptian elections? *Haaretz*, 25 November.

Ma Li Rong (马丽蓉) (2007). 西方霸权语境中的阿拉伯-伊斯兰问题研究 (The Arab-Islamic Question in the Context of Western Hegemony), Beijing: Current Events Press.

Ma Li Rong (马丽蓉) (2009). 全球化进程中清真寺功能影响研究 (The functions and influence of mosques in the globalization process), *Journal of Hui Muslim Minority Studies*, March, pp. 54–64.

Mabruk, Muhammad (2011). 5 maqa'id lil-Hurriya wa al-'Adala wa 2 lil-mustaqalin wa muq'ad lil-Wafd wa akhar lil-Nur bi jawla al-'iada bil-Gharbiya (Five seats to Freedom and Justice, two to independents, one to the Wafd and another to Nur in run-offs in Gharbiya), *Al-Ahram*, 14 January.

MacDonald, G. Jeffrey (2005). For investors with a conscience, options grow, *Christian Science Monitor*, 19 September.

Maged, Amani (2011). Islamist election map, *Ahramonline*, 24 November.

Mahdi, Muhsin (1964). Ibn Khaldûn's Philosophy of History: A Study in the Philosophic Foundation of the Science of Culture, Chicago: University of Chicago Press.

Maher, Hatem and Sherif Tarek (2011). Reformist judge, new MP Mahmoud El-Khodeiry on Islamist ascendancy, Palestine, *Ahramonline*, 15 December.

Marmar, Suzan (2012). Murtada Mansour about to ride Salafi support into Parliament, *Egyptvotes.org*, 14 January.

Martin, Patrick (2011). Islamists threaten to outmanoeuvre secularists in post-revolution Egypt, *Globe and Mail*, 29 July.

Masue, Muhammad Khalid, Brinkley Messick and David S. Powers, eds. (1996). *Islamic Legal Interpretation: Muftis and Their Fatwas*, Harvard: Harvard University Press.

Matheson, Virginia and A. C. Milner (1984). *Perceptions of the Haj: Five Malay Texts*, Singapore: Institute of Southeast Asian Studies.

Matthews, Owen (2005). How the west came to run Islamic banks, *Newsweek*, 31 October.

Maurer, Bill (2005). *Mutual Life, Limited: Islamic Banking, Alternative Currencies, Lateral Reason*, Princeton: Princeton University Press.

McDonnell, Mary Byrne (1986). The conduct of the hajj from Malaysia and Its socio-economic impact on Malay society: A descriptive and analytical study, 1860–1981, Ph.D. diss., Columbia University.

McManus, Doyle (2011). Mosque and state: Islamist parties are a legitimate political force, whether we like it or not, *Los Angeles Times*, 23 October.

McMillen, Michael J.T. (2000). A *rahn-adl* collateral security structure for project and secured financings. Available online at kslaw.com/library/pdf/mcmillencorporate.pdf (accessed 13 January 2013).

Mearsheimer, John J. (2003). *The Tragedy of Great Power Politics*, New York: W.W. Norton.

Metcalf, Thomas R. (2007). *Imperial Connections—India in the Indian Ocean Arena, 1860–1920*, Berkeley: University of California Press.

Michael, Maggie (2011). Christians under siege in post-revolution Egypt, *Associated Press*, 11 October.

Miliband, David (2011). Don't despair of Egypt's democracy, *Financial Times*, 14 October.

Mills, Paul S. and John R. Presley (1999). *Islamic Finance: Theory and Practice*, London: MacMillan Press.

Mitchell, Richard P. (1993). *The Society of the Muslim Brothers*, New York: Oxford University Press.

Moalla, Mansour (2012). Le Bourguisme pêut etre une solution en l'absence d'alternatives sérieuses, *Radioexpressfm.com*, 16 février.

Mohan, C. Raja (2012). *Samudra Manthan: Sino-Indian Rivalry in the Indo-Pacific*, Washington, D.C.: Carnegie Endowment for International Peace.

Morrow, Raymond A. (2010). Norbert Elias and figurational sociology: The comeback of the century, *Contemporary Sociology*, 38:3, 215–219.

Mosaiquefm.net (2012). Rached Ghannouchi: Les manifestations ne pourront pas déstabliliser le gouvernement, 10 April.

Moudoud, Ezzeddine (1985). L'impossible régionalisation «Jacobine» et le dilemme des disparités régionales en tunisie, *Canadian Journal of Regional Science*, 8:3, 413–438.

Mussher, Marwan (2011). Tunisia's lessons for the Arab world, *Carnegie Endowment Commentary*, 1 November.

Naqar, 'Umar 'Abd al-Razzāq (1972). *The Pilgrimage Tradition in West Africa: An Historical Study with Special Reference to the Nineteenth Century*, Khartoum, Sudan.

Natter, Katharina (2010). The failures of Egyptian agricultural policy, *Daily News* (Egypt), 20 June.

Nelson, Soraya Sarhaddi (2011). Islamist parties proliferate in post-Mubarak Egypt, *National Public Radio*, 15 November.

Newman, Richard J. (2004). Corporate kleptocracy: Why Conrad Black has Hollinger investors seeing red, *USNews.com*, 13 September.

Nomachi, Ali Kazuyoshi and Seyyed Hossein Nasr (2005). *Mecca the Blessed, Medina the Radiant: The Holiest Cities of Islam*, New York: Aperture.

Oakes, Timothy and Donald S. Sutton, eds. (2010). *Faiths on Display: Religion and Tourism in China*, Lanham, Maryland: Rowman & Littlefield.

Obaidullah, Mohammed (2005). *Islamic Financial Services*, Jeddah: King Abdulaziz University Islamic Economics Research Center.

One Hundred Seventh Congress of the United States of America, The Sarbanes-Oxley Act of 2002. Available online at http://www.sec.gov/about/laws/soa2002.pdf (accessed 16 April 2013).

Organization of the Islamic Conference and the Chinese Academy of Social Sciences, (2012). *China and the Muslim World: Cultural Encounters*, Beijing, 28–29 June. Available online at http://www.ircica.org/international-congress-on-china-and-the-muslim-world-cultural-encounters/irc902.aspx (accessed 13 January 2013).

Örücü, Esin, Elspeth Attwool and Sean Coyle (1996). *Studies in Legal Systems: Mixed and Mixing*, Dordrecht: Kluwer.

Ostrom, Elinor, Joanna Burger, Christopher B. Field, Richard B. Norgaard and David Policansky (1999). Revisiting the commons: Local lessons, global challenges, *Science*, 284:5412, 278–282.

Ottaway, David (2012). *Tunisia's Islamists Struggle to Rule*, Washington: Woodrow Wilson International Center for Scholars, April.

Partin, Harry B. (1967). *The Muslim pilgrimage: Journey to the center* (Unpublished doctoral dissertation), University of Chicago.

Pearson, Michael Naylor (2003). *The Indian Ocean*, London: Routledge.

Perdue, Peter C. (2010). *China Marches West: The Qing Conquest of Central Eurasia*, Cambridge: Harvard University Press.

Qian Xue Wen (钱学文) (2007). 中东、里海油气与中国能源安全战略 (*The Middle East, Caspian Oil and Gas, and China's Energy Security Strategy*), Beijing: Current Events Press.

Quraish, Khaled (2012). Fawz murashshaha al-Hurriya wa al-'Adala bi muq'ad al-fi'at wa al-Nur bi al-'umal fi al-Wadi al-Jadid (The Freedom and Justice candidate wins the professional seat and Nur wins the worker seat in the New Valley), *Al-Ahram*, 14 January.

Radwan, Islam (2012). Bakr wa 'Abd ul-Jawad wa Musa wa Qarshi fil-i'ada bil-da'ira al-thalatha fi Assyut (Bakr, 'Abd al-Jawad, Musa, and Qarshi in the run-offs in Assyut's third district), *Al-Ahram*, 14 January.

Radwan, Islam (2011). Copts and the Salafis in Asyut: 'One hand'? *Egyptvotes.org*, 19 December.

Radwan, Islam (2012). Fawz Khalaf bil-fi'at wa i'ada bayn Sadiq wa 'Abd al-Nasr 'ala al-'umal fil-da'ira Assyut (Victory of Khalaf in the professional seat and run-off of Sadiq and Abd al-Nasr for the worker seat in Assyut district), *Al-Ahram*, 14 January.

Rahman, Fazlur (1970). Islam and social justice, *Pakistan Forum*, 1:1, October–November.

Rahman, Fazlur (1982). *Islam and Modernity: Transformation of an Intellectual Tradition*, Chicago: University of Chicago Press.

Rahman, Fazlur (2009). *Major Themes of the Qur'an*, Chicago: University of Chicago Press.

Rallet, Alain (1995). Libéralisation de l'économie, problématique de développement régional et routines institutionnelles: le cas de la tunisie, *Revue Région and Développpement*, 2, 1–25.

Ramadan, Tariq (2005). *Western Muslims and the Future of Islam*, New York: Oxford University Press.

Rodinson, Maxime (1978). *Islam and Capitalism*, Austin: University of Texas Press.

Rodrik, Dani (2009). Making room for China in the world economy, *American Economic Review*, 100:2, 89–93.

Rosenau, James N. and Ernst-Otto Czempiel, eds. (1992). *Governance without Government: Order and Change in World Politics*, Cambridge: Cambridge University Press.

Rosly, Saiful Azhar and Mahmood M. Sanusi (1999). The application of bay' al-'inah and bay' al-dayn in Malaysian Islamic bonds: an Islamic analysis, *International Journal of Islamic Financial Services*, 1, July–September.

Sabri, Ahmad (2012). Taht al-'amtar, al-Ikhwan yahtifalun bi fawzihim bi maq'aidi al-da'ira al-thalatha bil-Iskandariya (In the rain, the Ikhwan celebrate their victory in two seats of Alexandria's third district), *Al-Ahram*, 14 January.

Salvatore, Armando (1997). *Islam and the Political Discourse of Modernity*. Reading: Ithaca Press.

Samti, Farah (2011). How the press perceives Hachmi Hamdi, *Tunisia-live.net*, 30 October.

Schimmel, Annemarie (1963). *Gabriel's Wing: A Study Into the Religious Ideas of Sir Muhammad Iqbal*, Leiden: E.J. Brill.

Schimmel, Annemarie (1993). *The Triumphal Sun: A Study of the Works of Jalaloddin Rumi,* Albany: State University of New York Press.

Sedlacko, Michal and André Marinuzzi (2012). Governance by Evaluation for Sustainable Development: Institutional Capacities and Learning, Cheltenham, U.K.: Edward Elgar.

Selim, Mohammad El-Sayed (2003). Globalization, multilateralism and the Islamic world, *IslamOnline.net*, 1 September.

Serageldin, Samia (2012). The dead Pope rises: Coptic conundrum in Egypt, *Salon.com*, 20 March.

Shadid, Anthony (2011). Islamists' ideas on democracy and faith face test in Tunisia, *New York Times*, 17 February.

Shadid, Anthony (2011). The old order stifles the birth of a new Egypt, *New York Times*, 22 November.

Shakespeare, Rodney (2006). An Islamic money supply as the means to integration, *Seventh Harvard University Forum on Islamic Finance*, Harvard Law School, 23 April. Available online at http://ebookbrowse.com/an-islamic-money-supply-as-the-means-to-integration-rodney-shakespeare-pdf-d172878214 (accessed 13 January 2013).

Shariati, Ali (2007). *Hajj: Reflections on Its Rituals*, translated by Laleh Bakhtiar, Chicago: Kazi Publications.

Shenker, Jack (2011). Cairo clashes mask a more insidious threat to a democratic future, *Guardian*, 10 October.

Shirayanagi, Kouichi (2011). Tunisian civil society demonstrates in full force in front of Constituent Assembly opening session, *Tunisia-live.com*, 23 November.

Shukrallah, Salma (2012). Confusion overshadows decision to elect Egypt's president before constitution, *Ahramonline*, 3 January.

Siddiqi, Mohammad Nejatullah (2006). Shariah, economics and the progress of Islamic finance: The role of Shariah experts, *Seventh Harvard University Forum on Islamic Finance*, Harvard Law School, 21 April. Available online at http://www.siddiqi.com/mns/Role_of_Shariah_Experts.htm (accessed 13 January 2013).

Siddiqui, Haroon (2001). Arab Islamists less scary than Republicans, *Toronto Star*, 10 December.

Simmel, Georg (1964). *Conflict and the Web of Group Affiliations*, New York: Simon and Schuster.

Sims, David (2003). "Urban slums report: The case of Cairo, Egypt," *UN-Habitat Global Report on Human Settlements*, pp. 195–228, Malta: Gutenberg Press.

Sirkin, R. Mark (2005). *Statistics for the Social Sciences,* Thousand Oaks, CA: Sage.

Slaughter, Anne-Marie (2004). *A New World Order*, Princeton: Princeton University Press.

Snouck Hurgronje, Christiaan (1911). Notes sur le mouvement du pèlerinage de la Mecque aux Indes Neerlandaises, *Revue du Monde Musulman*, 15, 397–413.

Snouck Hurgronje, Christiaan (1957). La pèlerinage à la Mekke, in *Selected Works of C. Snouck Hurgronje*, G.-H. Bousquet and Joseph Schacht, eds., Leiden, Netherlands.

Snyder, Francis (1999). *Global Economic Networks and Global Legal Pluralism*, Florence: European University Institute.

Stack, Liam (2011). Christians and Muslims in fatal clash near Cairo, *New York Times*, 9 March.

Strategypage.com (2010). Chinese general declares democracy the ultimate weapon, 19 August.

Sukma, Rizal (2009). A post-ASEAN foreign policy for a post-G8 world, *Jakarta Post*, 5 October 5.

Sun De Gang (孙德刚) (2007). 多元平衡与 "准联盟" 理论研究, 时事出版社 (Multi-polarity and the Theory of "Quasi-Alliances"), Beijing: Current Events Press.

Surowiecki, James (2004). *The Wisdom of Crowds: Why the Many Are Smarter Than the Few and How Collective Wisdom Shapes Business, Economics, Societies and Nations*, New York: Random House.

Taleb, Rachid (2000). Quelques aspects des relations villes-monde rural en tunisie, *uram-international.com*, 4 October.

Tarek, Sherif (2011) Liberals and democrats revel in Salafist electoral defeats, *Ahramonline*, 7 December.

Taylor, John B. (2002). Introductory remarks by John B. Taylor, Undersecretary for Intl Affairs, US Treasury, *Islamic finance 101 seminar*, Washington, D.C.: US Treasury Dept, 26 April. Available online at http://www.treasury.gov/press-center/press-releases/Pages/po3068.aspx (accessed 13 January 2013).

Teubner, Gunther, ed. (1997). *Global Law Without a State*, Brookfield, VT.: Dartmouth.

Thomas, Abdulkader, Stella Cox and Bryan Kraty (2005). *Structuring Islamic Finance Transactions*, London: Euromoney Books.

Turner, Bryan (1979). *Marx and the End of Orientalism*, London: Unwin Hyman.

Turner, Bryan S. (2004). Weber and Elias on religion and violence: Warrior charisma and the civilizing process, in *The Sociology of Norbert Elias*, S. Loyal and S. Quilley, eds., Cambridge: Cambridge University Press, pp. 245–264.

Turner, Victor (1995). *The Ritual Process: Structure and Anti-Structure*, Piscataway, New Jersey: Aldine Transaction.

Turner, Victor and Edith Turner (1995). *Image and Pilgrimage in Christian Culture: Anthropological Perspectives*, New York: Columbia University Press.

Uddin, Asma (2009). Parallel universe: Islam and democracy—Their relationship is all in how it's defined, *Islamica Magazine*, 19, p. 120.

Underdal, Arild and Oran R. Young, eds. (2004). *Regime Consequences: Methodological Challenges and Research Strategies*, Dordrecht: Kluwer.

Vogel, Frank E. and Samuel L. Hayes III (1998). *Islamic law and Finance: Religion, Risk, and Return*, Boston: Kluwer Law International.

Von Grunebaum, Gustave E. (2001). *Muhammadan Festivals*, London: Routledge Curzon.

Wall Street Journal (2011). Egypt's fading spring: While Tunisia votes, Cairo still lacks a democratic transition, 15 October.

Walt, Stephen M. (2011). Explaining Obama's Asia policy, *Foreign Policy*, 18 November.

Wang Gungwu (2005). China's cautious pride in an ancient mariner, *Yale Global*, 4 August.

Wang Ji Si (王缉思) (2012). "西进"，中国地缘战略的再平衡，环球时报 ("March West," Rebalancing China's Geostrategy), *Global Times*, October 17. Available online at http://opinion.huanqiu.com/opinion_world/2012-10/3193760.html.

Warde, Ibrahim (1998). Crony capitalism: the banking system in turmoil, *Le Monde diplomatique English edition*, November.

Warde, Ibrahim (2000). *Islamic Finance in the Global Economy*, Edinburgh: Edinburgh University Press.

Warde, Ibrahim (2001). The Prophet and the profits: Islamic finance, *Le Monde diplomatique English edition*, September.

Webster, Stephen C. and Glen Beck (2013). Education standards are a Chinese-Muslim conspiracy, Democraticunderground.com, March 29. Available online at http://www.democraticunderground.com/10022585696.

White, Hugh (2012). *The China Choice: Why America Needs to Share Power*, Collingwood, Australia: Black Inc.

Wolters, W., Nadi Selim Ghobrial and Marinus G. Bos (1987). Division of irrigation water in the Fayoum, Egypt, *Irrigation and Drainage Systems*, 1, 159–172.

Wolters, W., Nadi Selim Ghobrial, H.M. Van Leeuwen and Marinus G. Bos (1989). Managing the water balance of the Fayoum depression, Egypt, *Irrigation and Drainage Systems*, 3, 103–123.

Wong, Roy Bin (2001). Entre monde et nation: les régions Braudéliennes en Asie, *Annales*, 56:1, 5–41.

Wong, Roy Bin (2004). East Asia as a world region in the 21st century, *Nihon Kezai Shimbun*, 13 August.

Wright, Robin (2011). The Islamists are coming: But democracy and piety aren't always contradictions, *Foreign Policy*, 7 November.

Wu Bing Bing (吴冰冰) (2006). 从伊斯兰文明看文化自觉，回族研究 (Cultural Consciousness from the Perspective of Islamic Civilization), *Journal of Hui Minority Studies*, 1.

Wu Bing Bing (吴冰冰) (2011). 中东多极化是中国新机遇 (Middle East multipolarization is a new opportunity for China), *环球时报* (*Global Times*), 30 August.

Yang Yi (杨毅) (2012). 周边安全需要全方位战略， 环球时报 (Peripheral Security Requires a Comprehensive Strategy), *Global Times*, October 26. Available online at http://news.xinhuanet.com/world/2012-10/26/c_123875252.htm.

Yao Chun Jun (姚春军) (2009). 对新疆维吾尔宗教信仰者朝觐问题的心里探析 (A Psychological analysis of Uyghur Muslims' beliefs about the hajj), *Xinjiang Social Science*, 2, 52–57.

Yilmaz, Ihsan (2005). Muslim Laws, Politics and Society in Modern Nation-states: Dynamic Legal Pluralisms in England, Turkey and Pakistan, Aldershot: Ashgate.

Yin Gang (2008). Two Asias: The Middle East in an Asian century, *Bitter Lemons*, 8 May.

Younis, Jumanah (2011). Egypt's revolution means nothing if its women are not free, *Guardian*, 9 March.

Youssef, Abdel Rahman (2012). Copts, Islamists face off in Minya run-offs, *Daily News* (Egypt), 11 January.

Yu Keping (2009). *Democracy Is A Good Thing: Essays on Politics, Society, and Culture in Contemporary China*, Washington, D.C.: Brookings Institution Press.

Zakariya, Farid (2012). For conservatives, a Middle East divide, *Washington Post*, 10 October.

Zawya.com (2003). Noriba Bank launches new Sharia-compliant investment product, 8 December. Available online at http://www.zawya.com/story/Noriba_Bank_launches_new_Shariacompliant_investment_product-ZAWYA20050906082914/ (accessed 13 January 2013).

Zelin, Aaron Y. (2011). Ennahda's tight rope act on religion, *Foreign Policy*, 18 November.

Zhang Dainian (2002). *Key Concepts in Chinese Philosophy*, New Haven: Yale University Press.

Zhang Xin Ping and Li Wei Liang (张新平, 李维亮) (2004). 中亚与伊斯兰世界关系的地缘政治思考 (Geopolitical thinking on relations between Central Asia and the Islamic world), *Journal of the Northwest University for Nationalities*, 6, 66–71.

Zhu Wei Lie (朱威烈) (2007). 伊斯兰文明与世界, 世界政治 (Islamic Civilization and the World), *World Economics and Politics*, 7.

Index